LOST TO THE
WEST

LOST TO THE
WEST

∷∷

THE FORGOTTEN BYZANTINE EMPIRE THAT

RESCUED WESTERN CIVILIZATION

LARS BROWNWORTH

Originally published in hardcover in the United States
by Crown Publishers, an imprint of the Crown Publishing Group,
a division of Random House, Inc., New York, in 2009.

Cataloging-in-Publication Data is available on request
from the Library of Congress.

ISBN 978-0-307-40796-2

Printed in the United States of America

Maps by Anders Brownworth

20 19 18 17 16 15 14

First Paperback Edition

FOR ANDERS,

the great storyteller of our youth

N

BLACHERNAE
PALACE

PALACE OF THE
PORPHYROGENITUS

GATE OF
CHARISIUS

CHORA
CHURCH

GOLDEN HORN

LAND WALLS

MESE

LYCUS RIVER

GATE OF
ST. ROMANUS

LAND WALL

CHURCH OF
THE HOLY
APOSTLES

PANTOKRATOR
MONASTERY

THEODOSIAN

VALENS AQUEDUCT

GATE OF
RHEGIUM

CONSTANTINIAN

ST. POLYEUKTES

FORUM
CONSTAN

FORUM
BOVIS

FORUM OF
THEODOSIUS

MYRELAION
MONASTERY

OLD

FORUM
ARCADIUS

HARBOR OF
JULIAN

SECOND
MILITARY
GATE

STS. SERGIU
AND BACCH

VIA TRIUMPHALIS

ST. JOHN
OF
STUDIOS

SEA OF MARMARA
(PROPONTIS)

GOLDEN
GATE

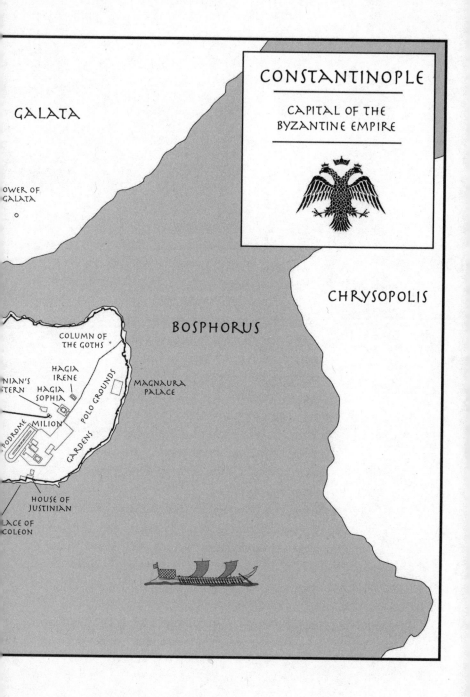

GALATA

OWER OF
GALATA

CONSTANTINOPLE

CAPITAL OF THE
BYZANTINE EMPIRE

CHRYSOPOLIS

BOSPHORUS

COLUMN OF
THE GOTHS

HAGIA
IRENE

NIAN'S
TERN

HAGIA
SOPHIA

POLO GROUNDS

MAGNAURA
PALACE

PODROME   MILION

GARDENS

HOUSE OF
JUSTINIAN

LACE OF
COLEON

CONTENTS

The interested reader can find a complete list of dynasties and emperors at the back of the book.

GUIDE TO MAPS

INTRODUCTION

I first met Byzantium in a pleasant little salt marsh on the north shore of Long Island. I had paused there to read a book about what was innocently called the "later Roman Empire," prepared to trace the familiar descent of civilization into the chaos and savagery of the Dark Ages. Instead, nestled under my favorite tree, I found myself confronted with a rich tapestry of lively emperors and seething barbarian hordes, of men and women who claimed to be emperors of Rome long after the Roman Empire was supposed to be dead and buried. It was at once both familiar and exotic; a Roman Empire that had somehow survived the Dark Ages, and kept the light of the classical world alive. At times, its history seemed to be ripped from the headlines. This Judeo-Christian society with Greco-Roman roots struggled with immigration, the role of church and state, and the dangers of a militant Islam. Its poor wanted the rich taxed more, its rich could afford to find the loopholes, and a swollen bureaucracy tried hard to find a balance that brought in enough money without crushing everyone.

And yet Byzantium was at the same time a place of startling strangeness, alluring but quite alien to the modern world. Holy men perched atop pillars, emperors ascended pulpits to deliver lashing sermons, and hairsplitting points of theology could touch off riots in the streets. The concepts of democracy that infuse the modern world would have horrified the Byzantines. Their society had been founded in the instability and chaos of the third century, a time of endemic revolts with emperors who were desperately trying to elevate the dignity of the throne. Democracy, with its implications that all were equal, would have struck at the very underpinnings of their hierarchical, ordered world, raising nightmares of the unceasing civil wars that they had labored so hard to escape. The Byzantines, however, were no prisoners of an oppressive autocratic society. Lowly peasants and orphaned women found their way onto the throne, and it was a humble farmer from what is now Macedonia who rose to become Byzantium's greatest ruler, extending its vast domains until they embraced nearly the entire Mediterranean. His successors oversaw a deeply religious society with a secular educational system that saw itself as the guardian of light and civilization in a swiftly darkening world. They were, as Robert Byron so famously put it, a "triple fusion": a Roman body, a Greek mind, and a mystic soul.

It's a better definition than most, in part because the term "Byzantine" is a thoroughly modern invention, making the empire attached to it notoriously difficult to define. What we call the Byzantine Empire was in fact the eastern half of the Roman Empire, and its citizens referred to themselves as Roman from the founding of Constantinople in 323 to the fall of the city eleven centuries later. For most of that time, their neighbors, allies, and enemies alike saw them in this light; when Mehmed II conquered Constantinople, he took the title Caesar of Rome, ruling, as he saw it, as the successor of a line that went back to Augustus. Only the scholars of the Enlightenment, preferring to find their roots in ancient Greece and classical Rome, denied the Eastern Empire the name "Roman," branding it instead after Byzantium—the ancient name of Constantinople. The "real" empire for them had ended in 476 with the abdication of the last western emperor, and the history of the "impostors" in Constantinople was nothing more than a thousand-year slide into barbarism, corruption, and decay.

Western civilization, however, owes an incalculable debt to the scorned city on the Bosporus. For more than a millennium, its capital stood, the great bastion of the East protecting a nascent, chaotic Europe, as one after another would-be world conqueror foundered against its walls. Without Byzantium, the surging armies of Islam would surely have swept into Europe in the seventh century, and, as Gibbon mused, the call to prayer would have echoed over Oxford's dreaming spires. There was more than just force of arms to the Byzantine gift, however. While civilization flickered dimly in the remote Irish monasteries of the West, it blazed in Constantinople, sometimes waxing, sometimes waning, but always alive. Byzantium's greatest emperor, Justinian, gave us Roman law—the basis of most European legal systems even today—its artisans gave us the brilliant mosaics of Ravenna and the supreme triumph of the Hagia Sophia, and its scholars gave us the dazzling Greek and Latin classics that the Dark Ages nearly extinguished in the West.

If we owe such a debt to Byzantium, it begs the question of why exactly the empire has been so ignored. The Roman Empire fractured—first culturally and then religiously—between East and West, and as the two halves drifted apart, estrangement set in. Christianity was a thin veneer holding them together, but by 1054, when the church ruptured into Catholic and Orthodox halves, the East and West found that they had little to unite them and much to keep them apart. The Crusades drove the final wedge between them, engendering lasting bitterness in the East, and derision in the West. While what was left of Byzantium succumbed to Islamic invasion, Europe washed its hands and turned away, confident in its own growing power and burgeoning destiny. This mutual contempt has left Byzantium consigned to a little-deserved obscurity, forgotten for centuries by those who once took refuge behind its walls.

Most history curricula fail to mention the civilization that produced the illumination of Cyril and Methodius, the brilliance of John I Tzimisces, or the conquests of Nicephorus II Phocas. The curtain of the Roman Empire falls for most with the last western emperor, and tales of heroism in Greece end with the Spartan king Leonidas. But no less heroic was Constantine Dragases, standing on his ancient battlements in 1453, or Belisarius before the walls of Rome. Surely we owe them as deep a debt of gratitude.

This book is my small attempt to redress that situation, to give voice to a people who have remained voiceless far too long. It's intended to whet the appetite, to expose the reader to the vast sweep of Byzantine history, and to put flesh and sinew on their understanding of the East and the West. Regrettably, it can make no claims to being definitive or exhaustive. Asking a single volume to contain over a thousand years of history is taxing enough, and much must be sacrificed to brevity. In defense of what's been left on the cutting-room floor, I can only argue that part of the pleasure of Byzantium is in the discovery.

Throughout the book I've used Latinized rather than Greek names—Constantine instead of Konstandinos—on the grounds that they'll be more familiar and accessible to the general reader. I've also used a personality-driven approach to telling the story since the emperor was so central to Byzantine life; few societies have been as autocratic as the Eastern Roman Empire. The person on the imperial throne stood halfway to heaven, the divinely appointed sovereign whose every decision deeply affected even the meanest citizen.

Hopefully, this volume will awaken an interest in a subject that has long been absent from the Western canon. We share a common cultural history with the Byzantine Empire, and can find important lessons echoing down the centuries. Byzantium, no less than the West, created the world in which we live, and—if further motivation is needed to study it—the story also happens to be captivating.

History isn't supposed to hinge on the actions of a single man. Vast impersonal forces are supposed to sweep humanity along on an irresistible tide without regard to individual lives. But on a crisp fall day in AD 324, history hung on the shoulders of a man named Constantine as he climbed up a hill overlooking the Bosporus. Striding confidently forward, spear firmly in hand, he led a solemn procession of astonished courtiers. He had come following a divine voice—although whether it was that of an angel or of God himself he didn't say. The turmoil of the recent civil wars was at last over. Once again the world lay at rest beneath the wings of the Roman eagle, but Rome itself, with its malarial streets and pagan past, was no longer worthy to be the capital of the world. So the young emperor had gone to Troy, that fabled cradle of the Roman people, and started work on a new capital. It was there, in the shadow of the ruined Trojan gates, that the voice first came to him. Priam's ancient city, it said, was a city of the past, and so it should remain. His destiny—and that of his empire—lay elsewhere. Over the Hellespont it beckoned him, and he followed to the thousand-year-old city of Byzantium. That night he dreamed of an old woman who suddenly became young again, and when he awoke, he knew that on this spot he would make his capital. Rome, old and decrepit, would, like the woman in his dreams, be refreshed here on the shores of the Propontis.

So at least runs the legend, and the empire centered on Constantine's New Rome would indeed grow vibrant once again. Refounded on a new, eastern, Christian axis, it would last for over a millennium, a shining beacon of light in a dark and turbulent world. Looking back, historians would claim that so much had changed in the moment of the city's founding that the Roman Empire itself had been transformed into something else, and Byzantine history had begun.

But the roots of this new world didn't begin with Constantine. The empire that he seized control of in the first decades of the fourth century had been profoundly changing for a generation, both politically and religiously, and Constantine merely put the finishing touches on its transformation. His vision and energy may have built the impressive edifice of Constantinople, but the reforms of his predecessor, Diocletian, provided the brick and mortar. And it is with Diocletian that the story of Byzantium properly begins.

LOST TO THE
WEST

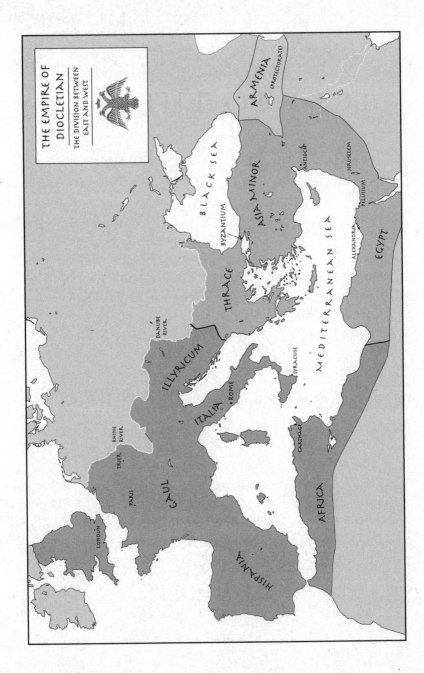

THE EMPIRE OF
DIOCLETIAN
THE DIVISION BETWEEN
EAST AND WEST

ARMENIA (PROTECTORATE)

BLACK SEA

ASIA MINOR

ANTIOCH

JERUSALEM

PELUSIUM

ALEXANDRIA

EGYPT

BYZANTIUM

THRACE

MEDITERRANEAN SEA

DANUBE RIVER

ILLYRICUM

SYRACUSE

ITALIA

ROME

RHINE RIVER

TRIER

CARTHAGE

PARIS

GAUL

AFRICA

LONDON

HISPANIA

1

::

DIOCLETIAN'S REVOLUTION

The long-suffering people of the third-century Roman Empire had the distinct misfortune to live in interesting times. For three centuries before Constantine's birth, Roman architects, engineers, and soldiers had crisscrossed the known world, bringing order and stability to the barbaric, diverse lands beyond the frontiers of Italy. In the wake of the mighty *Pax Romana* came more than fifty thousand miles of arrow-straight, graded roads and towering aqueducts, impervious alike to the mountains and valleys that they spanned. These highways were the great secret of empire, providing access to markets, ease of travel, and an imperial mail system that could cover more than five hundred miles in a single day. Graceful cities sprang up along the major routes, complete with amphitheaters, public baths, and even indoor plumbing—a visible testament to the triumph of civilization. But by the third century, time had ravaged the empire's glory, and revolts had stained its streets with blood. Those impressive Roman roads that had so effectively exported the empire now became its greatest weakness as rebel armies and barbarian hordes came rushing in. No one—not even the ephemeral emperors—was safe in those uncertain times. In the first eight decades of the century, twenty-nine men sat on the imperial throne, but only one escaped murder or capture to die a natural death.

Apathy and enervation seemed to be everywhere, sapping the strength of once solid Roman foundations. The military, too busy playing kingmaker to maintain itself, fell victim like everything else to the sickness of the age. In 259, the proud Emperor Valerian led his soldiers against the Persians, and suffered one of the greatest humiliations in Roman history. Captured by the enemy, he was forced to endure the indignity of being used as a footstool by the gleeful Persian king. When the broken emperor at last expired, the Persians had him flayed, dyeing the skin a deep red color and stuffing it with hay. Hanging the gruesome trophy on a wall, they displayed it to visiting Roman ambassadors as a constant reminder of just how hollow the myth of the invincible legions had become.

Such public humiliation was galling, but Roman writers had been lamenting the decay of the national character for years. As early as the second century BC, Polybius blamed the politicians whose pandering had reduced the republic to mob rule, Sallust railed against the viciousness of political parties, and Livy—the most celebrated writer of Rome's golden age—had written that "these days . . . we can bear neither our diseases nor their remedies."*

Now, however, a more ominous note crept in. The predictions of disaster gave way to glowing panegyrics celebrating the greatness and permanence of emperors who were plainly nothing of the sort. The men on the throne seemed like shadows flitting across the imperial stage, an awful confirmation that the gods had turned their backs on humanity. Barbarian enemies were gathering like wolves on the frontiers, but the generals sent against them more often than not used their swords to clear a path to the throne. The army, once a servant of the emperor, now became his master, and dynasties rose and fell with bewildering frequency.

The chaos of nearly continuous civil war made it hard to tell who the emperor actually was, but the tax collectors came anyway, with their unceasing demands for more money. The desperate shadow emperors tried to save money by reducing the silver content of their coins, but the resulting inflation crippled the economy, and most of the empire

---

*Ronald Mellor, *The Historians of Ancient Rome: An Anthology of the Major Writings* (New York: Routledge, 2004).

reverted to the barter system. Terrified by the mounting uncertainty, men took refuge in "mystery religions" that taught that the physical world was fleeting or evil, and put their hopes in magic, astrology, and alchemy. Life was full of pain, and the more extreme refused marriage or committed suicide to escape it. The very fabric of society was coming apart, and rich and poor alike prayed for deliverance.

Salvation came, unexpectedly enough, from Dalmatia. A tough soldier named Diocletian from that backward, rugged land of craggy peaks and lush forests rose up to claim the throne. Assuming power in the usual way by assassinating his predecessor and climbing over the bodies of rival armies, Diocletian was pragmatic enough to admit what others had only dimly suspected. The empire was simply too large to be successfully governed by one man in these troubled days. Its vast territory embraced the entire Mediterranean, stretching from the damp forests of Britain in the north to the blazing deserts of Egypt in the south, from the Rock of Gibraltar in the west to the borders of Persia in the east. Even if he spent his entire life in the saddle, Diocletian couldn't possibly react quickly enough to stamp out every crisis, nor could he dispatch surrogates to fight on his behalf; recent imperial history provided too many examples of such generals using their armies to gain the throne. If the wobbling empire were to be preserved at all, Diocletian needed to somehow shrink its enormous size—a task that had overwhelmed all of his immediate predecessors. Few leaders in history can have started a reign with such a daunting job, but the pragmatic Diocletian found an unorthodox solution: He raised an old drinking buddy named Maximian to the rank of senior emperor, or *Augustus,* and split the world in half.

It wasn't quite as revolutionary a decision as it sounded, especially because the empire was already divided linguistically. Long before Rome had dreamed of world conquest, Alexander the Great had swept east to India, crushing all who stood against him and forging the unwieldy territories into an empire. In his footsteps had come Hellenization, and though Alexander's empire had crumbled with his death, Greek culture seeped in and took root. Rome had spread from the west like a veneer over this Hellenized world, superior in arms but awed by the older culture's sophistication. Latin was spoken in the eastern halls of power, but not in its markets or homes. In thought and character, the East remained firmly Greek.

Handing over the western areas of the empire, where Latin was the dominant language, to Maximian, Diocletian kept the richer, more-cultured Greek east for himself. In theory, the empire was still one and indivisible, but each half would have a drastically different fate, and the rough line that was drawn between them still marks the divide between eastern and western Europe today. The full ramifications wouldn't become clear for another two centuries, but Diocletian had effectively divided the world into Roman and Byzantine halves.

Sharing power with another man was a dangerous game for Diocletian to play since it ran the obvious risk of creating a rival, but Maximian proved to be an extremely loyal colleague. Pleased by the success, and aware that two men were still not enough to stem the tide of invaders streaming over the frontiers, Diocletian divided power again by appointing two junior emperors (Caesars). These men were given full authority to lead armies and even issue laws, and greatly eased the burdens of administration by the senior rulers. Four men could now claim an imperial rank, and though for the moment they were remarkably efficient, only time would tell if this "tetrarchy" (rule of four) would be a team of rivals or colleagues.

Diocletian, meanwhile, was just getting warmed up. The lightened workload enabled him to carry out a thorough reorganization of the cluttered bureaucracy. Replacing the chaotic system with a clean, efficient military one, he divided the empire into twelve neat dioceses, each governed by a vicar who reported directly to his emperor.* Taxes could now be collected with greater efficiency, and the money that poured into the treasury could better equip the soldiers guarding the

---

*When the early church was developing a hierarchy, it naturally absorbed that of the empire around it. Thus Diocletian's reforms are still visible in the Catholic Church, in which bishops oversee a diocese and the pope is referred to as the "Vicar" of Christ.

frontiers. With budget and borders in hand, Diocletian now turned to the monumental task of stabilizing the crown itself.

The emperor understood better than any man before him just how precarious the throne had become. Numerous revolts had made the army loyal to the personality, not the position, of the emperor, and such a situation was inherently unstable. No one man, no matter how powerful or charismatic, could keep every segment of the population happy, and the moment some vulnerability was spotted, civil war would erupt. In earlier days, the royal blood of long-lived dynasties had checked ambition, but now that any man with an army could make himself emperor, something more was needed. To break the cycle of rebellion and war, Diocletian needed to make the *position* of emperor respected regardless of who occupied the throne.

This was the great struggle of the ancient world. Stability was needed for an orderly succession, but often such stability could only be achieved by a tyrant, and every dictator who justified his seizure of power further undermined the principle of succession. In any case, the idea of elevating the concept of the throne flew in the face of es- tablished tradition. The past five decades had seen emperors drawn from among the army, men who went to great lengths to prove that they were just like the men they commanded. They ate with their troops, laughed at their jokes, listened to their worries, and tried their best to hold on to their loyalty. Such a common touch was necessary; without it, you could easily miss the first flickers of unhappiness that might ignite into civil war, but it also reinforced the idea that emper- ors were just ordinary men. Mere mortals could be killed and replaced at will; Diocletian had to prove that emperors were something else entirely. If he failed to change that, then all that he had accomplished would be undone the moment he fell from power.

The Roman Empire had a long tradition of masking its autocracy behind the trappings of a republic. The first emperor, Augustus, had declined to even carry the title of emperor, preferring instead the in- nocuous "first citizen." For more than three centuries, the Roman le- gions had proudly carried standards bearing the legend SPQR, as if

they served the will of the people instead of the whim of a tyrant.*
Now, however, Diocletian wanted to change all that. No longer would
the imperial authority be masked behind the worn veneer of the long-
dead republic. Displays of naked power would awe the populace,
whereas pretending to be the "first among equals" had tempted them
to revolt.

Religion gave him the perfect outlet for his new political theory.
Power and legitimacy didn't flow up from the people, it flowed from
the gods down—and Diocletian was more than just a representative
of Jupiter, he was a living god himself. Those who were admitted to
see him were made to prostrate themselves and avert their gaze from
the brilliance of his presence. It was an impressive spectacle, and Diocletian made sure to dress the part. There would be no more simple
military clothes for the divine master of the civilized world. A splendid diadem adorned his head—he was the first emperor to wear one—
and a golden robe was draped around his shoulders. Cloaked in
elaborate ceremonies borrowed from the East, where traditions of
divine rulers ran deep, Diocletian now removed himself from the
sight of ordinary mortals, a god among men, surrounded by the impenetrable layers of the imperial court.

Propping up the wobbly throne with the might of Olympus was a
stroke of brilliance that had nothing to do with arrogance or self-
importance. In a world of chronic revolts, there was nothing like the
threat of a little divine retribution to discourage rebellion. Now revolts were acts of impiety, and assassination was sacrilege. At a stroke,
Diocletian had created an autocratic monarch, a semidivine emperor
whose every command had the full force of religion backing it up.
Though the faith behind it would change, this model of imperial
power would be the defining political ideology of the Byzantine
throne.

The pagans of the empire accepted it all willingly enough. They
were pantheistic and could easily accommodate a divine emperor or

---

Senatus Populusque Romanus (the Senate and the People of Rome).

two—they had in fact been deifying their dead rulers for centuries. Unfortunately for Diocletian, however, not all of his citizens were pagan, and his claims of divinity brought him into sharp conflict with the fastest-growing religion in the empire.

It wasn't in the least bit surprising that Romans were abandoning the traditional gods. The recent reforms of Diocletian had undoubtedly made things somewhat easier, but for the vast majority of citizens, life was still on the whole miserably unjust. Oppressed by a heavy tax burden, made worse by the corruption of half a century of chaos, the common man found no protection in the tainted courts and had to watch helplessly as the rich expanded their lands at his expense. Crushed into hopelessness, more and more people took refuge in the different mystery cults, the most popular of which was Christianity.

Against the arbitrary injustice of the world all around them, Christianity held out hope that their suffering wasn't in vain; that the seeming triumph of their grasping tormentors would be reversed by an all-powerful God who rewarded the just and punished the wicked. They weren't alone in a dark and fallen world, but could be nourished by the hand of a loving God who sustained them with the promise of eternal life. This physical world with all its pain was only fleeting and would pass away to be replaced by a perfect one where sorrow was unknown and every tear was wiped away. The old pagan religion, with its vain, capricious gods and pale, shadowy afterlife, could offer nothing so attractive.

When the imperial officials showed up to demand a sacrifice to the emperor, most Christians flatly refused. They would gladly pay their taxes and serve in the army or on committees, but (as they would make abundantly clear) Christianity had room in it for only one God. No matter how powerful he might be, the emperor was just a man.

This rejection of Diocletian's godhood struck at the very basis of imperial authority, and that was one thing the emperor wasn't prepared to tolerate. These dangerous rebels—godless men who denied all divinity—had to be wiped out. An edict demanding sacrifice to the emperor on pain of death was proclaimed, and the Roman Empire launched its last serious attempt to suppress Christianity.

The effects were horrendous, especially in the east, where the edict was enforced with a terrible thoroughness. Churches were destroyed, Christian writings were burned, and thousands were imprisoned, tortured, or killed. But despite the fervor with which they were carried out, the persecutions couldn't hope to be successful. Pagans and Christians had been more or less coexisting for years, and the suffering of the church was met with sympathy. There were the old stories, of course, the whispered tales of cannibalism and immorality, of Christians gathered in secret, eating their master's flesh and drinking his blood, but nobody really believed them anymore. Most pagans refused to believe that a religion that encouraged payment of taxes, stable families, and honesty in trade could be full of dangerous dissidents, threatening the security of the state. Christians were neighbors and friends, common people like themselves, struggling as best they could to make it in a troubled world. Christianity in any case couldn't be swept under the rug or persecuted out of existence. It had already spread throughout the empire and was well on its way to transforming the world.

Diocletian was fighting a losing battle against Christianity, and by AD 305 he knew it. A twenty-year reign had left him physically exhausted, and the glittering prestige of office no longer compensated enough. Nearing sixty and in declining health, the emperor had seen his youth slip away in service to the state and had no desire to spend what years remained under such a burden. Stunning his coemperors, he took a step unprecedented in Roman history, and announced his retirement. Typically of Diocletian, however, it was no mere abdication. It was, in its own way, as ambitious as anything he had ever attempted: a stunningly farsighted thrust to reverse the tide of history.

The ancient world never quite figured out the question of succession. The Roman Empire, like most in antiquity, had traditionally passed the throne from father to son, keeping control of the state in the hands of a small group of families. The great weakness of this system was that if the dynasty failed to produce an heir, the empire would convulse in a bloody struggle until the strongest contender prevailed. Whatever successive emperors might say about their divine right, the truth was that their legitimacy rested on physical strength, superior brains, or a well-placed assassination. Only in the written constitutions of the Enlightenment would political regimes find a solution to this basic instability. Without it, every reign was reduced at its core to the principle of survival of the fittest—or, as Augustus, wrapped up in the cloak of the republic, had more eloquently put it, "*carpe diem*"—seize the day.

Rome never really figured out a stable means of succession, but it did come close. Two centuries before Diocletian, in what must have seemed an idyllic golden age to the war-torn empire of his day, a succession of brilliant, childless rulers had handpicked the most capable of their subjects and adopted them as heirs. For nearly a hundred years, the throne passed from one gifted ruler to the next, overseeing the high-water mark of Roman power and prestige, and offering a glimpse of what could be accomplished when qualifications to high office were based on merit instead of blood. But this oasis of good government was only due to the fact that none of the adoptive emperors had sons of their own, and in the end heredity proved to be its Achilles' heel. Marcus Aurelius, the last of the "adoptive" emperors, had thirteen children, and when he died he left the empire to his aptly named son Commodus. Drunk with power and completely unfit to rule, the new emperor convinced himself that he was a reincarnation of Hercules, took the title *Pacator Orbis* (pacifier of the world), and renamed Rome and the months of the year in his honor. The Roman people endured their megalomaniacal ruler for twelve long years as his reign descended into depravity, before a senator finally took matters into his own hands and had the emperor strangled in his bath.* Once again, enlightened rule gave way to dynastic chance.

---

*Among other depraved acts, Commodus amused himself by clubbing thousands of amputees to death in the arena.

Diocletian's final announcement, therefore, was a revolution nearly fifteen centuries ahead of its time. This was not simply the abdication of a tired old man; it was a full-blown attempt at a constitutional solution to the question of succession. Both he and Maximian would be stepping down at the same time; their respective Caesars, Galerius and Constantius the Pale, would become the senior emperors, appoint their own Caesars, and complete the smooth transfer of power. Not only would this ensure a clean, orderly succession without the horrors of a civil war, it would also provide the empire with experienced, capable rulers. No man could become Augustus without first having proven himself as a Caesar.

Laying down the crown and scepter, Diocletian renounced his power and happily settled down to plant cabbages at his palatial estate in Salonae, on the Adriatic coast.* His contemporaries hardly knew what to do with a retired god, and history has proved in its own way just as mystified about his legacy. He ended chaos and restored stability—perhaps enough to have earned the title of a second Augustus—but had the misfortune to be eclipsed—in every sense of the word—by the man who nineteen years later rose to power. Diocletian had cut the Roman Empire free from the moorings of its past, but the future lay with Constantine the Great.

---

*When begged to return as emperor, Diocletian responded wryly that the temptations of power couldn't compete with the enjoyment of farming. The modern city of Split in Croatia is enclosed within the walls of his palace.

2

CONSTANTINE AND THE CHURCH ASCENDANT

Seneca saepe noster. [Seneca is often one of us.]
—TERTULLIAN

The tetrarchy deserved to survive a good deal longer than it did. There was, however, a rich historical irony in the way it collapsed, since Diocletian had gotten the idea from Roman history itself.

Longing for the stability of those golden years before the Roman juggernaut began to wobble, Diocletian had resurrected the adoptive system, but he should have known better than to pick two men with grown sons. Maximian and Constantius the Pale's sons, Maxentius and Constantine, considered the throne their birthright and eagerly expected a share of imperial power. But when Maximian reluctantly followed Diocletian into retirement, both boys were left with nothing. Once the sons of living gods, Constantine and Maxentius were left as nothing more than private citizens, feeling bitterly betrayed.

Determined not to let events pass him by, Constantine joined his father's campaign in Britain against the Picts. Easily subduing the barbarians, they both retired to York, where it became apparent that Constantius was pale because he was dying of leukemia. He'd been the most modest of the tetrarchs, largely ignoring the religious persecution of his more zealous eastern colleagues, and was wildly popular with the army, whose ranks included many Christians and sun worshippers. When he died on July 25, 306, an ambassador informed his heartbroken men that a distant Caesar named Severus would take his place. But the soldiers in the field had no intention of listening to some court bureaucrat. Most of them had never heard of Severus and didn't care to find out who he was. They had a younger, more vibrant version of their beloved leader much closer at hand. Raising Constantine up on their shields, the army hailed him as Augustus, and plunged the Roman world into war.

The island of Britain had not often intruded itself on the imperial consciousness, but Constantine's elevation was a shout heard in the empire's remotest corners, undoing at a stroke everything that Diocletian had been trying to establish about the succession. Encouraged by the way he had claimed power, others started to push against the limits forced upon them by Diocletian, eager to seize by force what was denied by law. Maxentius, still smarting from being passed over, seized Rome, tempting his father out of retirement to bolster his credibility, and successfully fought off every attempt to oust him. To the bewilderment of contemporaries and the annoyance of students studying the period ever since, there were soon six men claiming to be Augustus.

Mercifully, the confusion didn't last for long. As vast as the empire was, it wasn't large enough for six rulers, and the multiplying emperors helpfully started to kill one another off. By 312, there were only four of them left, and Constantine decided that the moment was right to strike. He had largely held his peace while the empire imploded, and now the tetrarchy was in hopeless shambles, both emperors in the West had seized power illegally, and the East was distracted with its own affairs. There was little possibility of outside interference, and only Maxentius was standing between him and complete control of the West. Carrying the standards of his patron god Sol Invictus ("unconquerable sun") before him, Constantine assembled forty thousand men, crossed the Alps, and descended on Italy.

As usual with great men, Constantine had both impeccable timing and remarkable luck. Maxentius's popularity was at an all-time low. Claiming that he was seriously short of money, he had ruthlessly taxed the Roman population, but then had used the funds to build a massive basilica in the Forum complete with a monumental statue of himself, provoking the exasperated citizens to revolt.* Order was finally restored by the slaughter of several thousand civilians, but Maxentius's popularity never recovered. When he heard of Constantine's approach, the frightened emperor was no longer sure of the city's loyalty, so he left the safety of Rome's walls and crossed the Tiber River by the old Milvian Bridge. Setting up camp a few miles away from the city, Maxentius consulted his soothsayers to see what the omens were and was assured that they were favorable. The next day would be his *dies imperii*—the six-year anniversary of his assumption of power. There could be no more auspicious time to attack.

Across the plain, Constantine, waiting with his army, also searched for signs of divine favor. The soothsayers and magicians thronging around Maxentius's camp unnerved him, and he was uncertain of how he should negate their influence. Priests representing every god in the pantheon had stared at the entrails of animals or the flights of birds and assured him that he would receive the blessings of divine favor, but surely his enemy was hearing the same lofty promises.

There in the dust of an army camp, with the bustle of military life swirling around him, Constantine knelt down and said a prayer that would change the course of history. As he himself would tell the story years later, he looked up at the sky and begged that a true God would reveal himself. Before his astonished eyes, a great cross of light appeared, superimposed over the sun that he had previously worshipped, bearing the inscription IN HOC SIGNO VINCES—"conquer by this sign." Stunned by this vision, the emperor wasn't quite sure of how to proceed, but when night fell, it was all helpfully explained in a dream. Christ himself appeared, showing the same sign, and

---

*It's still there, although today it's known as Constantine's basilica. After he entered Rome, the victorious Constantine replaced Maxentius's statue with one of himself, put some finishing touches on the building, and claimed it for his own.

instructed the emperor to carry it before him as divine protection. When he woke up, Constantine dutifully created new banners, replacing the traditional pagan standards with ones displaying a cross, topped with a wreath and the first two letters of Christ's name. Carrying them confidently before them, his outnumbered troops smashed their way to a complete victory. Maxentius's army fled back to Rome, but most of them drowned while trying to cross the old Milvian Bridge. Somewhere in the chaos, Maxentius, weighed down with armor, met a similar fate, falling into a river already choked with the dead and dying. His corpse was found the next day washed up on the shore, and Constantine proudly entered the city carrying his rival's head on a spear. Hailed by the Senate when he entered the Forum, the emperor conspicuously refused to offer the traditional sacrifice to the pagan god of victory. The tyrant was dead, he proclaimed, and a new age had begun.

The boast was more sagacious than Constantine realized. Though it would only become apparent later, the battle of the Milvian Bridge was a major turning point in history. By wielding the cross and sword, Constantine had done more than defeat a rival—he had fused the church and the state together. It would be both a blessing and a curse to both institutions, and neither the Christian church nor the Roman Empire would ever be the same again.

Oddly enough, despite the tremendous impact he would have on Christendom, Constantine never really made a convincing Christian. He certainly never really understood his adopted religion, and it seemed at first as if he had merely admitted Christ into the pantheon of Roman gods. The images of Sol Invictus and the war god Mars Convervator continued to appear on his coins for years, and he never gave up his title of *Pontifex Maximus*—chief priest of the old pagan religion. Gallons of scholarly ink have been spilled debating whether his conversion was genuine, but such speculation is beside the point. The genius of Constantine was that he saw Christianity not as the threat that Diocletian did, but rather as a means to unify, and the re-

sult of his vision that fateful day—whether genuine conversion or political opportunism—was a great sea change for the empire and the
church. Christianity's great persecution was over. From now on, the
once-oppressed faith would be in the ascendancy.

The pagan Senate didn't quite know what to make of their new
conqueror. He was clearly a monotheist, but which kind was not exactly certain, so, like politicians of any era, they decided to play it safe
and erect him a victory arch complete with an inscription vaguely referring to "divinity" aiding him in his just war. Perfectly pleased with
this ambiguity, Constantine issued an edict of toleration in 313, legal-
izing Christianity, but stopping short of making it the exclusive religion of the empire. Though Christianity was an easy fit for him—his
mother, Helena, was a Christian, and his own worship of the sun reserved Sunday as a holy day—he had no interest in being a missionary.
The majority of his subjects were still pagan, and the last thing he
wanted to do was to alienate them by forcing a strange new religion on
them. Instead, he wanted to use Christianity to support his regime the
way that Diocletian had used paganism. The main goal was to unite
the empire under his benevolent leadership, and he wasn't about to
jeopardize that for the sake of religious zeal.

There was, however, an even more compelling reason to portray
himself as a model of religious toleration. While he had been busy
conquering Rome, the emperor Licinius had emerged victorious in
the East, and was now nervously watching his predatory neighbor. He
had good reason to be afraid. Not only were Licinius's eastern territories richer and more populous than their western counterparts, but
Christianity had been born there, providing a natural base of support
for the man who had so famously converted. For eleven years, there
was a tenuous peace, but Licinius was terrified of the ravenous appetite of Constantine, and his paranoia betrayed him. Accusing the
Christians in his territory of acting as a fifth column for his rival,
Licinius tried to suppress the religion, executing bishops, burning
churches, and restarting Diocletian's persecutions.

The foolish eastern emperor had played right into his enemy's hands. Constantine had been hoping for just such an opportunity, and he pounced immediately. Sweeping into the East, he pushed Licinius's larger army over the Hellespont, destroying the trapped navy that the scrambling emperor left behind. After weeks of further maneuvering, the two armies met on September 18, 324, just across the Bosporus from the Greek colony of Byzantium, and in the shadow of that ancient city Constantine won a complete and shattering victory.

At fifty-two years of age, he was now the sole ruler of the Roman Empire, and to commemorate his success he gave himself a new title. After his victory at the Milvian Bridge, he had added "the Greatest" to his impressive string of names, and now he included "the Victor" as well. Humility had clearly never been one of the emperor's virtues, but Constantine was a master of propaganda and never missed an opportunity to promote himself. These instincts had served him well, allowing him to mask his thirst for power behind a disarming veneer of tolerance and kill off his rivals while retaining the guise of the people's champion. He had come to the rescue of his Christian subjects without persecuting his pagan ones, always maintaining a careful neutrality. Now that there were no more pagan enemies to fight, however, he could reveal a more open patronage of Christianity. His mother, Helena, was sent on a pilgrimage to the Holy Land—the first such trip in history—founding hostels and hospitals along the way to assist the generations to follow. In Bethlehem, she built the Church of the Nativity over the site of Christ's birth, and at Golgotha, in Jerusalem, she miraculously discovered the True Cross upon which he had been crucified. Leveling the temple of Venus that had been built by the emperor Hadrian on the site, she raised the Church of the Holy Sepulchre over the empty tomb.

While his mother was busy becoming the first pilgrim, Constantine carried out several reforms that would have far-reaching consequences. The confusion of civil war had disrupted markets and farms as the working classes fled for the comparative safety of the cities, and the emperor tried to stabilize the situation by forcing the peasant farmers to stay on their land. Going even further, he locked members of guilds—from bakers to hog merchants—in their occupations, forcing sons to follow their fathers. In the East, which had always been more stable and prosperous, this legislation was rarely enforced and had little effect, but in the chaotic, turbulent West, it was heavily pushed, and the result was the feudal system, which would take deep root and not be overthrown for a thousand years.

In the short term, however, a comforting stability returned to the shaken empire. Fields were harvested, markets resumed their operations, and commerce began to flourish.

Constantine was interested in more than just the material well-being of his subjects, and as the finances of his empire improved, he began to cautiously nurture his new faith. Pagan sacrifices were banned, sacred prostitution and ritual orgies were outlawed, and temple treasuries were confiscated to build churches. Crucifixion was abolished, and even gladiatorial contests were suppressed in favor of the less-violent chariot races. He had united the empire under his sole rule, and now Christianity would be united under him as well.

Just as the empire came together politically, however, a new and deadly heresy threatened to permanently rip it apart. It started in Egypt when a young priest named Arius started teaching that Christ was not fully divine and was therefore inferior to God the Father. Such a teaching struck at the heart of the Christian faith, denying its main tenet, which held that Christ was the incarnate word of God, but Arius was a brilliant speaker, and people began to flock to hear him speak. The church was caught completely off guard and threatened to splinter into fragments. Sporadically persecuted and until recently driven underground, the church was decentralized, a loose confederation of local congregations scattered throughout the empire. As the successor of Saint Peter, the bishop of Rome was given a special respect, but he had no practical control, and as the New Testament writings of Paul attest, the different churches had a strong tendency to go in their own directions. With no real hierarchy and little organization, the church had no means of definitively responding to Arius's teachings, and the controversy soon raged out of control.

It's typical of Constantine's soldier mentality that he thought he could simply order the warring factions to stop fighting. Completely misjudging the depth of feeling involved, he wrote to the bishops in Egypt with a painful naïveté, telling them that their differences were "insignificant" and asking them to just work them out and live in harmony. When it became apparent that they could do no such thing, he decided on a radical solution. The problem with Christianity, he thought, was that it suffered from a distinct lack of leadership. The bishops were like the old senators of Republican Rome—always arguing but never coming to a consensus unless threatened. Thankfully, Augustus had solved that problem for the empire, allowing the senators to continue to talk but dominating them by his presence when things needed to get done. Now it was Constantine's job to rescue the church. Under his watchful gaze, the church would speak with one voice, and he would make sure the world listened.

Announcing a great council, Constantine invited every bishop in the empire to attend, personally covering the cost of transportation and housing. When several hundred clerics had arrived at the Asian city of Nicaea, the emperor packed them into the main cathedral and on May 20, 325, opened the proceedings with a dramatic plea for unity. Constantine wasn't particularly concerned with which side of the argument prevailed as long as there was a clear victor, and he was determined to swing his support behind whichever side seemed to be in the majority. The council started off with minor matters, discussing the validity of baptisms by heretics and setting the official manner to calculate the date of Easter, before turning to the burning question of the relationship between the Son and the Father. At first all went smoothly, but when it came time to write up a statement of belief, neither side seemed inclined to compromise, and the proceedings threatened to break down.

The main problem was that the proposed word used to describe Christ in Greek was *homoiusios*—meaning "of *like* substance" with the Father. This was, of course, the Arian position that the two members of the trinity were similar not equal, and the other bishops objected to it strenuously. Seeing that the Arians were clearly in the minority, Constantine turned against them and proposed a solution. Dropping an "i," he changed the word to *homousios*—meaning "of *one* substance" with the Father. The Arians were upset with this ringing condemnation of their view, but with the emperor (and his soldiers) standing right there, they could hardly show their displeasure. The Arian bishops started to waver, and when Constantine assured them that equality with the Father could be interpreted in its "divine and mystical" sense, they bowed to the inevitable. The emperor had given them a way out—to interpret *homousios* however they wanted to—and the Arians left the council to return to their homes with their dignity intact. Arius was condemned, his books were burned, and Christian unity was restored.

The Nicene Creed that Constantine had overseen was more than a simple statement of faith. It became the official definition of what it meant to be a Christian, and defined what the true (orthodox) and universal (catholic) church believed. Even today, it can be heard in all Protestant, Orthodox, and Catholic churches, a dim reflection of a time when Christianity was unified. In the East, where the Byzantine Empire survived, the Council of Nicaea defined the relationship between secular and religious leaders: The bishops alone could decide on church matters, and the emperor's role was that of an enforcer. Constantine was the sword arm of the church, rooting out heresy and guarding the faith from schism. His successors would try to manipulate unity to varying degrees, but the underlying principle remained unchanged. The emperor's duty was to listen to the voice of the whole church; what that voice said was for the bishops to decide.

Now that Constantine's enemies—both theological and military—lay vanquished at his feet, he decided to build a suitable monument to his glory. He had already embellished Rome, adding the finishing touches to a massive basilica and seating a gigantic forty-foot-high statue of himself inside it. Now he added several churches and donated a palace on the Lateran Hill as a church for the pope. Rome, however, was filled with too many pagan ghosts to be the splendid center of his reign, and they couldn't be overcome with a thin Christian facade. Besides, Rome wasn't the city it had been, and the empire no longer rotated around it.

Far away from the empire's frontiers, Rome had long since ceased to be a practical capital, and had only been sporadically visited by the short-lived emperors of the third century. In the interests of military efficiency, Diocletian had insisted that his court travel with him, declaring that the capital of the empire wasn't in a particular city, but rather wherever the emperor happened to be. He was only saying out loud what had long been the uncomfortable truth. Unable to base themselves miles away from the troubled frontiers, emperors had gone their separate ways, and power had followed in the imperial wake. Diocletian himself, busy in his eastern court of Nicomedia, only set foot in the eternal city once, and his reforms reduced it to a symbolically important backwater.

Constantine was determined to give the drifting empire new roots and began looking for a fresh start. He would later claim (as usual) that he was led by a divine voice to the ancient city of Byzantium, but surely no prophetic voice was needed to pick the site. Nearly a thousand years old, the Greek colony was perfectly situated halfway between the eastern and western frontiers. Possessing a superb deepwater harbor, the city could control the lucrative trade routes between the Black Sea and the Mediterranean that brought amber and wood from the far north and oil, grain, and spices from the east. Surrounded on three sides by water, its natural defenses were so obvious that the founding fathers of a nearby colony were ridiculed as blind for having failed to recognize the superiority of its splendid acropolis. Most important to Constantine, however, the gentle slopes of Byzantium had witnessed his final victory over Licinius, where he had achieved his life's dream.* There could be no better spot to build an edifice to his greatness.

Trailed by all the courtiers who regularly cling to those in power, Constantine climbed one of Byzantium's hills and cast his eyes over the simple Greek colony that he would transform into the capital of the world. This was to be more than just another imperial city; it was to be the center of Christ's government here on earth, the beating heart of Christendom. He had chosen a site with seven hills to mimic the famous seven hills of Rome, and on this site, unfettered by a pagan past, he would build *Nova Roma*—New Rome—that would refound the empire on a Christian, eastern axis.

There was more than a touch of arrogance to this desire to establish a city in a single lifetime. Rome, after all, wasn't built in a day. But Romulus didn't have the resources of Constantine. The emperor was the master of the civilized world, and he was determined to move heaven and earth to finish his masterpiece. Artisans and resources from the length and breadth of the empire were marshaled for the project, and the city seemed to spring up almost overnight. Slopes once covered by grass soon sported baths and columns, universities and forums, even a magnificent palace and a vast hippodrome. Senators wanting to remain close to the halls of power were tempted east by the excitement of new opportunities, and were loaded with honors and installed in an expansive new Senate House. More than just the rich came, however. Constantinople was a new city as yet unclogged by centuries of tradition and blue blood, and therefore tremendous social mobility was possible. Public grants were made available to the poor who flocked to the Bosporus, and enough free grain was provided to feed more than two hundred thousand inhabitants. Water was provided by public cisterns, multiple harbors supplied fresh fish, and wide avenues led through squares dotted with beautiful sculptures culled from all over the empire.

---

*Constantine's association with the city actually went back to 292, when he had been kept there with his mother, Helena, as a hostage of the eastern emperor, Galerius,

The energy of the city was palpable, but despite its flash and youth, New Rome was born old. The famous serpent column commissioned to celebrate the Greek victory over the Persians in BC 479 was brought from Delphi, an Egyptian obelisk from Karnak was set up in the Hippodrome, and the forum was packed with statues of famous figures from Alexander the Great to Romulus and Remus. They gave the city a feeling of gravitas, rooting it in the familiar traditions of antiquity and (Constantine hoped) providing an unsurpassed prestige. The speed of its completion took the watching world's breath away. Only six years after construction began, the new capital was ready for dedication.

The emperor had already given the people of his new city bread, and now he made sure they would have their circuses as well. Official factions were appointed to oversee the festivities, sponsoring lavish chariot races in the Hippodrome while handing out clothing and money to the spectators.* The assembled populace was treated to an array of events, each more astounding than the last. Graceful gymnasts leaped over wild animals or astonished the crowd by walking along wires suspended high above the ground, bears were goaded into fighting each other, and painted actors delighted with lively pantomimes or bawdy songs. After the displays, the cheering senators and assembled dignitaries who filled the marble seats closest to the track could join citizens from all strata of society in a grand new bathhouse that the emperor unveiled in the central square of the city. The wealthiest, of course, had private baths in their mansions sprawling between the triumphal arches that lined the Mese—the central thoroughfare of the city—but even they couldn't fail to be impressed with the sheer opulence of Constantine's new public buildings.

The city that would become an empire was officially dedicated on May 11, 330, and though Constantine had named it Nova Roma, it

---

*This was the origin of the famous Blue and Green Circus Factions that would soon dominate the Hippodrome and play such a large role in Justinian's reign.

was always known as Constantinople in his honor.* The celebrations were lavish on a scale only the master of the known world could bestow and they culminated with a strange mix of pagan and Christian services. Accompanied by priests and astrologers, the man who had set himself up as the defender of Christianity processed to the center of his forum, stopping before the great column that he had erected in his own honor. The tall structure was surmounted fittingly enough with a golden statue taken from the temple of Apollo and recarved to look like Constantine. Crowned with a halo of seven rays (which, according to rumor, contained the nails used in the Crucifixion), the impressive figure gazed confidently toward the rising sun, dreaming of the glorious future that awaited. At the base of the column, the emperor presided over a solemn ceremony, dedicating the city to God while the most sacred items he could find from both the pagan and Christian past were buried below it. At a moment chosen by his astrologers, the relics were interred in great porphyry drums brought from the Egyptian desert and sunk below the column. There the sacred cloak of Athena, the ax that Noah had used to make the ark, and the baskets from the feeding of the five thousand would lie incongruously together through the centuries.† As far as his soul was concerned, Constantine clearly preferred to hedge his bets.

For the rest of his reign, the emperor tried hard to maintain a political and religious harmony. Under his firm hand, a measure of prosperity returned, but at times his ruthlessness bordered on petulance. Annoyed that his oldest son, Crispus, was wildly popular, Constantine accused him of trying to seduce his stepmother, Fausta. Not bothering to give his son a chance to protest his innocence, the emperor had him executed, then decided to kill Fausta by scalding her to death in her

---

*From 323 until the empire was destroyed more than a thousand years later, the citizens of Constantinople would meet in the Hippodrome every May 11 to commemorate the city's birth.

†Where presumably they still are. In time, the column itself came to be seen as a sort of relic, and each New Year's Day (September 1) the citizens would gather at the base of it and sing hymns.

bath. He had spilled too much blood to unify the empire under his rule to brook any rivals—especially within his own family.

When it came to his dealings with the church, however, this decisiveness was nowhere to be found. Bored by theological speculation, he cared only that Christians were united behind him, and this led to an irritating habit of backing whichever side he thought was in the ascendancy.

The main problem was that a council—even one as prestigious as Nicaea—could establish doctrine, but it couldn't change the minds of the common men and women who made up the body of the church. Arius may have been branded a heretic by a group of bishops, but that did nothing to diminish his effectiveness as a speaker, and he found warm support throughout the East, where people continued to convert to his cause. His Egyptian congregation had been given a new bishop—Athanasius, the fiery champion of the mainstream position—but they continued to prefer Arius's sermons. If Constantine had stood firmly by the decisions of his own Council of Nicaea, all would have been well. With strong leadership from the top, the Arian heresy would have withered away soon enough, but Constantine decided that public opinion had swung behind Arius, so he reversed his position and condemned Athanasius. When the accused man came to Constantinople to plead his case, the emperor was so impressed by his oratory that he reversed the ruling again and condemned Arius. By this time the citizens of Alexandria must have been suffering whiplash from wondering which of the two men was their bishop.

Things only got worse. Arius, doing his level best to ignore the fact that he had been deposed, started his own church, and an embarrassingly large number of Alexandrians soon supported him. Constantine responded by trying to tax them into obedience, announcing that any professed Arian would have much higher rates. This didn't seem to have much effect, and before long the Arian faction at court talked the vacillating emperor into reversing himself once again. Athanasius, in what by now must have been a familiar drill, was deposed and sent into exile. Thanks to Constantine's wavering, the situation was now hopelessly confused and continued to deteriorate even after Arius's rather lurid death.*

Constantine had no patience for the confusing religious problems, and before long his mind started to wander to thoughts of military glory. In his younger days, Christians had flocked to his banner when threatened by Licinius, and perhaps another military campaign would bring the church back into line. Casting about for a suitable opponent, his eye caught Persia, the favorite enemy of Rome. The Persian king Shapur II had just invaded Armenia, and a campaign to conquer and Christianize the fire-worshipping Persians would serve perfectly.

There was no love lost between the two empires, and Shapur II had much to answer for. The dyed skin of a Roman emperor still hung in a Persian temple and captured Roman standards still decorated its walls. The time had come to avenge these insults. Gathering his army, Constantine set out just after Easter in 337, but only made it as far as Helenopolis (modern-day Hersek), the city named after his mother, before he felt too sick to continue. The waters of a nearby thermal spa failed to improve his condition, and by the time he reached the suburbs of Nicomedia, he knew he was dying.

The emperor had always played it safe with religion, postponing his baptism in the belief that a last-minute consecration, with its cleansing of sin, would give him a better chance of entering paradise with a clean slate. Now, feeling his last breath approaching, he threw off the imperial regalia and donned the white robes of a new Christian. Vacillating between the sides of Nicaea to the end, he chose the city's Arian bishop, Eusebius, to perform the baptism. A few days later, on May 22, the first Christian emperor expired.

Even in death, he managed to trumpet his self-importance. He had taken to calling himself the "equal of the apostles"—though he

---

*While walking in the Forum of Constantinople, Arius was suddenly seized with a desire to relieve himself. Squatting down in the dust behind a column, his intestines spilled out, along with his liver and kidneys, killing him almost instantly.

certainly considered himself superior to them—and his burial left no doubt about how he saw himself. In a departure from the usual Roman tradition of cremation, he was laid in a magnificent sarcophagus in the sumptuous Church of the Holy Apostles that he had built in Constantinople. Arrayed around him were twelve empty caskets—one for each disciple—with himself as the Christ figure at the center. It was one last bit of propaganda worthy of the man who had couched his brutal and opportunistic maneuvering as a divinely inspired mission. Despite having murdered his wife and eldest son, he was venerated as a saint—quite an impressive feat for a man who was both deified as a pagan god and baptized by a heretic.

Aside from the unpleasantness of his character, few rulers in history have had such an impact on history. He had found an empire and a religion fractured and hopelessly divided, and bestowed on both an order that would serve them well. His limited understanding of Christianity made the divisions within it much worse, but his adoption of the faith set off a cultural earthquake that began a sweeping and permanent social transformation. In the West, he laid the feudal foundations of medieval Europe by making peasant jobs hereditary, and in the East, the faith he professed would become the binding force of his empire for the next thousand years. In time, the city that he founded would grow to become the great bulwark of Christendom, protecting an underdeveloped Europe from countless Asiatic invasions.

By the time of Constantine's death, the transformation that had started with Diocletian had come to its final fruition, and the old Roman Empire began to pass away. The capital on the Bosporus was founded on a Latin model, its bureaucracy and planning echoing that of Rome, but transplanted on an eastern shore, this New Rome had already begun to change. The Greek, Christian culture around it was beginning to take hold.

3

::

THE PAGAN COUNTERSTROKE

> *Tell the king, on earth has fallen the glorious dwelling, and the water*
> *springs that spoke are quenched and dead. Not a cell is left the god, no*
> *roof, no cover. In his hand the prophet laurel flowers no more.*
> —WILMER C. WRIGHT, *Julian: Volume III*

The empire might have been profoundly transforming itself, but its citizens were oblivious to the change. They had called themselves Roman at the start of Constantine's reign, and they would still be calling themselves Roman 1,123 years later when Constantinople finally fell. On the evening of May 22, 337, they were only aware that Constantine's thirty-one-year reign was over. It had been the longest one since Augustus, and had ushered in sweeping changes. Christianity had struck its first blow against paganism for the soul of the empire, but that war was by no means over.

Despite his formidable reputation as a defender of the faith, the world Constantine left behind wasn't by any means a Christian one. Strictly speaking, the Roman Empire was still officially pagan, and the government continued to pay for the upkeep of temples and priests of the old state religion. Constantine had done nothing more than legalize Christianity, but from the beginning it was clear that the new faith was the wave of the future. There were many in the empire who watched the growing influence of this strange new faith with fear, and writers and historians alike bemoaned the decay of traditional values. The old gods had nourished Rome for a thousand years, and moralists ominously warned that only disaster could come of abandoning them now. The temples were still full, despite the crowded churches, and there were many who prayed for a champion of the old gods who would save the empire from the enervation of the Christians. Only twenty-four years after Constantine's death, that leader arose.

It's one of those quirks of history that the last pagan emperor was a member of the empire's first Christian dynasty. Perhaps not surprisingly, Constantine had put very little thought into who would follow him on the throne. Showing his usual preoccupation with himself, he left detailed instructions about his funeral but didn't bother to address the succession. Each of his three surviving sons (with a distressing lack of originality, all had been given different variations of the name Constantine) assumed that he would become emperor, and the result was an awkward three-way division of the empire. Constantius II, the most able of the boys, took the precaution of killing off anyone with a drop of his father's blood, sparing his cousin Julian only because at five years old the child didn't seem much of a threat.

The massacre may have prevented any further diminution of the brothers' power, but though the empire was large, it wasn't large enough to contain the three monumental egos, and they started fighting almost immediately. Born into the luxury of the palace, they had been raised by an army of attendants, surrounded since birth by the cloying ceremonies of royalty. Educated by swarms of tutors, flattered by the attentions of courtesans, they had little time or opportunity to develop brotherly bonds, and this led to a troubled family dynamic, to say the least. Within three years, the oldest brother had invaded the territory of the youngest, and the empire convulsed once again into a civil war.

While Constantine's sons were busy killing each other, their cousin Flavius Claudius Julianus, better known to posterity as Julian the Apostate, was spending his childhood under virtual house arrest reading the Greek and Roman classics. By temperament a quiet, serious scholar, he was perfectly content to remain in his comfortable exile and showed no aspirations to join his family on the dangerous imperial stage. When he turned nineteen, Julian successfully obtained permission to travel abroad to pursue his studies, and he spent the next four years journeying from Pergamum to Ephesus, sitting at the feet of philosophers and falling under the spell of the vanishing classical world. By the time he reached the famous School of Athens, he had secretly rejected Christianity and converted to a form of paganism called Neoplatonism. Keeping his apostasy carefully hidden under an appearance of piety, he reassured his worried teachers that his faith was as strong as ever, even as he inducted himself into numerous pagan cults.

Julian's youthful travels came to an all-too-abrupt end. Constantius II had outlasted his brothers and united the Roman world under his sole rule, but he found that the empire had too many enemies for one person to face alone. When he had been consolidating power, his family had seemed a threat, to be eliminated or neutralized as quickly as possible. But now that he was established on the throne and the heavy responsibilities of office were weighing him down, blood seemed to be the best chance at loyalty after all. Barbarians were overrunning Gaul and someone had to be sent to stop them, but Constantius II was pinned down dealing with the ever-present threat of Persia. Searching for someone within his own family to send was somewhat embarrassing since he had been instrumental in killing virtually everyone related to him, but there was still one available candidate. Hoping that Julian had learned the virtue of forgiveness during his extensive education, Constantius II summoned his young cousin to Milan.

Julian would have liked to live out his time in quiet study, but an emperor's summons could hardly be ignored. Pausing only long enough to visit the ancient site of Troy, he nervously presented himself before his cousin. The last family member to appear in front of Constantius II had been executed, and after hearing his fate Julian wasn't sure that he had fared any better. Raised to the rank of Caesar, the former scholar was sent to Gaul to restore order on the Rhine frontier. To accomplish this arduous task, he was given only 360 men who (as he dryly put it) "knew only how to pray" and not to fight.*

Julian was hardly an impressive commander himself. Ungainly and somewhat awkward, he had never led anyone in his life and was openly ridiculed by the court. The West was in chaos that daunted even an experienced campaigner like Constantius II, and it would most likely take years to straighten out. No one put much faith in the serious and introverted new Caesar.

Decked out in an uncomfortable military uniform, the former student gathered up his books, and on December 1, 355, he set out on his unlikely mission. Against all expectations, he turned out to be a brilliant general. In five years of campaigning, he pacified the province, liberated twenty thousand Gothic prisoners, expelled the barbarians, and even crossed the Rhine four times to destroy the Alamanni in their own territory. Sending the conquered Germanic king to Constantinople in chains, the victorious junior emperor retired to Paris for the winter.

Such daring exploits were the last thing Constantius II wanted to hear about. Julian had left him as an awkward student, a quiet, non-threatening youth widely mocked by the court, and had somehow transformed himself into a skilled general and administrator, adored by his army and citizens. He had shown no signs of disloyalty, but Constantius II had seen too many pretenders in his time to just sit back and wait until he was betrayed. The sooner this emerging threat was dealt with the better. Claiming to need Julian's money and troops for a campaign against Persia, Constantius II wrote to his cousin demanding that the Caesar levy taxes on Gaul and immediately donate half of his army to the Persian campaign.

Word of the emperor's demands reached Julian in the winter of

---

*True Roman that he was, Julian was also disgusted by the Germanic beer that was consumed in such large quantities by the locals. Referring to the offending brew, he wrote: "I recognize thee not; I know only the son of Zeus [referring to Dionysus, the god of wine]. He smells of nectar, but you smell of goat."

359 and was greeted with horror and disbelief. Many of Julian's soldiers had joined explicitly on the condition that they would never be sent east, and the thought of marching thousands of miles to fight under another banner while their families were exposed to barbarian raids sparked a strange mutiny. Surrounding Julian's palace during the night, his soldiers hailed him as Augustus, and pleaded with him to defy Constantius II.* After claiming to have received a sign from Zeus, Julian at last agreed. Hoisting him up on a shield in the ancient Germanic fashion, the soldiers shouted themselves hoarse, splitting the Roman world once again between two masters.

The world was not to be split for long. Julian's actions obviously meant war, so he dropped the pretense of his Christian faith and sent manifestos to every major city in Greece and Italy declaring his intention to restore paganism. Word of the shocking apostasy sped throughout the West, but it failed to reach Tarsus, where Constantius had fallen seriously ill. Julian had timed his revolt perfectly. Unaware of his cousin's new faith, Constantius magnanimously named Julian as his successor and dismissed his doctors. A few days later, the forty-year-old emperor was dead, and a pagan once more took up the reins of the Roman Empire.

Julian was on the Adriatic coast when he heard of his cousin's death, and he traveled to the capital so fast that a rumor started that his chariot had grown wings. The first emperor to have been born in Constantinople arrived in his native city on December 11 and was greeted with a thunderous welcome. Nearly every inhabitant poured out into the streets and acclaimed Julian, in the words of one eyewitness, "as if he had dropped from heaven."† Senators hurried to

---

*The irony here, of course, is that the soldiers who rebelled at the prospect of being summoned east ended up following Julian to Constantinople and then Persia, a clear example of the respect the emperor commanded in his men.

†Marcellinus Ammianus. W. Hamilton, ed. and trans. *The Later Roman Empire (AD 354–378)* (New York: Penguin Classics, 1986).

congratulate him as jubilant crowds thronged the alleys cheering and clapping. Most of them had only heard rumors of their young emperor, whispered stories of military greatness that had trickled down from the frontiers. Their first glimpse of him striding confidently through the city seemed a vision of Julius Caesar himself, returned to lead the empire to a new golden age.

The view from the throne, however, wasn't quite so rosy. Everywhere he looked that bright December day Julian saw vice, debauchery, and unrestrained decay. The reign of Constantine's sons seemed to have unleashed bribery, gluttony, and every kind of corruption. Imperial offices were bought and sold with alarming ease, and even the army had grown soft and undisciplined. Ostentatious displays of wealth hid the decay under a glittering facade, and extravagance seemed to have replaced governance.

For Julian, true reactionary that he was, the source of his empire's sickness wasn't hard to see.* Augustus had dressed in simple robes and called himself a humble "first citizen." Now emperors went about in silken robes encrusted with jewels, hidden from their people by eunuchs and a cloud of incense. Where once they had conferred with generals to conquer the world, now they spent their time meeting with cooks, planning ever more elaborate culinary delights. Worst of all, they had thrown off the old Roman martial virtues of honor and duty and adopted Christianity with its feminine qualities of forgiveness and gentleness. No wonder emperors and armies alike had grown soft and weak. Marching through the Great Palace of Constantinople, Julian cut a great swath through the clutter, tossing out the cloying attendants and firing hundreds of barbers, cooks, chamberlains, and household servants who had pampered the previous occupants of the throne.

---

*In his attempt to roll back the clock, Julian took to sitting among the senators while they deliberated—as Augustus had done—claiming that even he was not above the law. He had no intention, however, of returning to the more collegial rule of the late republic. In his fanatical quest to destroy Christianity, he was among the most heavy-handed of emperors.

These imperial tics, however, were only the symptoms of imperial decay. The real source of the contagion as far as Julian was concerned was Christianity. Persecution had clearly not worked in the past, and he saw no need for it now. Internal feuds had racked the religion for decades, and all he had to do was to encourage it to destroy itself. Publishing an edict of toleration, he invited all the exiled Christians back to their homes and sat back to watch the Arian and Nicene factions tear each other apart. Paganism, he was sure, was the superior religion, and, given a choice, his people would willingly return to it. After quickly lifting the ban on pagan practices, he crisscrossed the empire, reopening temples and conducting so many sacrifices that his bemused subjects nicknamed him "the Butcher."

It was all to no avail. Paganism was a spent force only dimly half-remembered by its former adherents, and no amount of public prodding would bring it back. Impatiently, Julian decided to turn up the pressure by announcing that pagans were to be preferred over Christians for the appointment of public offices. When this failed to have the desired effect, he made it known that violence against Christians would not be prosecuted. After several bishops had been lynched, the emperor escalated it even further, forbidding Christians from teaching in the empire's schools.

Most of the best philosophers and teachers were by this time Christian, and their disenfranchisement came as a severe blow to Byzantines of every class. Even Julian's friends thought he had gone too far, and his usually flattering biographer, Ammianus Marcellinus, called it "a harsh measure better buried in eternal silence."* But none of these Draconian measures, animal sacrifices, or scolding letters exhorting his pagan subjects to resume their faith seemed to have any effect. Something else was needed.

Constantine had Christianized the empire by winning the battle

---

*Marcellinus Ammianus. W. Hamilton, ed. and trans. *The Later Roman Empire (AD 354–378)* (New York: Penguin Classics, 1986).

of the Milvian Bridge, and Julian thought that he could therefore reverse it with a great victory for paganism. An appropriate enemy was
readily available in the hostile power of Persia, which was even now attacking the cities of the East.* The campaign against them was long
overdue. Julian's famous uncle had wanted to crown his career with a
great victory against Persia, and now Julian would complete that
task—not to vindicate Christianity, but to destroy it.

In the spring of 362, he set off on a tour bound for Antioch, the
glittering metropolis of the East, to plan his campaign. When he
reached the city, its citizens welcomed him with open arms. Used to
the splendor and luxury of the imperial court, they were soon bitterly
disappointed by the austere emperor and his endless censorious
speeches castigating them for their lack of faith. Plummeting popularity and barely muted grumbling, however, had no effect on Julian, and
he continued his attempt to revive paganism. Messengers were sent to
Delphi, with instructions to ask the oracle for a prophecy. Delphi was
the most famous oracle in the Roman world, and its priestess's chew-
ing on laurel leaves and inhaling fumes had been relaying Apollo's
messages for over a thousand years, but the ancient world was gone,
and the answer the oracle gave was the last one ever recorded. "Tell
the king," she said, "on earth has fallen the glorious dwelling, and the
water springs that spoke are quenched and dead. Not a cell is left the
god, no roof, no cover. In his hand the prophet laurel flowers no
more."† It was a fitting epitaph—had he only known it—to Julian's attempt to repaganize the empire.

The emperor, however, stubbornly refused to give up. If paganism wouldn't recover, then Christianity must be crushed. Christ had

---

*The Persians looted their way across the frontier, but were unable to sack the
major Roman city of Nisibis. Thanks to the prayers of a local bishop, an army of
gnats and mosquitoes came to the rescue, biting the trunks of the Persian elephants and driving them mad.

†Wilmer C. Wright, *Julian: Volume III* (Cambridge: Harvard University Press,
2003).

prophesied that the Jewish temple wouldn't be rebuilt until the end times, and in order to disprove this and cast Jesus as a false prophet, he ordered it to be rebuilt. Work started quickly enough, but an earthquake (and, according to Christian sources, "great balls of fire") shattered the foundations, forcing the terrified overseers to abandon the project. Tempers were rising daily, and in Antioch the mood had become dangerously seditious. Matters weren't improved when the emperor paid a visit to inspect the city's famous temple of Apollo. Disgusted to learn that a Christian martyr had been buried within its precincts, Julian tactlessly ordered the body exhumed immediately. Outraged riots swept the city, and order was only restored when he forcibly arrested and executed several Christian agitators. A few weeks later, a pagan worshipper left candles burning unattended in the temple, and the entire structure caught fire and burned to the ground.

Blaming the conflagration on the city's Christian population, Julian closed their cathedral and confiscated their gold plate, using it to pay the soldiers he was gathering. By this point, the city was on the brink of revolt, and he was even losing the support of his pagan subjects. Mocked openly in the streets for his beard and his anti-Christian measures, every day seemed to bring both sides closer to the breaking point.* Finally, in March 363, Julian's great army was ready, and to everyone's immense relief he gave the order to march east.

The campaign against Persia had all the markings of a tragedy even before it began. The idealistic young emperor was determined to find the glory that would refurbish the tattered standard of his religion in a vain and unnecessary war, regardless of the cost. Nothing

---

*Constantine and his sons had set recent imperial style by remaining clean-shaven, but Julian, perhaps in homage to the philosopher-emperor Marcus Aurelius, proudly wore one. He passed his time in Antioch writing two books: *Misopogon* and *Against the Galileans.* The first, translated as "Beard Hater," was a withering attack on the people of Antioch, while the second was a scathing critique of Christianity.

seemed to go right, but Julian stubbornly pressed on. The Persians offered little resistance, doing their best to keep out of the way of the superior Byzantine force, but the locals diverted rivers to flood the army's path, and it was high summer before Julian reached the Persian capital of Ctesiphon. Julian's Gaulish troops were unused to the heat, and Ctesiphon's high walls couldn't be taken without a long siege. With the burning sun beating down on them, constant harrying attacks, and rumors of a large Persian army approaching, Julian was reluctantly persuaded to abandon the attempt.

For ten days, the army stumbled back, suffering incessant skirmishes as their enemies became increasingly bold. Then, on the morning of June 26, the Persians suddenly attacked. Showing his customary bravery, Julian leaped out of his tent and went crashing into the thick of the fray without pausing to fully strap on his armor. There, in the chaos of the battle, he was struck in the side with a spear. His men rushed to him, lifting him up from where he had collapsed in the dust. The spear was quickly pulled out, releasing a gush of blood, and he was carried back to his tent. The wound was washed with wine, but the tip had pierced his liver, and Julian knew it was fatal. There in his tent, with the sounds of battle already receding, he closed his eyes and stopped fighting. Scooping up a handful of his blood, he threw it towards the sun and, according to legend, died with the words *"Vicisti Galilaee"** on his lips.

The words were wiser than the dying emperor meant them to be. The old religion was disorganized and decentralized, a fashionable relic for the cultural elite. It couldn't compete with the personal revelation of Christianity for the hearts and minds of the masses, and its complex jumble of gods and rituals ensured that it was too divided for its partisans to cohesively unite behind it. Even had he lived, Julian wouldn't have been able to change that—the old world that he had

---

*"Thou hast conquered, Galilean"—a reference to the triumph of Christianity.

fallen in love with in his youth was irretrievably gone. Hopelessly romantic and frustratingly stubborn, the emperor had squandered his energy and imagination foolishly trying to revive a moribund religion at the expense of the one that would define the empire for the next thousand years. Rome and its polytheistic days belonged firmly in the past, and even Julian's pagan subjects seemed bewildered by his numerous sacrifices. As one of them dryly put it, "Perhaps it was better that he died, had he come back from the east there would soon have been a scarcity of cattle."*

His body was brought, ironically enough, to Tarsus, the birthplace of Saint Paul, and the last pagan emperor was laid to rest with all his immense promise unfulfilled. At his death, the Constantinian line came to an end, and the gods of Mount Olympus were consigned to decorative mosaics and whimsical scenes on palace floors to amuse bored emperors.

The vast pagan literature of the classical world, however, didn't pass away. It was too deeply ingrained in Roman culture, too entwined with intellectual thought, to be so lightly cast off. The future was with Christianity, but no one who considered him- or herself Roman could completely reject the classical world. Unlike their western counterparts, early Byzantine church fathers recognized the benefits of pagan philosophy, arguing that it contained valuable insights and that careful reading would separate the wheat of moral lessons from the chaff of pagan religion.† Byzantine universities, from Constantinople to the famous Academy of Athens, would preserve and cultivate classical writing throughout the empire's history, and even the Patriarchal Academy in Constantinople taught a curriculum that included study

---

*Ammianus Marcellinus. *The Later Roman Empire (AD 354–378)*, W. Hamilton, ed. and trans. (New York: Penguin Classics, 1986), p. 298.
†The most famous example of this was the fourth-century father Saint Basil of Caesarea, who wrote a treatise entitled *To Young Men, on How They Might Derive Profit from Pagan Literature*.

of the literature, philosophy, and scientific texts of antiquity. This sharply contrasted with the West, where waves of barbarian invasions would shatter civilization and break the bonds with the classical past. In thought and in power, the future was with the East; from now on the world would be ruled from Byzantium.

4

BARBARIANS AND CHRISTIANS

Of all the problems that faced the Roman Empire at the end of the fourth century, none was more serious than the barbarian threat. Ever since the days of Augustus, Roman armies had learned to be wary of the dark German forests and blood-curdling cries across the frozen Rhine. For nearly three hundred years, the barbarians had remained just beyond the borders of the empire, occasionally making raids across the frontier, but for the most part were restrained by their ever-shifting alliances and fear of Roman arms. By the time of Julian the Apostate's death, however, all that had begun to change. From the east came a new and terrifying power, wild Huns so barbaric that the frightened Germanic tribes ignored the decaying imperial forces guarding the frontiers and came flooding across. This time, however, they came as settlers, not invaders, and the prize they sought was land, not gold. The influx of new people, unwilling to assimilate, provoked an identity crisis within the Roman world and stretched the creaking empire to its breaking point. The pressure would redefine what it meant to be a Roman and nearly bring down the classical world.

The particular genius of Rome had always been in its conception of citizenship, a fact made more extraordinary since it came of age in a world which more often than not restricted citizenship to individual cities. Fifth-century Greece, which had so dazzled the Mediterranean with its brilliance, remained at its heart a patchwork collection of city-states, and for all its glory could never quite transform a Spartan into an Athenian or an Athenian into a Spartan. Locked firmly behind their walls, the cities were unable to refresh themselves, and after a few remarkable generations the luster all too quickly burned itself out. The Romans, on the other hand, had expanded the concept beyond the narrow confines of a single city, spreading citizenship in the wake of its legions. Athens in all its splendid exclusivity had remained just a city; Rome had embraced the world.

Yet for all the empire's inclusiveness, the Romans tended to look down their noses at the peoples just beyond their borders. Those outside of the Roman orbit lacked citizenship and were therefore barbarians, uncivilized regardless of their cultural achievements. Of course, the astute among them realized that their own ancestors had once been considered as barbaric as the tribes beyond the Rhine and were perfectly aware that a few centuries in the imperial melting pot had made Romans of them all. The most recent flood of newcomers, however, seemed different. The empire had always been able to absorb new people into its expanding body, and the immigrants had proved more often than not to be a source of strength, but times had changed. The empire was now on the defensive, and the Germanic peoples crossing its borders wanted its land, not its culture. They were coming on their own terms, unwilling to be absorbed, speaking their own languages, and retaining their distinct cultures. The influx of new blood was no longer the source of strength it had always been. For many of those watching the traditions of millennia getting swept away, the strangers seemed like a frightening wave threatening to overwhelm the empire.

It would have been difficult at the best of times to absorb the sheer volume of newcomers, but, unfortunately for the empire, this massive wave of immigration came at a time when remarkably shortsighted rulers sat on the imperial throne. There had been a depressing decrease in quality ever since Julian's death. His immediate successor had left a brazier burning in his tent one night and suffocated only eight months into his reign, and this left the throne to a pair of rather boorish brothers named Valentinian and Valens, who split the empire between them and tried to shore up the crumbling frontiers. Valentinian, the older of the two, managed to keep the West together for eleven years, while at the same time maintaining a restraining influence on the brash young Valens, but he could never control his own temper and suffered a fatal aneurysm in the midst of a characteristic rant. His sixteen-year-old son, Gratian, inherited the throne but was too young to assert himself, and this left the mercurial Valens as the driving force behind imperial policy.

With the Roman stage conspicuously empty of statesmen, the Visigoths and Ostrogoths asked permission to settle in Roman territory. They had left the frozen lands of Germany and Scandinavia behind and had come in search of new lands, something the fertile Eastern Empire seemed to have in abundance. They promised to provide troops in exchange for land, and the emperor obligingly agreed, allowing two hundred thousand Goths to cross into imperial territory and lumber toward their new homes in Thrace.

In theory, Valens's plan to bolster the depleted imperial army with Germanic troops and at the same time repopulate devastated lands was an excellent idea, but it was doomed from the start. There was no way that the eastern government could handle such a staggering influx of immigrants, and Valens hardly even bothered to try. Shipments of food promised to the Goths arrived rotten or of such low quality as to be barely edible. Local merchants fleeced the starving newcomers, and several magistrates even started kidnapping them and selling them into slavery. Provoked beyond endurance, the Goths erupted in revolt.

Valens, whose shortsighted policies had largely been responsible for the debacle in the first place, wrote to his nephew Gratian to plan a joint campaign and set off in August 378 along the Via Egnatia with an army forty thousand strong, determined to teach the newcomers a lesson. As he approached the Gothic camp near Adrianople, he got an erroneous report that the Goths numbered only ten thousand, and he decided to attack at once without checking to see if the report was true. Throwing caution to the wind in his desire to prevent Gratian from sharing in the glory of vanquishing the Goths, he plunged forward with the entire army. It was a disastrous mistake. The day was unseasonably hot, and the Romans were parched, exhausted from their long march, and in no condition to fight. The Ostrogothic cavalry mercilessly swept down on them, easily splitting their ranks and cutting off all hope of escape. By the time the carnage ended, Valens, two-thirds of his army, and the myth of Roman invincibility lay trampled under the blood-soaked Gothic hooves.

It was the worst military disaster in four centuries, and it opened the floodgates of invasion to every barbarian tribe on the frontier. The eastern government was brought to its knees, its armies shattered and its emperor dead. Unafraid of Roman arms, the Goths rampaged through the East, attacking its major cities and even threatening Constantinople itself. Terrified peasants fled from their farms at the approaching hordes, watching from the hills as the horrifying foreigners destroyed their homes, sending a lifetime of work up in flames. Civilians huddled behind the walls of their cities and prayed for deliverance, but the imperial government was listless in the wake of Valens's death. If a savior didn't arrive soon, the mighty Roman Empire seemed destined to dissolve under the strain.

Desperate situations have a way of thrusting greatness upon seemingly ordinary people, and in its hour of need, a retired general arrived to save the empire. His name was Theodosius, and though he was only in his early thirties, he already possessed a formidable military education. Born in Spain to an army family, as a youth he had cut his teeth putting down rebellions in Britain and campaigning on the lower Danube. By the time of the disaster of Adrianople, the empire could boast no finer general, and the western emperor, Gratian, raised him to the rank of emperor, charging him with restoring order to the eastern half of the empire.

The task was nearly impossible, and there was no shortage of people telling him so, but Theodosius threw himself into the job with a refreshing sense of energy and purpose. To replace the nearly twenty thousand veterans who had been lost, he started a massive recruitment drive, pressing every able-bodied man into service—even those who had mutilated themselves in hopes of escaping. When this still failed to produce enough men, the emperor resorted to the dangerous precedent of enlisting Gothic renegades, swelling his ranks with barbarian troops. The gamble worked, and in 382, after a long and bitter struggle, Theodosius forced the Goths to sign a peace treaty with the Roman Empire. Confirming the previous arrangement, Theodosius allowed the Goths to settle on Roman land in exchange for contributing twenty thousand men to the imperial army. This continued the dubious precedent of letting a sovereign nation settle inside the empire's frontiers, but Theodosius could congratulate himself on having staved off the collapse of the East, as well as having solved his manpower needs all in one blow. A few voices were predictably raised, objecting to the "barbarization" of the military, wondering aloud if absorbing such a strong Germanic element into the army didn't create more of a threat than it replaced, but they were easily ignored in the face of political realities. After all, immigration had always been a source of strength to the empire, and some of its greatest emperors had been from territories as diverse as Africa and Britain. Even Theodosius's native Spain had once been called barbaric, and it was now just as Roman as Augustan Italy.

Such were the things that men said to comfort themselves, but these barbarians had no reason to become Roman and never would. The Goths who joined the imperial army served under their own commanders, spoke their own language, and maintained their own customs. They had no reason to blend in and so failed to become Romanized, remaining a semiautonomous group within the borders of the empire. Within a generation, they would completely dominate the government and push Europe toward the terrible chaos of the Dark Ages. Though he had no way of knowing it at the time, Theodosius had signed the death warrant of the Roman West.

Barbarian pressure wasn't the only thing transforming the classical empire into medieval Europe. In addition to the Gothic treaty, the year 382 saw the beginning of the final triumph of Christianity within the empire. It started, remarkably enough, with a terrible sickness. Traveling to Thessalonica, Theodosius fell so seriously ill that his ministers despaired of his life. Like all the Christian emperors, he had delayed his baptism, hoping to wipe away his sins at the last moment and enter the judgment hall with a clean slate. The local bishop was summoned, and in a hasty ceremony he baptized the dying emperor. To the great astonishment of his attendants, the emperor made a full recovery, and by the time he reached Constantinople, he was a profoundly changed man. As an unbaptized Christian, Theodosius could afford to ignore his conscience, since he could count on his eventual baptism to wash away whatever foul deeds he had committed. Now that he was a full communicant member of the church, however, he had placed himself beneath the spiritual authority of the bishops. No longer could he cavalierly order the execution of innocents or ignore the heresy that was ripping the church apart. It was his sacred duty to restore both temporal and spiritual peace. To ignore either one would put his soul at risk.

Nearly every emperor after Constantine—even Julian, in his own way—had been a supporter of the Arian heresy, and this imperial patronage had kept the rift in Christianity alive and well. Determined to put an end to it once and for all, Theodosius summoned a great council of the church to meet at Constantinople and offer an explicit condemnation of Arianism. After some deliberation, the bishops did so, giving a ringing endorsement of the Nicene Creed, and giving Theodosius official sanction to move against the heresy. The emperor acted with all the firmness that Constantine had never shown. Arians were compelled to surrender their churches, and without imperial support their congregations quickly disappeared. Within the empire, only the Goths remained stubbornly Arian, but although they soon came to dominate the West, they never made a serious attempt to convert their Christian subjects. After a disastrous sixty years of infighting, the Arian controversy was at last over.

Having put the church in order, Theodosius was soon convinced to move against the dying embers of paganism. Though it had deep roots throughout the empire, for most citizens, paganism had long since been reduced to a collection of venerable traditions without any significant religious meaning. But since the temples were public property, they continued to be maintained at the public's expense, and the awkward fact of Christian emperors funding pagan rituals horrified the emperor's fiery religious adviser, Bishop Ambrose of Milan.

This wasn't the first time the bishop had attempted to enlist imperial support in stamping out the last traces of the ancient religion. A few years before, the bishop had convinced the emperor Gratian that it was embarrassing for a Christian emperor to be carrying around the title *Pontifex Maximus*—chief priest of the state religion—prompting Gratian to go striding into the Senate House of Rome and publicly declare that he was renouncing the title.* Unfortunately for Ambrose, Gratian was killed soon after, and the provoked senators tried to revive their religion by putting a pagan on the throne. Theodosius quickly overthrew the man, uniting the empire under his leadership, but the episode convinced the bishop that paganism was a dangerous force that had to be actively destroyed. For the moment, the rather mild Theodosius ignored his thundering sermons, but a clash between the two was inevitable.

It was set off when one of Theodosius's generals was lynched during an uprising in Thessalonica, and to punish the city, the furious emperor trapped seven thousand citizens in its hippodrome and slaughtered them. When he heard the news, Ambrose was mortified and marched into the palace to tell Theodosius that no matter what the provocation, a Christian emperor didn't go about killing innocent civilians. When Theodosius ignored him, feeling fully justified in

---

*Although Gratian was the last emperor to use the title *Pontifex Maximus*, it didn't disappear into the mists of history. In 590, Pope Gregory I adopted it in his role as "chief priest of Christianity," and from it we get the title "pontiff." Literally, it is translated as "bridge builder," because the *Pontifex Maximus* bridged the gap between the world of the gods and the world of man. Constantine had kept the title because he saw himself as the "Bishop of Bishops"—a title that the pope also assumed.

enforcing his authority, Ambrose turned up the pressure by denying him communion or entrance to a church until he performed penance. After several months of endangering his soul without the sacrament, Theodosius caved in. Dressing in sackcloth and sprinkling ashes over his head, he publicly apologized and submitted to the bishop. Unlike the absolute authority of Diocletian's pagan rule, it appeared as if there were limits to what a Christian emperor could do—even one appointed by God. In the first great contest between church and state, the church had emerged victorious.*

Theodosius was appropriately chastened, and he began to take a harder line against the last vestiges of paganism. The Olympic Games, held in honor of the gods for the last thousand years, were canceled, and the Delphic Oracle was officially suppressed. In the Forum of Rome, the eternal fire in the Temple of Vesta was snuffed out, and the vestal virgins were disbanded, provoking outraged citizens to warn of terrible repercussions and divine retribution. For the most part, however, such protests were rare. Though it would cling to some semblance of life for the better part of a century, paganism was clearly moribund.† Christianity had triumphed, and the coup de grâce came in 391, when Theodosius made it the only religion of the Roman Empire.

Despite the historical importance of his actions, Theodosius was in no way a revolutionary. By making Christianity the state religion, he had merely put the finishing touches on a movement that had begun at the Milvian Bridge. Christianity had become so entwined with the Roman way of life that for barbarians and Romans alike, to be a

---

*Seven hundred years later, Pope Gregory VII would famously repeat the clash with Henry IV of Germany. Once again, the result was the same. Henry trudged humbly through the snow—barefoot—to offer his submission.

†The pagan temples on the acropolis of Constantinople survived until the beginning of the sixth century, and other practices continued even longer. As late as 692, the church found it necessary to forbid peasants from invoking the name of Dionysus while pressing grapes or from using bears (or other animals) to predict the future.

Christian and to be a Roman were essentially the same thing. Christian theologians adopted the intellectual traditions of the classical past and made them their own. Clement of Alexandria described the church as emerging from the two rivers of biblical faith and Greek philosophy, and Tertullian quipped, *"Seneca saepe noster"*—"Seneca is often one of us."

Even the ceremonies of the church and the court had begun to mirror each other. Priests and courtiers dressed in luxurious vestments, elaborate processionals and singing choirs heralded the beginning of services, and incense and candles were carried as a sign of honor. Where the court had its emperor, the church had its bishops, and both were accorded the same outward signs of respect. There was a comforting sameness to it all, a familiarity that reassured each celebrant of the divine order. Even the imperial propaganda reflected the theme. In the Hippodrome, Theodosius set up an obelisk, carving the base with images of himself flanked by his subordinates much in the same way Christ had been depicted with his disciples. Every citizen, from the most erudite to the illiterate, could clearly see that the heavenly kingdom was mirrored here on earth.

There were no doubts in the Roman mind that the divine was smiling on their empire. Even the economy had been improving for nearly a century. Relative political stability had allowed fortunes to once again be amassed. Traders carried their wares unmolested along the great land routes, and ships once again safely plied the waters of the Mediterranean. Farmers could bring their produce to the great urban centers and find revitalized markets awaiting them. The Roman Empire might not be as prosperous as it once had been, but its citizens could still dream that the golden days of the past could yet return.

There were, however, troubling signs on the horizon. Most of the money from taxes had been drawn from the nobility, and these families were exhausted. As more and more of them fled their burdens by joining the clergy or embracing the monastic life in the deserts of Egypt or Asia Minor, the government responded by leaning more heavily on the poor and working classes. Successive governments would raise taxes and try to bind peasants to the land, arguing that this was necessary to keep society running smoothly, but the end result for many was grinding poverty. The West in particular suffered from the exactions, and though the East had always been richer, it now almost seemed as if they were two different worlds. How long, astute citizens wondered, would it be before the distance between Rome and Constantinople was too great to be bridged?

5

A Dreadful Rumor from the West . . .

Theodosius had been strong enough to control the Germanic elements in the empire, but those who succeeded him were not, and barbarians soon dominated virtually every level of government. Even the army was unrecognizable; the traditional Roman infantry had given way to barbarian cavalry, and the orderly legions were now a strange, heterogeneous mix with each group sporting different armor and speaking a different language. Emperors were dutifully crowned in the East and the West, but the men who commanded the unwieldy armies held the real power. A series of petty, barbarian strongmen rose to prominence in Constantinople, appointing puppet emperors and squandering any chance to revive imperial power in their desire to maintain control. Ignoring the enemies pouring over the frontiers, the foolish rulers of Constantinople looked with fear and loathing at the brilliant half-Vandal general named Stilicho, serving under the weak emperor Honorius, who was now the master of Rome. To the detriment of the entire Roman world, they insisted on seeing him as their true enemy.

It was fortunate that the West had Stilicho, for it was now fighting for its life. The winter of 406 was the coldest in living memory, and far to the north of Rome, the Rhine River froze completely over. Germanic barbarians, hungering for the warmth and riches of the Mediterranean, came streaming across the porous frontiers and had soon overrun Gaul and pushed into Spain. Stilicho raced from North Africa to the Rhine, putting down revolts and fighting off invasions along the way. Twice he came to the East's defense by driving away the Goths, and twice he was labeled a public enemy for his trouble. If the two halves of the empire had been able to put aside their differences and maintain a united front against the threats confronting them, they could perhaps have pushed back the Dark Ages for a few centuries, but the East was consumed by petty squabbles and was more fearful of the powerful Stilicho than the barbarian threat. When a new Visigothic king named Alaric united the Goths and went rampaging through the East, suspicions between the two governments were so bad that instead of fighting Alaric, Constantinople encouraged him to invade Italy.

Stilicho was strong enough to shield the West from the Goths, but for all his military brilliance, he made for a lousy politician. For years, he had ignored the treacherous court at Ravenna and the poisonous intrigue at Rome, too busy off fighting for the empire, and in any case trusting that his obvious service to the state would see him through. The Senate, however, composed as it was of illustrious names who held little real power, despised the general and deeply resented the fact that a half-barbarian upstart held power over them. Ever since Stilicho had destroyed the Sibylline Books, the conservative, pagan senators had hated him with frightening intensity.* When the general appeared before them and asked them to come up with the four thousand pounds of gold needed to buy off the Visigothic threat, they erupted in outrage.

It wasn't surprising that Stilicho had decided to bribe Alaric instead of going to war against him. The general had been fighting a

---

*The Sibylline Books were a collection of prophetic verse bought by the legendary last king of Rome, Tarquin the Proud. Though the originals were destroyed in a fire in the first century BC, replicas were kept in a vault beneath the temple of Apollo on the Palatine. At great moments of crisis the senate would consult them to determine what religious observances were needed to avert catastrophe.

desperate battle to maintain the West's integrity for years, but his exhausted, underpaid army couldn't be everywhere at once. With his overcommitted troops stretched to the limit, paying off the Visigoths was the only sensible solution, but to the senators sitting safe in Rome this seemed like an unnecessary humiliation.* In such a charged atmosphere, it was easy for one of them to convince the weak emperor Honorius that Stilicho had betrayed Rome's glorious prestige with his shameful request and must be executed. Guards were quickly sent to arrest him, escorting the stunned general out of the church service he was attending, and killing him safely out of the sight of his troops.

The Senate didn't have long to relish its spiteful triumph. With the great champion of the West gone, Italy was defenseless before the terrible Goths. After crossing the Alps in a matter of months, the gleeful Alaric drew up his army before the gates of the empire's ancient capital. The citizens of Rome refused to believe the evidence of their eyes, trusting in the formidable reputation of the city that had ruled the world. Defiantly, they promised the Goths that each citizen would fight to the death before a single barbarian crossed the threshold. Alaric simply laughed at their bluster, murmuring "The thicker the hay, the easier to mow." He threw his army at the walls, and in late August of 410 the unthinkable happened. For the first time in eight hundred years, an invading army entered Rome.

The Senate had only itself to blame as it watched the Goths climbing over the seven hills. For three days, the barbarians sacked the Eternal City, even breaking into the mausoleum of Augustus and scattering the imperial ashes. As these things generally went, the pillaging was not especially brutal, but it had a profound impact that sped out in shock waves to every corner of the empire. Saint Jerome, writing from Bethlehem, put into words the surreal horror that everyone felt: "A dreadful rumor has come from the West. . . . My voice sticks in my

---

*One of them is said to have remarked, *"Non est ista pax sed pactio servitutis"*—"That is no peace, but a mere selling of yourselves into slavery."

throat. . . . The City which had taken the whole world was itself taken."*

The shock of seeing this supposedly inviolate city at the mercy of barbarians hopelessly shattered the western view of the empire as a divinely ordered state. Here was the first great crack in worldviews between the East and the West. Safe in Constantinople, the East eventually would recover from the trauma and regain its faith in the universal and divine claims of the empire. In the West, however, such beliefs were no longer possible. Rome was revealed to be merely a mortal creation, and no government or state this side of paradise could truly claim to be divinely ordained. Christians were not citizens, but rather pilgrims traveling through a world that was not their home, and any empire—whether based in Rome or Constantinople—was only transitory. Such divergent beliefs at first seemed almost insignificant, but they would soon grow into a great cultural divide that would split the old empire more thoroughly than any barbarian army could have.

The Romans could take some grim satisfaction from the fact that Alaric didn't enjoy his triumph for long. A few months after his victory, the barbarian king expired of a fever, but the damage to the imperial reputation had already been done.† The legions were powerless, and no city seemed safe from the waves of barbarism engulfing the empire. The eastern emperor Theodosius II was so alarmed that he immediately ordered huge new walls built around Constantinople. Rising forty feet high and nearly sixteen feet thick, these powerful defenses of stone and brick would throw back every hopeful invader for the next thousand years. The sack of Rome may have deeply scarred the Roman psyche, but it had also created the most impressive defen-

---

*Charles Christopher Mierow, *The Letters of St. Jerome* (Westminster: Newman Press, 1963).

†He was buried with his loot in the bed of a river that had been diverted for that purpose. When the body had been interred, those who dug the grave were killed and the river was allowed to resume its course, forever hiding the resting place of the conqueror of Rome.

sive fortifications ever built in the ancient or medieval worlds. The empire would seldom know peace in the long years to come, but at least the defenses of its capital city would be secure.

The West had no such luxury. Honorius had fled the moment the Goths were spotted, and with the weakness of Rome revealed, he officially moved the capital to the more defensible Ravenna. But even in a new city, the western emperor was powerless to stop the decay and could only watch as the provinces fell away. The Visigoths and Franks overran Gaul, Spain flared up in revolt, and Saxon invaders swarmed into Britain. The anxious British wrote to Honorius begging for help, but the answer they received made it all too clear that the imperium was failing in the West. "Look after your own fates," the emperor advised.* He could hardly do otherwise; the imperial armies were everywhere on the retreat, and Britain was abandoned to its long and futile fight against the Saxons.† Rome still had the wealth of North Africa, but by the time Honorius finally expired of edema of the lungs in 423, the Vandals had wrested most of it from his control.

The eastern government did what it could to help its dying counterpart, but it had its own problems with a terrifying new enemy. Descending from the central Asian steppe in a wild, undisciplined horde, the Huns came crashing into imperial territory, destroying everything in their path and spreading terror and death wherever they went. Unlike the other peoples the empire dismissively called uncivilized, the Huns were barbarians in every sense of the word. Wearing tunics sewn from the skin of field mice, they never bathed or changed clothes, slept on their horses under the open stars, and ate their food raw. To the people of the empire, this wild, screaming horde seemed

---

*Such advice was typical of the rather pathetic Honorius. When informed that Rome had fallen, he thought at first that something had happened to his pet rooster Roma and was relieved to find that it was *only* the city that had been sacked.

†The invading Saxon horde eventually extinguished classical civilization in Britain, but before it did, a Romanized British leader made a last stand to hold the darkness at bay. He failed, but the attempt inspired the legend of King Arthur.

like some kind of awful divine punishment, and their terrible leader, Attila, was known throughout Europe as "The Scourge of God."

Brushing aside the frantic imperial armies sent against him, Attila sacked every major city from the Black Sea to the Propontis and extracted humiliating treaties from Constantinople that allowed him to cross the border at will. With the government completely cowed and promising him two thousand pounds of gold per year to maintain his good graces, Attila seemed content to leave the empire in peace, but a few months later the entire Roman world learned the frightening news that the Huns were on the march again. This time, however, the Romans only had themselves to blame. In order to escape a forced marriage to an unpleasant Roman senator, the emperor's sister Honoria had foolishly sent a letter—along with a ring—to Attila asking him for help. Whether or not she was asking for marriage, the great khan chose to interpret it as a proposal and informed the terrified emperor that he was coming "to claim what was rightfully his."

Crossing into Gaul, Attila unleashed his horde, while the frightened Roman army scattered, and its commanders looked on helplessly.* There was nothing now that could spare the empire's ancient capital, and the panicked city watched the horizon and prayed that Attila would turn away. The long absence of emperors from Rome had left a power vacuum, and with no secular leaders rising to the occasion, more and more of these temporal responsibilities had been filled by the only real leader left in the city—the pope. When Attila arrived, there were no glittering troops or majestic emperors to shield the city from his fury, just the lonely figure of Pope Leo who trudged out on foot to meet him. There, in the dust of an army camp, the pontiff—armed only with his intellect—met with the barbarian to try to turn the long-expected blow aside.

---

*The citizens of the little town of Aquileia fled at Attila's approach to the safety of the nearby lagoon. Recognizing the superb defensive position it offered, they elected to stay put, laying the foundations of what would become the mighty Republic of Venice. Its oldest island, Torcello, still has a crude stone chair dubbed by the locals "Attila's throne."

There is no record of their conversation, but whatever Leo said, Attila turned his soldiers around and left Italy, leaving the city of Romulus unexpectedly intact.* He stopped long enough to add another child bride to his harem and spent the night feasting and drinking heavily. When he failed to appear the next morning, his warriors broke into his bedroom and found him dead. During the night, an artery had burst and the Scourge of God had expired from a glorified nosebleed. Singing songs to the "terror of the world," his men buried him in three coffins—one of gold, one of silver, and the last one of iron. Howling with grief, they tore their clothes and gashed their faces, all to the glory of the man before whom kings and emperors had groveled. Far away in Constantinople, the emperor dreamed of a broken bow and knew the mighty Attila was dead. The empire could breathe again.

---

*Attila was known to be extremely superstitious. Perhaps the crafty Leo simply pointed out that the conquest of Rome had proved quite lethal to the last man (Alaric) who had attempted it.

6

::

THE FALL OF ROME

The death of their great enemy sent the Roman world into wild jubilation, but it did nothing to alleviate the true danger. Valens had let them inside the frontiers, Theodosius had allowed them to stay, and now the barbarians had turned both of Theodosius's sons into puppet emperors. For the moment, the barbarians were content to stay behind the throne, but how long before they decided to rule on their own? If the emperors didn't break free soon, the empire would dissolve from within into petty barbarian kingdoms.

The western emperor Valentinian III attempted to escape first. Flushed with excitement in the wake of the Hun's departure, he rashly decided to assassinate his barbarian master, Flavius Aetius. He carried out the deed personally, naively assuming that his freedom could be purchased with a simple thrust of the sword. The barbarian yoke, however, couldn't be thrown off so easily. The death of one man didn't diminish the barbarian influence, and Valentinian hadn't done anything to inspire his citizens' loyalty. Early the next year, two of Aetius's men angrily cut the emperor down in broad daylight while the imperial bodyguard just watched impassively.

The assassination threw Rome into an uproar, and, in the chaos, Valentinian's widow made the terrible decision to appeal to the Vandals for help. Only too happy to come swooping down on the beleaguered city, the barbarians immediately appeared with a large army and demanded that the gates be opened. For the third time in four decades, the old capital was at the mercy of its enemies, and though

Pope Leo once again trudged out to plead for mercy, this time he was in a far weaker position. As Arian Christians, the Vandals didn't have the faintest intention of listening to a pope, but, after an extended negotiation, they did agree to spare the lives of the inhabitants. For two weeks, they sacked the city, methodically stripping everything of value that they could find, even the copper from the temple roofs.* When there was nothing left, they departed from the shattered city with their loot, carrying off the empress and her daughters for good measure, to their North African capital of Carthage.†

After the reverses of the past few years, this most recent sack of the city wasn't quite as shocking as the first, but it did convince the watching eastern court of the dangers of trying to shake off their barbarian masters. It was a lesson that Aspar, the Sarmatian general who currently had Constantinople securely under his thumb, hoped his courtiers had learned well.‡

Aspar's Arian religion had made him far too unpopular to seize the throne himself, but he'd found a tame proxy in the person of a rather bland, safely Christian lieutenant named Leo. The general had simply had him crowned and settled down to rule the empire from his perch behind the throne.§

Leo was the perfect choice for a puppet. Somewhat "elderly" at fifty-six, he was a deferential, undistinguished man with two daughters, but he had no son to follow him on the throne. His reign would most likely be short, and with no pesky heirs to challenge the general, he would serve as the perfect conduit for Aspar's power. The

---

*In our word "vandal," we can distantly hear the horror of the Roman world at the thoroughness of this sack.

†The Roman population didn't reach its imperial peak again until the twentieth century.

‡The Sarmatians were an Iranian seminomadic group that eventually settled in modern Georgia in an area called Ossetia.

§Leo was the first emperor to be crowned by the patriarch, infusing Christian elements into the coronation ceremony. Fifteen centuries later, this basic service is still in use.

barbarian general was well connected, with a long career of service to the empire, a glittering reputation, and personal control over half the army. Even had Leo wanted to, there seemed little chance that with only a worthless title, the emperor could pose a threat to the general's authority.

Confident in his own security, Aspar failed to realize that he had dangerously miscalculated. Leo had both the ability and, more important, the *will* to lead, and he didn't intend to remain a figurehead for long. The new emperor wasn't rash enough to move against his master at once. Assassinating Aspar—even if it were possible—would only accomplish his own early death, and in any case, where one overlord was cut down, another would inevitably rise to take his place. What Leo needed was a permanent solution to be rid of barbarian masters forever, and for that he had to strike at the true source of Aspar's power—his control of the army.

Looking around for a military counterbalance to his overpowerful general, Leo found a perfect candidate in a man named Tarasicodissa. He was the leader of a tough mountain people from southern Asia Minor called the Isaurians, and since he wasn't a native of the capital, he depended completely on the emperor for advancement. Traveling with a small group of men to the capital, Tarasicodissa managed to find evidence of treason by Aspar's son, providing the emperor a perfect opportunity to publicly scold his barbarian master. Tarasicodissa was rewarded with both the hand of Leo's daughter and a post equal to Aspar's. The suddenly respectable Isaurian mercifully Hellenized his name to the more acceptable Zeno and soon became the darling of Constantinople's polite society.

With Aspar humiliated and on the defensive, Leo was temporarily free to direct imperial policy on his own. Realizing that the western half of the empire was on the verge of collapse, he launched an ambitious plan to aid it by conquering the Vandal kingdom of North Africa. Returning the province to the Western Empire would go a long way toward restoring both its solvency and its prestige, and, more important, it would punish the Vandals for their sack of Rome. The fact that it would also flex his growing power and prestige was, of course, an additional benefit, and Leo was determined to spare no expense. Emptying the entire eastern treasury, the emperor liquidated 130,000 pounds of gold to muster and equip over a thousand ships with four hundred thousand soldiers.

To command one of the largest invasion forces ever attempted, Leo chose one of the worst commanders in history. His name was Basiliscus, and his main qualification was being Leo's brother-in-law. Against any other leader, the Vandals would have stood no chance; but under Basiliscus, the overwhelming odds just made for a more spectacular collapse. Landing forty miles from Carthage, Basiliscus somehow managed to wreck his fleet and largely destroy his army within five days. Panicking in the middle of a battle, the wretched general left the remains of his grand force to fend for itself and fled to Constantinople.

When he reached the capital, Basiliscus very sensibly hid in the Hagia Sophia, which was soon surrounded by an angry mob calling for his head. Leo was also in a lynching mood, but the timely intervention of the empress Verina managed to save Basiliscus, and Leo exiled him to Thrace instead of beheading him. His incompetence had left the East nearly impoverished and had extinguished the last hope of the West. His mischief, however, was not yet completed, and, though disgraced and exiled, he would return to haunt the empire again.

The only silver lining in the disaster was that it enabled Leo to finally break completely free from his barbarian master. Since Aspar was the de facto head of the military, he was quite unfairly blamed for the entire debacle, and his reputation plummeted. Seeing his opportunity, Leo lured Aspar to the palace and had him quietly assassinated, barring the doors so that no help could come.* It was a less-than-honorable solution, but Leo was at last free. Zeno was now the most powerful general in the army, and he was completely loyal to the

---

*Palace eunuchs carried out the deed, but the emperor earned the nickname "Leo the Butcher."

crown. Against all odds, Leo had broken the barbarian hold on the throne.

He was not, however, to enjoy his triumph for long. Three years later, in 474, Leo died of dysentery, and the throne passed to his son-in-law Zeno. The new emperor had handled his heady rise to power well enough, but his fellow Isaurians had let it go straight to their heads and were now getting on everyone's nerves by strutting around Constantinople as though they owned the place. As if this weren't bad enough for Zeno, he was also saddled with rather atrocious in-laws. Leo's family could never quite reconcile themselves to the fact that a jumped-up provincial had risen so quickly, and Leo's wife, Verina, in particular had been horrified by her daughter's marriage to the un-couth Isaurian. For a few years, the Empress Mother managed to maintain a cordial disdain for her daughter's husband, but it turned to outright hatred when her only grandson—Zeno's seven-year-old son—died of an illness. For the rest of her life, Verina blamed the heartbroken Zeno for the boy's death and did everything in her power to undercut him.

Slightly less dangerous an enemy than Verina was her worthless brother Basiliscus, who never let incompetence stand in the way of his dreams, and who was busy scheming to seize the throne himself. He had largely destroyed his own credibility with his shameful conduct against the Vandal kingdom of Africa, but this had done nothing to damage his unshakable belief that he should be sitting on the throne. Time, he was sure, had glossed over the mistakes of the past, and though he had never been particularly close to his sister, he was quite willing to make common cause with her against their mutual enemy. The vengeful siblings somehow attracted the support of a disgruntled Isaurian general named Illus, and the three of them hatched a plan to overthrow their despised relative.

Waiting until Zeno was busy presiding over the games at the Hippodrome, Verina sent a frantic messenger to tell him that the people, backed by the Senate, had risen against him. Zeno had grown up far from the busy life of the capital, and for all his success he never really felt at home in the cosmopolitan city. He was painfully aware of how unpopular he had become, and the roar of the crowd around him was quite indistinguishable from the cacophony of revolt. Not bothering to check if his citizens were actually rising against him, the terrified emperor fled with a handful of followers and what was left of the imperial gold reserve to his native Isauria.

Constantinople now belonged to Verina, the mastermind of the rebellion, and she planned to have her lover crowned immediately, but it turned out that toppling an emperor was a good deal easier than making a new one. The army may have not raised a finger to help Zeno, but they balked at handing the throne over to an unknown whose only qualification was that he was sleeping with Verina. Only a member of the imperial family could become emperor, and the army turned to the one candidate readily available—Basiliscus. Incredibly, the man who had almost single-handedly destroyed the military capability of the East and doomed the West with his disastrous African campaign now found himself hailed by the army as the supreme leader of the Roman Empire.

The new emperor soon proved that his stewardship was on par with his generalship. His first action was to allow a general massacre of every Isaurian in the city—despite the fact that Isaurian support had been vital in his bid for the throne. He then turned to his sister, rewarding her part in the revolt by having her lover executed and forcing her into retirement. Having thus mortally offended his coconspirators, Basiliscus sent an army to crush Zeno and secure his position on the throne. To lead this all-important expedition, the emperor made the baffling choice of the Isaurian general Illus, apparently without considering that his recent slaughter of Isaurians in the capital might make Illus a less than perfect candidate to go fight his countrymen. Indeed, Illus marched straight to Zeno and switched sides, encouraging the emperor to return to Constantinople at once and reclaim his throne.

Meanwhile, Basiliscus was busy eroding any support he had left in the capital. Appointing the dubiously named Timothy the Weasel as his personal religious adviser, he let the man talk him into trying to force the church to adopt the heretical belief that Christ lacked a human nature. When in response the patriarch draped the icons of the Hagia Sophia in black, the annoyed emperor announced that he was abolishing the Patriarchate of Constantinople. This action proved so offensive that it touched off massive riots and caused a local holy man named Daniel the Stylite to descend from his pillar for the first time in three decades.* The sight of the saint wagging his finger frightened Basiliscus into publicly withdrawing the threat, but that did little to restore his popularity.

By the time word came that Zeno was approaching with a large army, tensions in the capital were explosive. Basiliscus defiantly promised a valiant defense, but there was no one willing to waste any more time fighting for him. The Senate threw open the gates, and the population poured out into the streets, cheering Zeno as he triumphantly entered. Basiliscus fled with his family to the Hagia Sophia, but was led out by the patriarch after exacting a promise that none of his blood would be spilled. True to his word, Zeno had the fallen emperor sent off to Cappadocia, where he was enclosed in a dry cistern and left to starve.

Only two years had passed since that terrible night when Zeno had been forced to flee the city, but the world had irrevocably changed in his absence. In the moment of Constantinople's weakness, the dying embers of the Western Empire had finally been snuffed out. A barbarian general named Odoacer, growing tired of the charade of puppet emperors, decided to rule Italy in his own right. Smashing his way into Ravenna, where the teenage Romulus Augustulus was cowering,

---

*Stylites were Christian ascetics who tried to escape the temptations of the world by ascending pillars to literally withdraw from it. These hermits commanded immense respect, and though the practice fell out of fashion by the seventh century, stylites could still be found in the eastern deserts well into the twelfth century.

Odoacer decided at the last moment to spare his life, choosing instead to send the young emperor into exile.* On September 4, 476, Romulus Augustulus obediently laid down the crown and scepter and went to live with his family in Campania. Though no one thought him important enough to bother recording when or where he died, his abdication marked the end of the Western Roman Empire.

It's unlikely that anyone at the time noticed such a watershed moment in history. Barbarian generals overthrowing emperors had become distressingly routine for Roman citizens, and for most inhabitants of the former empire, life on the morning of September 5 was no different than the day before. The civil service and the law courts functioned as they always had, merchants and artisans continued to travel down the wide Roman roads, and nothing seemed to suggest a sharp break with the past. Nor, in fact (despite later claims to the contrary), had the Roman Empire actually fallen. A perfectly legitimate Latin-speaking Roman emperor sat on his throne in the East, and what fragments remained of western power withdrew to southern France to keep the flickering imperial power alive as best they could.† The only real change was that Odoacer didn't feel like appointing a new emperor. He very sensibly decided that there was no use in going through the bother of ruling through a puppet when he could simply pay lip service to Constantinople and rule in his own right.

Sending the western imperial regalia to the East along with a letter congratulating Zeno on recovering his throne, Odoacer asked only for permission to rule the West in his name. The eastern emperor, of course, had no intention of legitimizing a barbarian strongman, but he

---

*The name "Augustulus" means "little Augustus," either in reference to his age or importance. Some writers sarcastically called him the "little disgrace," but it seems somehow fitting that the last emperor of Rome had the same name as its founder and first emperor. In an odd twist of fate, the same would be true of the Eastern Empire, whose last emperor was Constantine XI.

†In fact, the West technically also still had a legitimate emperor in the deposed Julius Nepos, who had been overthrown the previous year by Romulus Augustulus's father.

could hardly go charging out to rescue the western throne when his own was so shaky. Prudently dodging the issue, he let Odoacer continue with the charade of ruling as a surrogate and concentrated on putting his own house in order.

Not surprisingly, Basiliscus had left the East in a mess. In addition to making himself hopelessly unpopular, in his two short years on the throne the wretched emperor had managed to mortally offend the Ostrogoths, who were now running amuck in the Balkans. Zeno solved the problem temporarily by bribing their powerful king, Theodoric, to enter imperial service, but after putting down a few revolts, Theodoric got bored and reverted to his favorite activity of plundering. Zeno desperately needed to find some sort of solution quickly, and, fortunately for the empire, he came up with a truly inspired plan.

The tacit approval from the East had convinced Odoacer that he could do what he pleased without fear of retribution, and the insufferable barbarian soon dropped the pretense of being the loyal vassal and began calling himself "King of Italy." The imperial armies were too weak to avenge this obvious insult, but the clever emperor saw a way to solve two imperial headaches at the same time. Sending for the rampaging Gothic king, Zeno gave him his blessing to lead his entire people—men, women, and children—into Italy to rule it in the emperor's name. Thus Theodoric got official sanction to rule a land more promising than the impoverished Balkans—and with it the gravitas of legitimacy—and the East would see Odoacer punished without the loss of a single eastern soldier. Most important of all, Constantinople would be rid of the Goths forever.

Within five years, Theodoric had battered Odoacer into submission and brought Italy welcome peace and a remarkably efficient government. He ruled for thirty-three years, and though he was independent of even the remotest imperial control, to the end of his life, the only face on his coins was that of the emperor of the East.

Zeno never lived to see the triumph of his strategem. He was obviously in declining health and survived just long enough to see his young son and heir die of illness before succumbing to dysentery himself. After such a turbulent reign, many of his subjects couldn't help but remember him with disgust or at best ambivalence, but he deserved more than that. After inheriting the empire during its blackest days, he had guided the ship of state through the upheavals that brought down the West and left the empire stronger than when he found it. Thanks to his tenacious hold on power, the East had survived its first serious test, and the barbarian yoke had been thrown off forever. The empire's foundation may have been shaken, but it had endured and was now ready to regain its strength.

There were certainly no shortages of problems for the empire to overcome. The years of chaos and weakness had taken their toll on virtually every level of society, commerce was crippled by heavy taxes, and the imperial treasury still hadn't recovered from Leo's disastrous African campaign. Zeno's legacy, however, provided a secure throne to work from, and over the next three decades the empire experienced a remarkable recovery. Bribery and corruption were rooted out, money was collected more efficiently, and taxes were generally lowered. Commerce, freed from the burdens of excessive taxation, once again flourished, and wealth came pouring into the cities and markets of the empire. A population increase followed the improving economy, and the empire began to prosper on an unprecedented scale. The memories of the fifth century's turbulence began to fade like a bad dream, and a new generation of Byzantines began to take up the reins of power. For the first time since Diocletian, the empire was facing no serious military or political threats, and despite the volatility of the past centuries, it hadn't lost a single inch of imperial territory. Brimming with self-confidence, the empire was strong, secure, and ready for explosive growth. It only needed an emperor who was willing to dream.

7

∴∴∴∴∴∴∴∴∴∴∴∴∴∴∴∴∴∴∴∴∴∴∴∴∴∴∴∴∴∴∴∴∴∴

THE RISE OF PETER SABBATIUS

The seventy-year-old man who sat on Constantinople's throne in 518 was hardly emblematic of the winds of change that were blowing through the Eastern Empire, but he was nevertheless a living example of the upward mobility possible in the sixth-century Roman world. Justin's life began in a small peasant home in Thrace, and he spent his youth tending the few sheep his parents could afford. When he turned twenty, he decided to leave the crushing poverty of his homeland and set off for Constantinople with nothing more than the clothes on his back and a few biscuits in his knapsack. Arriving in the city, he found a job in the army, and, thanks to a healthy mix of hard work and ability, he rose to become commander of the palace guard. This job conveniently placed him at the head of the only real troops in the city, and when Zeno's successor expired, Justin found himself ideally placed to seize power. With a few strategic military parades and a generous donation of a pound of silver to each soldier to maintain their support, he was cheerfully hailed as Augustus by the people of Constantinople.

At first glance, he was hardly a good choice for the throne. Poorly educated and now "elderly," he had no administrative experience and didn't seem remotely qualified for the heavy burdens of state. He did, however, have one important advantage—his brilliant nephew Peter Sabbatius.

Peter had been born thirty-six years before, during the last years of the reign of Zeno, and had left the dusty Macedonian town of his

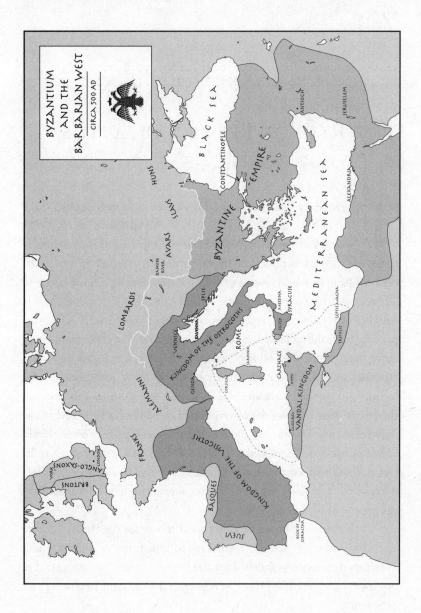

BYZANTIUM AND THE BARBARIAN WEST

CIRCA 500 AD

birth to seek his fortune in the city where his uncle was rising fast. Recognizing the boy's extraordinary ability, Justin adopted him as a son, providing him the finest education available, steeping his mind in the classical texts and intellectual climate of the capital. Peter was so moved by his uncle's generosity that he adopted his name in gratitude. From that time on he was known simply as Justinian.

Keenly aware of the new power and wealth of the empire, Justinian was determined to adopt a more aggressive foreign policy. The barbarian kingdoms that had inherited the western half of the empire had been allowed to flaunt their independence for long enough. The emperors of Constantinople, busy as they were clinging onto their own thrones, may have been too distracted to respond in the past, but stability had returned and the imperial star was once again in the ascendancy. The time had come to deliver those suffering under the shifting, chaotic oppression of barbarian overlords. No longer would Roman pride be crushed under the brutish barbarian heel. The time had come to return to the West.

The opening salvo in Justinian's great reconquest was the restoration of relations with the papacy. Relations between Rome and Constantinople had become somewhat strained thanks to a recent heresy teaching that Christ was divine but not fully human.* Various patriarchs and councils had ruled against it, but the priests and monks of the East were stubbornly independent and determined to make up their own minds on religious matters. Tired of the endless theological speculation, the pope broke off relations, hoping to force his eastern brothers to admit the error of their ways.† Justinian couldn't repair

---

*Called Monophysitism (single nature), this heresy stemmed from several bishops who vigorously defended the church from the teachings of Arius. So intent were they on denying the claim of an inferior, human Christ that they went as far in the other direction.

†Pope Felix III actually excommunicated the patriarch of Constantinople, but since no one was brave enough to deliver the sentence in person, the questionable decision was made to pin the letter of anathema to the back of his robes when he wasn't paying attention.

the damage overnight, but he could lay the groundwork. Appointing firmly Christian ministers, Justinian had his uncle send a letter to the pope asking for the regrettable schism to be healed so that the church might be united again. Satisfied that the eastern half of the church had recovered its bearings, the pope at once agreed.

The warming relations between pontiff and emperor sent shock waves rippling throughout the barbarian kingdoms of the West, especially in Theodoric's Italy, where the shrewd Gothic king was fully aware that he ruled Italy only because Constantinople had other things on its mind. Theodoric knew that as an Arian ruling a Christian population, his position was weak. If his subjects found common cause with their coreligionists in Constantinople, Theodoric's kingdom was doomed. Where spiritual victories appeared, armies would soon follow, and Rome for all its decay had not forgotten its imperial glory. If the empire was once again casting its attention toward its ancestral capital, he had no doubt the citizens of Rome would throw open the gates.

If Theodoric had spies in Constantinople, they would have given him the comforting news that Justinian, the guiding star of imperial policy, was increasingly distracted by the attractions of the Hippodrome. Like any city in any age, Constantinople had its fanatical sports fans who would occasionally engage in acts of hooliganism and generally considered the success of their teams to be more important than life itself. Called the Blues and the Greens after the colors they would don to show their support, the factions were mostly made up of youths and members of the lower classes who had few other ways to vent their energy. Showing up at the Hippodrome to watch the chariot races, they would sit in their own sections and try to drown out the opposing side with mildly insulting chants. Most emperors and their families maintained a careful neutrality when it came to the rowdy circus factions, spouting bland assertions of support depending on the company they were in, but Justinian, with his typical disregard for tradition, made no attempt to hide his passionate support for the Blues.

A day at the chariot races was more than just entertainment. The vast network of Blue supporters allowed Justinian to keep a finger on the pulse of the city and alerted him to possible threats from public disturbances. There was never a shortage of people willing to ingratiate themselves with the heir apparent by sharing information, and one of them, a star ballet dancer named Macedonia, introduced Justinian to a beautiful ex-actress named Theodora. The daughter of a bear keeper and an actress, Theodora was nearly twenty years his junior and had grown up on the stage—a profession synonymous with prostitution in the sixth century.* The gulf between them was so large, and the occupation of actress so frowned upon, that there was even a law forbidding someone of senatorial rank from marrying a lady of the stage. It would have been hard to pick a less appropriate mate for a future emperor, but the moment he set eyes on her, Justinian fell madly in love.

Despite their different social status, it proved to be an inspired match. Theodora's prodigious energy and intelligence matched Justinian's, and the two of them were soon inseparable. Easily overcoming the legal barriers to marriage by pressuring his uncle to amend the offending law, Justinian soon married his new love and turned his formidable mind back to foreign policy.

The emperor Justin was as always content to be led by his brilliant nephew, and Byzantium looked outward with an expansive new confidence. Dissidents crushed by the tyrannies of foreign oppression suddenly found they had a powerful ally in Constantinople, and emissaries flocked to the capital. The glittering new power and prestige drew neighboring powers into the Byzantine orbit, and one diplomatic triumph seemed to follow the next. Client kings tired of the oppressive Persian rule began to break away, transferring their allegiance to Constantinople, despite the furious protests of the Persian king.

---

*Theodora herself seems to have specialized in a particularly obscene form of pantomime involving geese. Such details of her life, however, come from the lurid pen of Procopius, who had reason enough to hate her, and should probably be taken with a large grain of salt.

The long arm of Justinian's ambition even reached the southern tip of the Arabian Peninsula, where the Jewish king of Yemen had recently massacred his Christian subjects by throwing them into a ditch and setting them on fire. Offering to provide transport ships to aid in crossing the Red Sea, Justinian induced the Christian king of Ethiopia to retaliate and avenge the disaster. Within two years, a Christian king was installed on the Yemenite throne, and the empire was given access to trade routes from the Red Sea to India.

Most of these accomplishments came at the expense of Persia, and the annoyed king sent an army into modern Georgia to prevent any more vassals from defecting. This ham-fisted measure provoked the annoyed Justinian into more direct action, and he persuaded his uncle to send a Byzantine army to raid Persian Armenia. It wasn't a large force, and it was remarkable only for a single man that Justinian contributed from his personal bodyguard. At the moment, he was simply an unknown soldier, but he would soon show himself to be the most brilliant general in imperial history. Like Justinian, his origins were humble, but kingdoms and kings would one day tremble at the name of Belisarius.

By the end of 526, as the two ancient enemies slowly rumbled to war, Justin's health started to seriously decline, and the Senate asked him to crown Justinian as coemperor. He did so on April 1, 527, in a magnificent ceremony that seemed more a coming-out party than a simple coronation. By the end of the summer, Justin was dead of an old war wound, and Justinian and Theodora stood as the sole rulers of the Roman Empire.

8

NIKA!

The new imperial couple could hardly have been more different from the old regime. They were both young—he in his forties and she in her twenties—and if they were never exactly popular, they at least seemed like a breath of fresh air to the populace. The coronation had been an extravagant affair, unlike anything seen during the stingy days of Anastasius, and there were those who hoped it was a sign that a glorious new age was dawning.

Justinian certainly wasn't like other men who had held the imperial throne. Alone of the Byzantine emperors, he dreamed on a truly imperial scale, unable to abide the abomination of a Roman Empire that didn't include Rome. He had been steeped since youth in the classical view that just as there was one God in heaven, there was only one empire here on earth. His authority as the sole Christian emperor was absolute, and his duty was to mirror the heavenly order. This was a sacred trust, and the fact that half of the empire lay in heretical barbarian hands was an insult he couldn't let pass. It must be made whole again, and be filled with monumental public works that would endure through all the ages as a testament to the splendor of his reign.

Of course, ambitions as grand as these needed to be paid for somehow, and though his two penny-pinching predecessors had left the treasury bursting at the seams, Justinian had already proven how quickly he could burn through state funds. Six years earlier, he had managed to disperse more than thirty-seven hundred pounds of gold to pay for the decorations of the lavish games in honor of his consulship, and by the second year of his reign, he had already begun a monumental building program that had started construction on no fewer than eight churches. He had many virtues, but clearly restraint and frugality were not among them.

The money for all these projects inevitably came from taxes, and Justinian was fortunate to have on hand a ruthless individual named John the Cappadocian who seemed capable of squeezing money out of a stone. Uneducated and devoid of any charm, John streamlined the tax system, closed loopholes, and attacked corruption with a doglike tenacity. His favorite targets were the rich, who had long escaped their due with privileges and exemptions, and he was perfectly willing to torture those he thought were trying to dodge their responsibilities. The provoked nobility raised an outcry, but the emperor was distinctly unsympathetic.

An upstart himself, Justinian had no patience for the patricians who looked down their long noses at him, and he had no intention of sparing their delicate sensibilities. As far as he was concerned, the aristocracy had been a plague on imperial history, forever battling the power of the emperor and clogging up the bureaucracy with their constant attempts to maintain the status quo. This was a time to try new ideas, not to be weighed down with the outmoded thinking of worn-out tradition. The way into his favor was to have impressive merits, not names, and he was determined to surround himself with pragmatic figures who would sweep aside the clutter of the stuffy imperial court. John the Cappadocian was admirably reforming the bureaucracy, and if the nobility were squirming in the process, so much the better.

The emperor was, in any case, already onto his next project. He had met an extraordinary lawyer named Tribonian who seemed to be a walking encyclopedia of Roman law. This was all the more impressive because Roman law was a confusing mess of nearly a thousand years of often-contradictory precedent, special exemptions, and conflicting interpretations, none of which were written down in any one place. In a typically ambitious move, Justinian decided to bring much-needed order to the situation by removing all the inconsistencies and repetitions, making the first comprehensive legal code in imperial history. The brilliant Tribonian was clearly the man for the job, and he attacked it with relish and an astonishing speed. In a mere fourteen months, he published the new *Codex*—the supreme authority for every court in the land, and the basis of most European legal systems today.* Law schools sprang up from Alexandria to Beirut, and the University of Constantinople soon produced legal scholars who exported the code throughout the Mediterranean world.

These glittering achievements, however, came with a cost. Tribonian and John were among the most hated men in the empire, and the fact that Tribonian was famously corrupt—and a pagan into the bargain—didn't help matters. Had the emperor been listening, he would have heard an ominous rumbling of dissent. The bruised egos of the powerful aristocracy demanded retribution, and the common man suffering under the cruel hands of the imperial tax collectors began to wonder if life wouldn't be a whole lot easier with another man on the throne.

Justinian was far too busy with foreign affairs to notice storm clouds on the domestic horizon. In 528, war had finally broken out with Persia, and he had been busy reorganizing the eastern army. The aging Persian king sent a huge army to flatten the Romans, but Belisarius defeated it with his characteristic flair, and he even managed to conquer part of Persian Armenia. It was the first clear victory on the Persian frontier in living memory, and it sounded the clarion call of imperial revival.

It also resulted in the fall of the Vandal king of Africa. He'd been maintaining an increasingly difficult balancing act for years, and this latest triumph of Byzantine arms had made his position nearly

---

*It's also, interestingly enough, the basis of the law practiced in the state of Louisiana.

untenable. On the one hand, he had to placate Justinian to keep the imperial armies away, but too much of an effort to keep the Byzantines happy would inevitably invite charges of betrayal by his own subjects. Most Vandals feared for their independence and wanted a tough stance from their leader, but the king chose this moment to unveil a new series of coins with the emperor's portrait on them. The ill-timed attempt to ingratiate himself with the eastern court cost him his crown. Aided by the outraged Vandal nobility, the king's cousin Gelimer easily overthrew him and seized the throne of Carthage.

From the start, Gelimer made it clear that he didn't intend to be intimidated by any bullying from Constantinople. When Justinian sent a letter protesting his usurpation, Gelimer told him to mind his own business, subtly reminding him that the last Byzantine military expedition against his kingdom had ended in a complete fiasco. If these blustering Byzantines wanted their land back, Gelimer announced, let them come and get it. They would find Vandal swords ready for them.

Justinian was slightly disappointed by the change in Vandal kings, since he was quite sure the right diplomatic pressure would have delivered North Africa back into the Roman fold without the loss of a single soldier, but Gelimer's warlike stance would do almost as well. The contemptuous letter provided an insult to be avenged, a useful bit of propaganda for the emperor and the perfect pretext to invade. The Vandal occupiers had plundered Roman land and thumbed their noses at Constantinople for long enough. Now they would find out what it meant to taunt the Roman wolf.

There was only one man who could be entrusted with the African campaign, but Belisarius was busy fighting on the Persian frontier. In 531, he managed to fight a much larger Persian army to a standstill, and, with his customary good luck, this proved to be the decisive conflict of the war. A few days later, the demoralized Persian king unexpectedly died, leaving a young but shrewd son named Chosroes to take his place. The new king desperately needed peace to consolidate his power, and hastily agreed to an "Everlasting Peace," leaving Justinian's favorite general free.* Nothing, it seemed, could now stop the reconquest of North Africa.

But Belisarius had barely arrived in Constantinople when a very different sort of war erupted. While Justinian was dreaming of glory in Africa, tensions in the capital had built to a fever pitch. Upset by the rising taxes and increasing corruption, the population had reached its boiling point when the emperor severely restricted the privileges of the Blues and the Greens in order to cope with a rise in factional violence. Not only had Justinian allowed his surrogates to fleece the citizens with cruel taxes, but now he was interfering in their sports as well. Games celebrating the ides of January were held to defuse the situation, but when the spectators caught sight of Justinian taking his usual seat, things began to get ugly. The anonymity of the crowd gave someone the courage to taunt the emperor, shouting out that he wished Justinian's father had never been born, and the stadium shook with the roar of approval. When Justinian furiously asked if they had gone mad to address him so, the mob exploded in a rage, bursting out of the Hippodrome intent on destruction.

Justinian beat a hasty retreat to the Great Palace, and, after a few hours of rioting, his imperial police managed to get control of the situation. Seven of the ringleaders were arrested and sentenced to death, but the large crowd that soon gathered seemed to unnerve the executioners, and they managed to botch the final two hangings. The first attempt was embarrassing enough, as the rope broke and both men were found to be still breathing, but when the hangmen tried again, the entire scaffold collapsed. Naturally, such excitement drew a larger crowd, and in the uproar that followed, several monks from the nearby monastery of Saint Conon managed to spirit the condemned men to safety.

The commander of the imperial guard was hesitant to pursue

---

*It was called the Everlasting Peace because, unlike most treaties with Persia, it was open-ended and didn't provide a time limit when hostilities could resume. Unfortunately, "eternity" turned out to be only eight years.

them, fearful that forcing his way into a sacred building would touch off a riot, so he elected to starve them out instead. If this plan was meant to ease tension, however, it backfired badly as a large mob quickly surrounded the soldiers and loudly demanded that the two men—one Blue and one Green—be pardoned immediately. The sight of heavily armed soldiers besieging a monastery seemed the very embodiment of tyranny to the populace, a bitter betrayal of everything they had been promised. Justinian's coronation had hinted of imperial largesse, of bread and circuses and enlightened rule by a supporter of the Blues who was one of them and understood their passions. Now, however, they found their emperor as austere as any of his predecessors, and his heavy-handed threatening of unarmed monks revealed him as the worst sort of tyrant.

Justinian tried to defuse the situation by announcing new games, but when the Hippodrome opened for the races three days later, tempers were even worse. When the emperor arrived to take his place in the imperial loggia, the normal babble of the crowd swelled to a deafening roar. The traditional practice of the Blues and the Greens was to try to drown each other out by shouting *"Nika!"* ("Conquer!"), followed by the name of their favorite charioteer, but by the end of the races they were united against the emperor. Thirty thousand throats screamed the single word in unison, unleashing their pent-up rage at Justinian in a horrifying crescendo. For a moment, the emperor tried to brave the terrifying sound as the very ground beneath him seemed to tremble, but the palpable fury threatened to sweep him off his feet. He was but a single man, a lone figure against the rage of the crowd, and he prudently turned and fled into the recesses of the imperial palace, slamming the doors shut behind him.

The crowd spilled out into the streets, looking for ways to vent their frustration. Finding the palace impregnable, they stormed the city prisons, swelling their numbers with freed convicts. Justinian once again sent out the imperial police, but by now things were slipping completely out of control. Women flung roof tiles and pottery from upstairs windows onto the heads of guards, and the mob erected barricades in the streets. Hooligans set fire to shops, and before long the wind had spread it, burning a nearby hospital to the ground with all its patients inside. Order might have been restored if the powerful aristocratic families had rallied behind the throne, but they had always considered Justinian a pretentious upstart and in any case hated him for the policies of John the Cappadocian. As far as they were concerned, the emperor had sowed every bit of what he was about to reap. This was the perfect opportunity to replace him with one of their number.

Providing the rioters with weapons, the patricians joined the looters in the streets, watching as half the city went up in flames. The next day, the mob returned to the Hippodrome and demanded the immediate dismissal of the hated Tribonian and John the Cappadocian. A severely alarmed Justinian acceded to their demands on the spot, but the aristocracy was now in control, and they would accept nothing less than his abdication.

In the excitement of the moment, neither the patricians nor the mob were quite certain of exactly how to proceed. Half of them wanted to wait to see if Justinian gave up the crown, while the other half wanted to force his hand by storming the palace. Finally, a senator got up and urged immediate violent action. If the emperor was allowed to escape, he warned, he would sooner or later return at the head of an army. The only thing to do was to overwhelm and kill him before he could slip away. This advice carried the day, and the crowd began eagerly heaving against the walls of the imperial palace.

The noise was deafening, and, inside the palace, Justinian's advisers were trying to make themselves heard over the terrifying din. They still had access to the harbor, and most were shouting for the panicked emperor to flee the city while there was still time. Justinian was just about to order the ships prepared when Theodora, who had held back while the men argued, rose and silenced them with perhaps the most eloquent speech in Byzantine history. "I do not care," she said, "whether or not it is proper for a woman to give brave counsel to frightened men; but in moments of extreme danger, conscience is the only guide. Every man who is born into the light of day must sooner or later die; and how can an Emperor ever allow himself to become a fugitive? If you, my Lord, wish to save your skin, you will have no difficulty in doing so. We are rich, there is the sea, there too are our ships. But consider first whether, when you reach safety, you will not regret that you did not choose death in preference. As for me, I stand by the ancient saying: royalty makes the best shroud."*

With those words ringing above the muted roar of the crowds outside, there could obviously be no thought of retreat, and Justinian and his advisers were infused with some much-needed spine. If his throne were to be saved, he clearly needed to go on the offensive, but the troops in the city had already proven untrustworthy. There were other options, however. A large group of Scandinavian mercenaries had recently arrived, and, as luck would have it, Belisarius, the greatest general in Byzantine history, just happened to be in the city awaiting his deployment to Africa.

Quickly taking command of the situation, Belisarius gathered his men and slipped out into the streets. Most of the rioters were still in the Hippodrome howling for Justinian's death, unaware of the changing mood in the palace or of the danger of congregating in one place. An elderly eunuch named Narses, who was the commander of the imperial bodyguard, blocked the exits of the Hippodrome while Belisarius and his men burst in, catching the infuriated crowd completely by surprise.† At first, the mob hurled themselves at the heavily armed sol-

---

*Theodora, or perhaps Procopius (the historian writing it down), is misquoting here a famous maxim once given to the tyrant of Syracuse, Dionysius the Elder: "Tyranny makes the best shroud." Considering how it turned out, though, most citizens of Constantinople would probably consider the distinction unnecessary. Procopius, *History of the Wars: The Persian War Books I & II* (New York: Cosimo, 2007).
†Eunuchs had a valued place in Byzantine society. Their condition disbarred them from the throne, and they could therefore be uniquely trusted for high office. In a world of constantly shifting alliances and unceasing intrigue, eunuchs were loyal, distinguished, and wielded a considerable amount of power. Although the practice was officially frowned upon, fathers would often castrate younger sons to ensure them a lucrative career in the civil service.

diers in a frenzy, but they stood no chance against the swords and armor of Belisarius's men, and the angry shouts were soon replaced by the screams of dying men. When the killing finally stopped, the Hippodrome resembled a ghastly charnel house, with the bodies of thirty thousand citizens lying where they had fallen. The Nika revolt was over, and as looters carefully stripped the bodies of valuables, an eerie quiet descended on Constantinople, broken only by the occasional crash of a burning building.

Justinian was shaken by the riots, and though he soon felt secure enough to reinstate the hated ministers of finance and law, he kept a careful grip on their excesses with the common man. The nobility, however, were another matter entirely. Their arrogance and staunch belief that one of their own members should be sitting on the throne was unforgivable, and he was determined that in the wake of the riots, his victory over them would be complete. Nineteen senators were executed, their sprawling palaces were torn down, and their bodies were thrown into the sea. The nobility who escaped were hardly any luckier. John the Cappadocian was unleashed on them, harassing them mercilessly to tap their fortunes for the state, and, for the rest of Justinian's reign, they were too busy trying to save themselves to cause him any further trouble.

This victory over the nobility marked another break with the West that would prove important in the centuries to come. In those decentralized, shifting kingdoms, there was no one to stand against the encroaching power of the aristocracy, and the gains of strong individual kings vanished as soon as they vacated the stage. The great landowning nobility sapped the strength of numerous kings over the centuries, drowning any potential unity in a sea of petty squabbles. Caught between the warring sides as always were the poor, crushed in the grip of feudal lords and bound ever more tightly to their land. Constantinople, by contrast, to its great benefit, managed largely to keep its aristocracy in check, ensuring a surprising degree of social and economic mobility for its citizens that added immeasurably to the prosperity and strength of the empire.

Whether they knew it or not, the people of Constantinople had reason enough to thank their emperor, and, in the aftermath of the riots, they found that they had learned another lesson as well. A wise ruler would court his people, but this didn't mean that he sat on his throne by the grace of his subjects. Emperors could apparently not be made and unmade as easily as they had thought, and the corpses in the Hippodrome attested to the dangers of trying to push Justinian around. The building itself remained closed to games for several years, sitting in mournful silence as a testament to a chastened people. Never again would the fury of the Hippodrome haunt Justinian's reign.

9

::

OF BUILDINGS AND GENERALS

It was hardly an auspicious start to what would become the Byzantine golden age. For three days, smoke hung thickly over the devastated capital, and small fires flickered in the streets. The rioters had left a trail of destruction, reducing the main gate of the imperial palace, the Senate house, the public baths, and numerous houses and palaces to ashes in their wake. The center of the city seemed to be a blackened shell, and the flames had even claimed the city's cathedral of the Hagia Sophia and the neighboring Hagia Irene as well. Constantinople looked as if it had been looted by some ravaging barbarian horde, and the fact that its own citizens had inflicted such a wound hovered like a black cloud over the streets. Surveying the damage from the windows of his palace, Justinian nevertheless saw not a disaster, but a perfect opportunity. The destruction had cleared away the detritus of the past, making way for an ambitious new building program, which would transform the city—and the empire as well—into the glittering center of civilization.

Never before had the citizens of the Roman Empire seen such construction, at such a pace. The dusty city of the emperor's birth, Tauresium, was refurbished and renamed Justiniana Prime; hospitals and baths sprang up, and fortifications were strengthened. Bridges spanning mighty rivers were constructed, and inns were spaced along the major highways for the imperial post to change horses. The most impressive work, however, was saved for Constantinople. A sumptuous new Senate house, colonnaded with creamy white marble pillars and topped with fine carvings, rose near the city's central square to replace the burned one. Three statues of barbarian kings were set up, all bowing before a large column surmounted with an equine statue of Justinian in full military dress.* To the west of his column, the emperor built a massive subterranean cistern to feed the city's numerous fountains and baths and to provide fresh water for all of its inhabitants. Constantinople gleamed with new construction, but, for the emperor, this was merely the prologue. He now turned to the project which would surpass them all.

The Hagia Sophia was undoubtedly the most important structure that had been destroyed in the riots. Originally built by Constantius II to house the mystery of the Holy Communion, it had been demolished by rioters more than a century before when the great golden-tongued reformer Saint John Chrysostom had been exiled to Georgia. The emperor Theodosius II had rebuilt it eleven years later along the same rather uninspired lines, and most in the city assumed that the familiar outline would soon greet them once again. Justinian, however, had no intention of following the tired plans of an earlier age. This was a chance to remake the cathedral on a whole new scale, something worthy of his vision for the empire. It was to be nothing short of a revolution, equal parts art and architecture, the enduring grandeur of the emperor himself frozen in marble and brick.

Little more than a month after the Nika riots, construction began on the mighty showpiece of his reign. Choosing two architects who had more vision than practical experience, Justinian told them to create a building unlike anything else in the world. Sheer scale wasn't enough—the empire was full of grand monuments and immense sculpture. This had to be something different, something fitting for the new golden age that was dawning. Expense, he informed them, wasn't an issue, but speed was. He was already in his fifties, and he

---

*Justinian chose to portray himself in a Persian uniform to signify Belisarius's victories in the East. The column and statue, alas, no longer exist.

didn't intend to have some successor apply the final coat of paint and claim it as his own.

The two architects didn't disappoint. Rejecting the classical basilica form that had been used for three hundred years, they came up with a bold and innovative plan.* Building the largest unsupported dome in the world, they put it on a square floor plan and distributed its weight over a cascading series of half-domes and cupolas. The riches of the empire were poured into its construction. Each day, gold arrived from Egypt, porphyry from Ephesus, powdered white marble from Greece, and precious stones from Syria and North Africa. Even the old capital provided a quarry for the new, as columns that had once stood in the Temple of the Sun in Rome were carted off to adorn the rising church.

The building seemed to grow at a breathtaking rate. The architects split their crew of ten thousand men into two parts, placing one group at the south end and the other at the north end. Spurred on by the presence of the emperor—who daily visited the site—the two teams raced against each other, speeding up the building to a frenetic pace. In the end, it took only five years, ten months, and four days from the laying of the first stone to the completion of the building—a remarkable achievement in any age, much less one without modern machines.†

Stepping through the great doors reserved for the emperor and patriarch into the vast interior of the Hagia Sophia for the first time, Justinian was overwhelmed, struck by a vision of heaven made real in every graceful curve and sweeping arch.‡ The cavernous interior dome, 107 feet high and spanning nearly four acres, was decorated

---

*The two architects—and Justinian himself—were almost certainly thinking about their novel design before the Nika riots. Their first attempt (albeit on a much smaller scale) still exists in the nearby Church of Saints Sergius and Bacchus.

†By contrast, Westminster Cathedral took some thirty-three years to rebuild, Notre Dame more than a hundred, and the Duomo in Florence about 230.

‡Unlike Western cathedrals, the Hagia Sophia's domed shape makes its entire interior space visible from any of its seven main doorways.

with simple crosses and completely covered in gold, seemingly float-
ing above the ground as if "suspended from heaven itself on a golden
chain." Candles and lamps were hung from the upper galleries, out-
lining the interior in an unforgettable glow and casting soft light over
the glittering mosaics. From the floor rose multicolored columns
topped with intricate scrollwork and deeply carved with the complex
monograms of Justinian and Theodora. At the front of the church, a
massive fifty-foot iconostasis was hung with great silver disks en-
graved with images of Mary, Jesus, and the saints. Beyond lay the high
altar, sheltering an unrivaled collection of relics, from the hammer
and nails of the Passion to the swaddling clothes of Christ. Even the
wood surmounting the great imperial door was unlike any in the
world, composed as it was from an ancient fragment of Noah's Ark.
Marveling at the stunning panorama, Justinian stood silently, drinking it in. After a long moment, those closest heard him whisper, "Solo-
mon, I have surpassed you."

The emperor wasn't in the habit of making idle boasts, nor had he
forgotten his great dream of redressing the embarrassing situation of a Roman Empire that didn't include Rome. The aftermath of
the Nika revolt had given him a measure of domestic peace, and he
could now concentrate on his plan to reconquer the lost lands. Predictably, there were plenty of people telling him that it couldn't be
done. Chief among them was John the Cappadocian, who, like any
treasurer worth his salt, was looking at it from a financial standpoint
and didn't think it made economic sense. He remembered all too
clearly the disaster of Basiliscus's African invasion, which had crippled
the imperial economy for nearly sixty years. Pleading with Justinian
not to risk the empire's resources on an unnecessary campaign, he succeeded in getting the emperor to drastically reduce the size of the
force to be sent with Belisarius. On the one hand, this ensured that
the empire could survive the expedition's failure; but on the other, its
small size seemed to invite the very failure it was trying to avoid. It

hardly mattered to Justinian, however; he had an unwavering faith in the abilities of his general.

In the late summer of 533, Belisarius sailed with eighteen thousand men and, more important for posterity, his personal secretary, Procopius, who would write a firsthand account of the campaign. Arriving in Sicily to pick up new supplies, the campaign got its first lucky break when it was discovered that the Vandal fleet was away putting down a revolt in Sardinia, a diversion that Justinian had carefully encouraged. Belisarius moved quickly to take advantage of the opportunity. Disembarking on the coast of what is now Tunisia without seeing a single Vandal soldier, the Byzantines found a land ripe for the taking.

For years, the Vandal overlords had been alienating the native African population by trying to covert them to Arianism, and, after crushing numerous revolts, the paranoid barbarians had finally torn down the walls of their cities to prevent their seditious subjects from ever resisting again. So Belisarius arrived to find Africa's great cities shorn of their defenses and filled with a population that welcomed him as a deliverer.

Sixty-five years before, Basiliscus had dithered within sight of his ships until the Vandals had cut him to pieces, but Belisarius, with barely a tenth of his numbers, headed straight for Carthage—the only of all the Vandal cities to have maintained its walls. His aim was to draw Gelimer out and strike a quick knockout blow while surprise was on his side, but when he was only ten miles from the city, his scouts reported a massive Vandal army waiting just ahead in a carefully planned ambush. Prudence seemed to dictate a strategic withdrawal to a neutral ground, but Belisarius was anxious to come to grips with Gelimer. Trusting his instincts, the great general plunged ahead.

Most of Gelimer's veteran troops were off fighting in Sardinia, so the Vandal king had made the mistake of padding his numbers with raw recruits. This gave him an impressive-looking army, but since it was too large to be effectively commanded by a single person, he was forced to divide the command with his brother. Unfortunately for Vandal Africa, Gelimer's inexperienced brother was completely incompetent and proceeded to get his entire wing annihilated by blundering into the Byzantine vanguard. Gelimer tried to save the day by charging forward, but his troops took one look at Belisarius's terrifying Hunnish allies and fled, trampling their own forces in their haste to get away. Somehow Gelimer managed to rally his men, but just as the weight of his superior numbers was beginning to force the Byzantines back, he stumbled on the body of his brother and was overcome with grief. Refusing to budge until the body was given a proper funeral, Gelimer lost whatever momentum he had gained, and a sudden charge by Belisarius shattered the Vandal army.

The way to Carthage was now clear, and the victorious general entered the cheering city in triumph, taking possession of Gelimer's palace in time to eat the feast prepared for the Vandal king. The city's population turned out to greet him, scattering flowers before his horse and waving branches. Some feared looting and destruction like the last time a Roman army had taken Carthage, but Belisarius had instructed his men carefully.* This wasn't an occupation; it was a liberation. After more than a century under the barbarian boot, a treasured province was welcomed back into the Roman Empire. There was no swagger or requisitioning. Food was paid for at a fair price, and discipline was strictly enforced.

The conquering army didn't stay for long. Gelimer's veteran Vandal troops had returned from Sardinia, and the furious king was now marching with his surviving brother to retake his capital. By cutting the aqueduct that provided fresh water to the city, the Vandals forced Belisarius to abandon the city to face them. Choosing a vast plain that would give advantage to neither side, Belisarius drew up his forces for the decisive contest of the war.

The two sides heaved against each other, sweating under the

---

*That had been in 146 BC at the end of the Third Punic War, when Scipio Aemilianus had burned the city to the ground, sold the population into slavery, and scattered salt on the ruins.

blazing North African sun, and, imperceptibly at first, the heavily out-numbered but more-disciplined Byzantines began to push the Vandals back. Gelimer surged forward, trying to encourage his men, but history repeated itself as his brother was cut down in front of him in the vicious fighting. Paralyzed with grief, the king halted, and his wavering troops broke completely before the Byzantine charge. Vandal thoughts were now only of escape, and men clawed and flailed their way frantically through the confusion toward the distant mountains rising from the dusty African plain. Thousands of them were cut down in flight, soaking the battlefield with barbarian blood before Belisarius wearily called off the pursuit.

The victory shattered the Vandals so thoroughly that they virtually disappeared from history. Gelimer survived to flee into the mountains and fight on, but by the time winter was over, he realized it was a lost cause and surrendered. Belisarius entered the bustling city of Hippo in triumph and found there both Gelimer's vast treasury and the looted riches of Rome. Within a few months, Sardinia, Corsica, and Gibraltar had fallen, and his extraordinary victory was complete. The Vandal kingdom had been extinguished in little more than a year, and the watching world had been put on notice. The empire was returning to claim its own.

Leaving a subordinate to finish mopping up resistance, Belisarius gathered his spoils and the most prominent captives and sailed for Constantinople. Justinian greeted his general with euphoria. The stunning reconquest of North Africa had vindicated all his cherished dreams of reuniting the empire. He'd proved all the doubters wrong and added immense prestige to both empire and emperor. Somehow Justinian had to communicate his thanks and he characteristically chose an extravagant reward. Belisarius, he announced, would be granted a triumph.

There was no higher honor a Roman general could receive, but no triumph had been awarded outside of the imperial family since 19 BC. For Justinian, however, steeped as he was in history, such a fact was yet another witness that his reign signified the return of the glorious ancient empire.

The young general strode through the ecstatic crowds into the Hippodrome, his face painted red, and the bright sun gleaming off his armor. At his side—as was traditional—stood a slave holding a golden wreath above his head and whispering into his ear, "Remember, you are but a man."* Following him, beneath the fluttering insignias of the Vandal kingdom, came Gelimer, his family, and the best-looking specimens of Vandal prowess. Behind them, ranged out in a seemingly endless baggage train, came the spoils of war: solid-gold thrones, jewel-encrusted chariots, the silver menorah that Titus had seized from Jerusalem in AD 71, and all the treasures the Vandals had plundered from Rome. Entering the Hippodrome, the mighty procession found the entire population on its feet, as far above them Justinian and Theodora sat enthroned in the imperial box. The noise rose to a deafening crescendo as Gelimer tore off his royal robes and was forced to kneel in the dust before the emperor. Groveling with the ruins of his power around him, the fallen king was heard to whisper a verse from Ecclesiastes: "Vanity of vanities, all is vanity."

As much as Belisarius would have liked to stay in Constantinople and enjoy the rewards of his recent campaign, the emperor had other plans for him. As far as Justinian was concerned, the conquest of North Africa had only paved the way for the more symbolically important conquest of Italy, and there was no reason to delay. Ordering the fleet to be prepared immediately, the emperor sent Belisarius with seventy-five hundred men to take Sicily, while another general led the main army through Dalmatia into northern Italy.

The invasion was perfectly timed. The Goths were reasonably popular with the rank-and-file Italians, but the main chink in the armor of their support was religion.† The church had long been the

---

*This was originally done as a safeguard against rebellion, lest the fickle adulation of the crowd go to the hero of the moment's head.
†But then again, the malodorous Goths *were* barbarians, after all. The Italians loved to complain about their appalling taste in music, ridiculous trousers, and overabundance of hair grease.

vehicle for Roman culture and civic values—the clergy still dressed in their Roman aristocratic robes (now called vestments), even though their congregations had adopted barbarian dress—and this acted as a great dividing line between those who were civilized and those who were not. For all their warm relations with their subjects, the Goths were still Arian heretics who could never really be fully accepted.

Italy was clearly ripe for the picking, but first Belisarius had to conquer Sicily. This he did with his customary panache, sweeping through the island and overcoming the only Gothic resistance at Palermo by sailing his ships up to the city walls and having his men jump onto the battlements. The suddenness of Sicily's collapse completely unnerved Theodahad, the Ostrogothic king. When an imperial ambassador was shown into his presence, the king tremblingly offered to turn over Italy on the spot. For a moment, it looked as if the ancient heartland of the empire would fall as quickly as Africa.

It might indeed have done so, but unfortunately for the inhabitants of the peninsula (and subsequent Western history), the Byzantine general invading Dalmatia chose this moment to bungle his advance and was killed in an inconclusive battle. Since the army didn't have the authority to advance without its general, it withdrew to its winter quarters and refused to budge without further instructions. Suddenly, the Byzantine threat began to look less impressive, and Theodahad started to recover his nerve. Regretting his rash promises of surrender, he threw the imperial ambassadors into jail and prepared to resist, raising an army as fast as he could. The opportunity for a quick victory was lost forever, and Italy, still glowing in the sunset of the classical world, was plunged into the darkness of a ruinous war. The region would remain a bloodstained battlefield for centuries to come.

The entire Byzantine offensive momentum ground to a halt as even Belisarius, in Sicily, ran into delays. Just as he was about to cross into southern Italy, word reached him that a full-blown mutiny was sweeping across Africa. Months were lost while the general raced to put it down, and when he returned, it was to find his own men on the verge of revolt. By the time he had calmed them, autumn had begun, and the campaigning season was over.

The delays annoyed Belisarius as much as his men, and early the next year, he crossed the Strait of Messina, determined to make up for lost time. Theodahad hadn't bothered to build up the Gothic defenses, and virtually every city in the south fell in rapid succession. Each victory further reduced Ostrogothic morale, but it also required Belisarius to leave a garrison behind. By the time the general reached Naples, his forces were too small to take the nearly impregnable city by storm. There were more ways to enter a city than by frontal assault, however, and Belisarius's resourceful mind soon found one.

One of his men had been climbing up the old aqueduct to see how it was constructed and discovered a small, unguarded channel that still went into the city walls. Unfortunately, it wasn't large enough for an armored man, but Belisarius knew how to get around that. Noisily attacking another section of the wall, he used the clamor of battle to cover the sound of his workmen enlarging the hole. After the work was completed, Belisarius cheerfully retreated and waited till nightfall, then sent six hundred men through and launched an all-out attack. The guards were quickly overwhelmed, the gates thrown open, and, within a matter of hours, the most important Gothic city in the south was in his hands.

The fall of the city panicked the Goths into murdering their spineless king and abandoning Rome for the nearly impregnable Ravenna. Electing an energetic noble named Vitiges as their new monarch, they set to work improving their defenses in the new capital, leaving only four thousand men with the impossible task of manning and defending Rome's sprawling and dilapidated walls. A few weeks later, Belisarius arrived.

The imperial army was preceded by its formidable reputation, and by the time the first of the Byzantines came within sight of Rome's walls, the Gothic garrison had convinced itself that resistance was impossible. Thanks to careful negotiations beforehand by the great general, Pope Silverius had already invited Belisarius into the city, and the Goths thought only of preserving their lives. As the Byzantines marched into Rome through the Asinarian Gate, the Gothic garrison hastily marched out the other end of the city along the old Flaminian Way.

For the first time in nearly six decades, the Roman Empire had control of its ancient capital. Its citizens proudly welcomed the restoration of their ancient glory and shouted, "No longer will the tombs of the Caesars be trampled by the savages of the North!"* The keys of Rome were sent, together with a captured Gothic chieftain, to Constantinople, where they were displayed in their entire splendor before Justinian's throne.

It had been a remarkable year, but Belisarius knew better than to believe that the war was ended. With only a handful of men, he had managed to conquer Sicily, southern Italy, and Rome. The Byzantine success, however, was mostly smoke and mirrors. The moment Vitiges realized that the fearsome Belisarius was holding Rome with only five thousand men, the entire conquest would be in danger of crumbling. The triumphant entry into Rome became a desperate race to repair the walls before Vitiges learned the truth.

When the master of Ravenna found out that he had lost nearly half his kingdom to so few, he was enraged, and within three months a massive Gothic army was drawn up before the gates of Rome. Within moments of their arrival, they almost caught Belisarius and ended the struggle before it began. After fortifying the Milvian Bridge with a tower, the general had ridden out to survey the enemy positions, secure in the belief that the Goths couldn't cross the Tiber in time to endanger him. Unfortunately, the guards charged with defending the tower fled at the first sight of the enemy, and the Goths poured over the bridge unmolested. Belisarius found himself suddenly surrounded by their vanguard and cut off from the Flaminian Gate. Conspicuous on his bay horse, he flailed about trying to break free

---

*Edward Gibbon, *The Decline and Fall of the Roman Empire*, v. 4 (New York: Random House, 1993).

while Roman deserters pointed out his position to the Goths. He fought with desperate courage, shouting encouragement to his men and spurring his horse forward. The Goths, surprised by the ferocity of his attack, fell back, and Belisarius was able to slip back inside the city with his men.

With his face covered with blood, dust, and sweat, and his voice hoarse from shouting, he was almost unrecognizable and had to remove his helmet to stop a rumor that he had been killed. After reassuring his men, the exhausted commander visited every post, personally infusing his troops with his infectious optimism. Only when he had convinced himself that nothing more could be done did he allow his wife to lead him away to get some much-needed sleep.

Unaware how close he had come to victory, Vitiges ordered the cutting of all ten aqueducts to Rome, which for more than a millennium had supplied public fountains, plumbing, and the hydraulic mills that made the city's flour. Belisarius improvised by using the rivers that ran through the city to power the mills—ensuring a constant supply of flour and bread—and braced for the next attack. Vitiges had constructed huge towers to breach the Roman walls, and a few weeks later he put them into action. The fighting was desperate as the Goths attacked two sections of the wall simultaneously. Time and again they came within inches of overwhelming the defenders, but Belisarius seemed to be everywhere at once, firing arrows from the walls and hacking at the scaling ladders. By the end of the day, more than thirty thousand Goths were dead, and Vitiges' towers lay in a smoking ruin. Looking out over the walls, however, it was hard to see a dent in the waves of enemy soldiers. Belisarius knew that he would be hard-pressed to defend further attacks of this kind and hastily wrote to Justinian asking for reinforcements.

This wasn't the first time that the general had written requesting more men, and, at first, Justinian simply ignored him. Belisarius had humbled Africa with a mere handful of men, repeatedly performing miracles of improvisation to keep his campaigns going, and this caused the emperor to repeatedly underestimate the men and materials needed to retake Italy. But there was something else, a dim flicker of uneasiness in his queen, a gnawing fear that things were not quite what they seemed. Theodora began to suspect that the constant calls for a larger army were merely a ruse. Surely these barbarian opponents could be vanquished with the troops available. Perhaps the general was preparing to turn the sword against the master. The emperor finally sent a few thousand reinforcements, but Theodora remained suspicious. This general would need careful watching.

The new men tipped the balance in favor of Belisarius, and the general soon felt secure enough to go on the offensive. In the medieval world, siege warfare was often worse on the invading army than on the besieged. Exposed to the elements, running short of food, and trying to avoid sickness in unsanitary conditions, Vitiges was fighting a losing battle, and he knew it. Even the land he was encamped on seemed exhausted. It had long ago turned to a sea of mud, and his men were forced to wander farther and farther away in search of food. This left them dangerously vulnerable to counterattack, and each successful raid dented their spirits.

The mood in the Gothic camp wasn't improved when Vitiges got word that a Byzantine advance force had managed to slip out of Rome and capture the town of Rimini, only thirty-three miles from Ravenna. This entire struggle had been a vast exercise in futility for the Gothic king, and having his new capital in danger was the last straw. Cursing the winds that brought such an enemy to Italy, the disgusted king gave the order to retreat. Not even then, however, were the Goths allowed to leave in peace. Somehow guessing the timing of the withdrawal, Belisarius came roaring out from behind his walls and inflicted a thoroughly humiliating rout on Vitiges' panicked forces.

As the last Goth fled, he could perhaps have consoled himself with the fact that Italy hadn't seen a man of Belisarius's character since Hannibal had crossed the Alps more than seven hundred years before. With only a few thousand men, the Byzantine general had taken on a kingdom that numbered in the hundreds of thousands and managed to cripple its fighting ability within two years. In five years, with scarcely more men, he had subdued Africa and Italy and bent them to the imperial will.

Given a proper army and a little trust, there was no telling what Belisarius would have been able to do. The conquests of Spain and Gaul were tantalizingly within his reach; perhaps the Western Empire itself could be revived. With the imperium thus restored, Europe would have been spared the ravages of the Dark Ages, or at least the intensity of their destruction.

Unfortunately for the empire, it was never to find out. The brilliance of the general's success had planted seeds of jealousy and distrust in the mind of Theodora, and there they were about to bear a bitter harvest. Belisarius was too young, too talented, and far too popular to be trusted.

When Justinian received yet another letter asking for reinforcements, he sent seven thousand troops and a man named Narses to keep an eye on his brilliant general. Already in his mid-sixties, Narses was the perfect candidate for the job. Indisputably the most powerful figure at court, he was the same eunuch who had helped Belisarius put down the Nika revolt, and he could be implicitly trusted because his condition prevented him from gaining the throne himself.

The reinforcements were welcome enough, but as Justinian should have been able to foresee, the aging eunuch's presence completely undercut Belisarius's authority and nearly ruined the war effort. Generals who wanted to fast-track their careers quickly saw that Narses had the imperial favor; before long, the officers were hopelessly split between those loyal to Belisarius and those loyal to the eunuch. The only solution was to divide the already small force in half. While Narses kept the main Gothic army tied down, Belisarius left to mop up northern Italy.

Moving with his customary speed, Belisarius swept through the north, liberating Italian cities from the Gothic yoke. Most towns threw open their gates, eager to rid themselves of their heretical oppressors and rejoin the empire. The general was happy to accommodate them, but this led to the familiar problem of siphoning off his manpower with garrisons as the victories piled up. By the time the archbishop of Milan begged for Byzantine aid in liberating his city, Belisarius could spare only three hundred men. Sending the soldiers under the command of a subordinate, Belisarius continued on while the archbishop of Milan opened the city gates and massacred the Gothic garrison.

The ease of Milan's fall was gratifying to the Byzantines, but it provoked a furious response from the Gothic king. Milan was the crown jewel of Vitiges' kingdom, easily the largest city in Italy, and the moment he heard the news of its capture, he sent an army thirty thousand strong to retake it.

Somehow the beleaguered defenders got word to Belisarius, and he ordered the two closest generals to relieve the city. Now, however, the dangers of dividing the command were disastrously illustrated. The generals charged with coming to the city's rescue, perhaps fearing for their political careers, refused to move another inch without a countersignature from Narses; and while they dithered, Milan died. The desperate defenders had been reduced to eating dogs and mice; now, on the brink of starvation, they at last gave up and agreed to surrender to the Goths. The terms were horrendous. Milan was to be made an example of, a cautionary warning to the rest of Italy of what it meant to defy the Gothic sword. The women and children were rounded up and sold into slavery, the men were butchered on the spot, and the city was burned to the ground.

The shocking fate of one of the most beautiful cities in Italy was made far worse because it could have been easily prevented, but it at least convinced Justinian of the folly of undermining Belisarius's authority, and Narses was hurriedly recalled. At last, Belisarius had an undisputed command, and he was determined to strike a quick blow to end the war. Vitiges' forces still easily outnumbered his own, but by now the king was terrified of the general and refused to venture beyond the walls of Ravenna. If Belisarius could take the city with all of his enemies pinned inside, the war would be ended at a single stroke.

The news that the terrible Byzantine army was on the way threw

Vitiges into a panic, and he did the only thing he could think of to preserve his throne. A few weeks earlier, word had reached him that the Persian king Chosroes was threatening war on the Byzantine flank, and Vitiges now desperately wrote to the Persian monarch, hoping to enlist the aid of the empire's traditional enemy. If only the Persians could be persuaded to invade the East, the threat would force Justinian to recall his fearsome general and save the cornered Gothic king. Although Vitiges' messengers were caught and killed long before they came near Persia, luck was with the Goths. After eight years of struggle, Chosroes had finally established himself on the Persian throne and had no need for a Gothic invitation to invade. The Byzantine forces in the East had been noticeably thinned by the Italian campaign, and in any case he was quite sure that without Belisarius they would prove an easy match. Of course, there was the small matter of the "everlasting peace" with the empire that he had personally signed, but Chosroes wasn't one to let an inconvenient piece of paper get in the way of glory and tribute. Sending raiders knifing into Syria, the Persian king mobilized his army, determined to take full advantage of the empire's preoccupation with the West.

As Vitiges had hoped, the Persian threat hanging in the air was enough to scare Justinian into prematurely ending the Italian campaign. There was no telling how long the siege of Ravenna would take, and the emperor couldn't afford to have his best general pinned down besieging an already beaten enemy while the Persians ran free in the East. The only solution was to come to terms with Vitiges. In exchange for half of their treasury, the emperor was willing to let the Goths keep all their land north of the Po River.

When the two ambassadors carrying Justinian's terms reached Belisarius's camp, the general was horrified. Vitiges was a beaten man, and Ravenna was on the verge of collapse. Furiously, the general tried to reason with the imperial ambassadors, but they could hardly disobey Justinian's instructions. Seeing that it was hopeless, Belisarius bowed his head to the inevitable, but he refused to sign the treaty. He had no wish to put his name to such a shameful thing, and since Justinian hadn't ordered him to, he left it off as an act of defiance.

Once again, his famous luck saved the situation. Fearing one of Belisarius's ruses, the Gothic king refused to believe that the offer was genuine and sent it back to the Byzantine camp, saying that he wouldn't consider it until the general had signed it. Belisarius cleverly announced that he would only put his name to the document if Justinian himself ordered him to, forcing the imperial ambassadors to make the long return trip to Constantinople to get the emperor's response. Having temporarily rid himself of the meddlesome pair, Belisarius let the Goths know that there would be no further offers, and the announcement crushed what little hope remained to Vitiges. Sending messengers to secretly slip into the Byzantine camp under the cover of night, the Gothic king offered an intriguing proposal. If Belisarius would accept the crown of a revived Western Roman Empire, Ravenna's gates would be thrown open, and the Goths would bow at his feet.

There were few men better placed to see the advantages of such a situation than Belisarius. He'd been marching up and down Italy for the better part of five years, and with the Goths united behind him, there was no force in the East or the West capable of displacing him. The opportunity would have been irresistibly tempting to most of his officers, but Belisarius's loyalty never wavered. Feigning acceptance to Vitiges' terms, he entered Ravenna in May 540 and received the Gothic surrender. The streets were crowded with cheering Goths, as yet unaware of the deception. Writing to Constantinople, Belisarius informed Justinian of his actions, announcing that the war was over and Italy had been restored to the Roman Empire. The remarkably bloodless victory had been flawlessly executed, and Belisarius must have wondered if he would receive a triumph, or perhaps an even greater reward. In his mind, the way he had conquered Ravenna differed from a thousand other conquests only in the details, but accepting the Gothic crown—even as a ruse—was an unpardonable crime that awoke all the smoldering fears in Empress Theodora's mind.

From now on, it would be war between them, and Theodora was not one to easily forgive.

Those shadows, however, were not yet apparent to the conquering general. The next month, breathless ambassadors reached him, recalling him to Constantinople with the news that Chosroes had invaded. Loading the entire Gothic treasury as well as the presumably surprised Vitiges and his family onto transports, Belisarius left to obey the summons. It wasn't until the ships sailed out of the harbor that the Goths realized that they had been betrayed.

The general arrived in the East to find it in complete disarray. Chosroes had made the most of his four-month head start by heading straight for Antioch, the third-largest city in the Byzantine world. The emperor's cousin Germanus, who had been charged with the defense of Syria, had offered a large bribe to the Persians if they would leave Byzantine territory, but he had gotten bogged down in the details and petulantly decided to leave the city to its fate. The six thousand soldiers charged with guarding its expansive walls prudently fled at the approach of the massive invading army, and the Persians poured into the city.

Blue and Green street fighters desperately tried to stem the tide, but they were helpless against the tough, professional Persians, and the carnage was terrible. Soldiers ran through the streets burning and looting as they went, and when everything of value had been stripped away, Chosroes burned the city and sold its population into slavery. The Persian king had been right about Byzantine vulnerabilities all along, and he cheerfully continued his assault toward Syria. By the time the Persians arrived, however, things had drastically changed, and Chosroes abruptly halted his advance. A terrified Persian ambassador was brought into the Great King's presence and breathlessly advised his monarch to flee. "I have met a general," he said, "who surpassed all other men." Belisarius was in the East.

The general's arrival electrified the troops and immediately improved morale. News of Chosroes' presence in Syria arrived, but Belisarius had no intention of waiting around for him. Since the Persians had invaded the empire, he would return the favor. There was nothing like a little pillaging to raise the spirits and bring the Persian king scampering home. Chosroes had barely crossed into imperial territory when he discovered to his horror that Belisarius was burning his way toward the capital of Ctesiphon. It seemed as if the war with Persia would be ended with one bold strike.

10

:::

YERSINIA PESTIS

Chosroes came rushing home in a desperate defense of his cap-ital, but the Byzantine attack never happened. The year 541, as it turned out, was a high point for both Justinian's reign and the Byzantine Empire. In the West, Belisarius had returned both Africa and Italy to imperial control; in the East, he had pushed the Persians back and now seemed on the verge of conquering their capi-tal. The immense wealth of the Vandal and Gothic treasuries had added a shimmering veneer of impressive buildings in cities across the empire. Antioch had been rebuilt, and Constantinople gleamed with the crown jewel of the Hagia Sophia, the architectural marvel of the age. The Goths had elected a new king named Totila, but their king-dom was on the verge of collapse, and with the Persians scattered, it seemed as if no enemy could stand before the might of Byzantine arms. Even as Belisarius embarked for Ctesiphon, however, that enemy had arrived.

The port city of Pelusium, tucked into the eastern corner of the Nile Delta, had been a witness to some of the greatest invaders of the ancient world, from Alexander to Mark Antony. Augustus Caesar had once stood before its walls, and Pompey the Great had been murdered at its gates. Its most impressive conquerors, however, were rodents. By the time of Justinian, they had already had a long history with the city. In the eighth century BC, Sennacherib and the Assyrians were chased away when field mice chewed their bowstrings and the straps of their shields. The Persian king Cambyses II—apparently a good student of history—took the city in the sixth century by driving cats before the army, scattering the tiny defenders. The rodents, however, could only be kept out for so long, and in the spring of 540 they returned.

Traveling by boat from ports in Lower Egypt, rats carrying infected fleas slipped into the city and the dreaded *Yersinia pestis* made its terrible entrance on the world stage. Its most famous appearance would be in the fourteenth century, when it would be shudderingly remembered as the "black death," but the sixth-century outbreak—though more dimly remembered—was perhaps worse. The disease spread like wildfire to Alexandria, chief source of imperial grain, and from there to the rest of the empire.

Those struck by the contagion had little warning, and it spread with horrifying speed. Victims would awake with a headache and vague sense of weakness. If it spread to the lungs, painful swelling would occur along the lymph nodes, and death would come within a week; if it entered the blood, black patches would appear throughout the skin, and the victim wouldn't live out the day. There was no understanding of the contagion or how it spread, and therefore no protection. Moving with men and ships, it struck the most densely populated areas, occasionally carrying off as many as three-fourths of the population.

In Constantinople, the disease raged unchecked for four months with the horrifying casualty rate of ten thousand per day. The dead fell in such numbers that they overwhelmed the graveyards and had to be flung into an unused castle until the rotting corpses were spilling over the walls. The depopulated city ground to a halt, unable to maintain the rhythms of daily life under the strain. Trade sank to almost nothing, farmers abandoned their fields, and the few workers who remained did their best to flee the stricken city. When the plague at last abated, famine and poverty followed in its wake.

At first, the disaster didn't affect Belisarius, far away on the Persian frontier. Stories of tragic sickness were filtering through, but there was little he could do about it, other than resolve the trouble with Persia as quickly as possible. Racing east, however, came news that dramatically changed everything: Justinian himself was stricken.

The Byzantine army was thrown into chaos. Justinian had named no heir, and Theodora had been whispering her poisonous thoughts against the military in the emperor's ear for years. If he were to die now, the generals had little doubt she would appoint a successor without consulting them. They unanimously picked Belisarius as their choice for emperor and pledged to accept no decision made by Theodora without their input or consent.

As a childless queen, Theodora was acutely aware of her tenuous grip on power, and after a few months of governing the empire by herself, there were few more relieved than she when Justinian unexpectedly showed signs of recovery. It was then, newly secured in her position, that she received word of what the generals had decided in the East. Furious that they would dare dispute her authority, she immediately recalled Belisarius to the capital. Others may have been taken in by his claims of loyalty, but she had always known that he was a viper lusting for the throne. This newest outrage merely confirmed her darkest suspicions.

Enraged as she might have been, however, Theodora knew her limitations. Emperors and empresses had fallen from power by outraging public opinion, and she herself had come within an inch of exile during the Nika revolt. Belisarius was not as other men—his prestige was so great that to throw him into prison would most likely topple her from the throne. So, as much as she would have liked to execute him, she contented herself with stripping his command, seizing his property, and banishing him in disgrace.

Justinian recovered his health to find the empire crumbling around him. Perhaps a fourth of all those living around the Mediterranean had died, and the loss of so many potential soldiers and taxpayers had severely crippled imperial resources. The only consolation was that Persia was suffering as well. Trying to take advantage of his weakened enemy, Chosroes had raided Byzantine territory, but he had only succeeded in infecting his own men—and, on his return, the rest of Persia as well.

The West was in an even worse condition. Without Belisarius, the Byzantine reconquest had collapsed with frightening speed. Ironically enough, Justinian had only himself to blame for most of it. Scared by the power of a general who had never wavered in his loyalty, he had decided that no one officer would wield supreme command and split the leadership of the Italian campaign between no fewer than five of them. This foolish decision divided the diminished Byzantine resources among squabbling, incompetent generals who almost immediately fell to arguing instead of completing the conquest.

Imperial weakness could hardly have come at a worse time. The Goths at last had found a worthy king in the brilliant Totila, and he was determined to save his kingdom from the desperate situation his predecessor had left it in. Easily outmaneuvering the unwieldy Byzantines, Totila surged through Italy, promising deliverance from the heavy imperial tax collectors and an end to the unceasing war. Belisarius had been welcomed into Rome as a liberator, but now it was the Goths who would set the Romans free.

Within a year, Totila had undone most of Belisarius's work, and the hapless Byzantine generals wrote to Justinian, informing him that they were no longer capable of defending Italy. The reconquest, which had taken so much effort, seemed to be on the brink of slipping away, and the realization stung Justinian into action. Overriding the protests of his wife, he called once again for Belisarius.

The general had hardly deserved his disgrace, but with Theodora at his side, Justinian could never quite bring himself to trust his old friend, and the general was sent to Italy with only four thousand men. When he arrived, Belisarius found that the situation was virtually hopeless. His soldiers were deeply disillusioned, his commanders were uninspired, and the population was sympathetic to Totila and openly hostile to the Byzantines. Opening an offensive against the Goths was out of the question; it would be a miracle to hold those cities left in imperial control.

Somehow Belisarius managed to hold on to the center of Italy, but every day seemed to bring fresh disasters. Barbarian attacks on the frontiers grew more insistent, and the troops who didn't drift off to protect their homes seemed more eager to defect to Totila than to fight him. They hadn't seen regular pay since the onset of the plague, and the Gothic conquest had begun to seem inevitable. Hemorrhaging men and worried that he would soon be unable to protect Rome, Belisarius wryly wrote to the emperor, informing him of the deplorable situation and begging him to send more troops: "The soldiers already stationed . . . are discontented, fearful, and dismayed; at the sound of an enemy they dismiss their horses, and cast their arms on the ground. . . . If the war could be won by the presence of Belisarius alone, your preparations are perfect. . . . But if you desire to conquer, you must do something more than this."* Belisarius's refreshingly candid letter went on to say that he could rescue the situation only if his old veterans were sent to him.

From the start, the request seemed doomed. The messenger charged with delivering it decided to enjoy his time in the capital instead of going directly to the palace. Only after he had courted a woman and gotten married did he seek an audience with the emperor and fulfill his mission. The second obstacle was more formidable. Theodora had no intention of allowing Belisarius and his veterans to be reunited, and there was simply no money to equip new troops. A few reinforcements were scraped up and sent, but as always it was too little and too late.

Without real aid from Constantinople, Belisarius couldn't hope to raise enough men to defeat the Goths, and the war settled into a depressing stalemate. Rome seesawed back and forth between each army and was left a shattered ruin, desolate and nearly deserted.† By

---

*Edward Gibbon, *The Decline and Fall of the Roman Empire*, v. 4 (New York: Random House, 1993).

†The historian Procopius, who was probably there, claims rather unbelievably that only five hundred citizens were left.

548, Belisarius was desperate enough to send his wife, Antonina, to Constantinople to beg for aid. The plague had run its course and things seemed to be generally improving elsewhere for the empire, so the general hoped that now money and men could be found to turn the tide against the Goths. There was also a good reason to hope that his wife would prove a more able ambassador than the last man he had sent. A close friend of Theodora, she would be able to bypass whatever red tape was thrown in her way and quickly receive a direct audience with the empress. Antonina arrived in the city eager to see her friend, but she found instead everything draped black in mourning and Justinian overwhelmed with grief. Theodora was dead.

She had been a bulwark in those desperate early days of the Nika riots, but as the de facto leader of the empire, she had been disastrous. Convinced that Belisarius was as politically minded as she herself was, she had poisoned the mind of her husband against the one man who could have accomplished his dreams of reconquest. Even worse, while Justinian lay dying, she had made it her personal mission to restore Monophysitism throughout the empire, revitalizing the heresy just as the entire controversy was on the brink of disappearing.* This single act would do more damage than any barbarian army could have, badly weakening the loyalty of most of Syria and Egypt. A century later, when a new and hostile enemy arrived, they would be greeted as liberators against the religious oppression of Constantinople, and much of the East would be wrenched from the Roman orbit forever.

Devastated by his loss, Justinian recalled Belisarius in 549 and greeted him like a brother. Throwing his arms around the tired man who had been so faithful through the years, Justinian installed the general in a sumptuous palace and even erected a bronze statue in his honor. Belisarius was uncomfortable with such praise and soon faded quietly into the background, but there were few people in the empire who deserved fame more. Without him, Justinian's vast reconquests would have been unthinkable, and the smaller, reduced

---

*Monophysitism is the teaching that Christ was divine but not fully human.

state wouldn't have had the resources to withstand the coming turbulent centuries.

As Belisarius watched from the shadows of Constantinople, Totila besieged Rome, and its unpaid, demoralized garrison, tired of the taste of horse meat, threw open the gates after a brief show of resistance. With the fall of the ancient capital—the fourth time it had changed hands since the war began—Justinian was finally convinced that Italy could only be won by entrusting undivided command to a single general. Calling the elderly eunuch Narses to him, he outfitted a massive army and entrusted it to the courtier.

Already in his seventies, Narses was an odd choice as supreme commander, especially since his only military experiences had been butchering a few thousand unarmed citizens during the Nika riots and causing Belisarius to lose Milan twelve years before. But Narses was a shrewd diplomat who had spent a lifetime gliding among the turbulent waters of the imperial court, and there were few men in the empire who were better connected. As far as the emperor was concerned, age wasn't a concern. He was nearly seventy himself, and if age hadn't diminished his own energy, he didn't see why it should affect his new general.

Narses was equipped with all the supplies that had been denied to his predecessor to claim the victory that should have belonged to Belisarius. Sailing with nearly ten times the number of men granted to the great general, Narses brought with him all the money owed to the long-suffering Byzantine garrisons. When he arrived in Italy, scattering largesse, men flocked to his banner, swelling his ranks.

Just as the last transport ship left the imperial harbor, two ambassadors entered Constantinople bringing an intriguing message to the emperor. They were from Visigothic Spain and brought news of spreading chaos and a Roman revolt against the barbarian king. Under the command of a brilliant leader named Athanagild, the rebels had taken Córdoba and were now asking for imperial help to take Seville.

Almost any other man would have wished the men the best of

luck and rejected the entire ridiculous idea. The empire's resources were strained to the breaking point, its armies were bogged down in the ugly Italian morass, and the last thing it needed now was to commit to a far-flung province miles away from the overextended communication and supply lines. Justinian, however, couldn't resist the opportunity and instantly agreed. Spain was the last kingdom where a Christian, Roman population was ruled by a barbarian, Arian king, and it would be easy for the Byzantines to present themselves as the champions of the faith. The Spanish population would inevitably rally against their heretical overlords, Justinian thought, providing a perfect bridgehead for the eventual reconquest of the whole peninsula.

Those who had thought Narses too old and decrepit to lead a military invasion were stunned with the man Justinian chose to lead the expedition to Spain. Nearly ninety years old, Liberius was a general of long experience, and—despite his age—an excellent choice for a commander. Leading an army of only a few hundred men, the wily general would soon have the Spanish on their heels. Upon landing in Spain, he quickly came to Athanagild's aid and conquered Seville, but when the rebel leader was proclaimed king and nervously asked the Byzantines to leave, the shrewd general refused. Conducting a brilliant guerrilla war, he managed to play off the Romanized populace against their Arian overlords and reconquered the entire south of Spain for the empire.

The same month that Liberius set sail, Narses started the long march on Rome. Totila laughed when he heard that a eunuch was leading the imperial armies and let the barbarian Franks flood into northern Italy, hoping that they would eradicate the nuisance for him. As the Goths were soon to find out, however, there was an able mind concealed in Narses' frail body, and he effortlessly dodged the Franks by keeping to the coast.

Near the old Roman town of Busta Gallorum, Narses caught Totila and, in a bloody struggle, completely crushed the Gothic army, killing the king in the process. Impoverished Rome threw open its gates to the Byzantines, and Narses sent its keys—along with Totila's jewel-encrusted crown, golden armor, and bloody robe—to Constantinople as symbols of his triumph.

While the victorious Narses concentrated on driving the remnants of Gothic power from Italy, Justinian started preparing the conquest of Spain, but the plague returned to spoil his plans. For six months it raged, draining the already depleted empire, and the emperor was forced to give up his dreams of further conquest. As if to symbolize the hardships now afflicting Byzantium, that same year an earthquake caused the collapse of the half-dome above the high altar in the Hagia Sophia. What must have seemed a lifetime ago, the entire church had been built in six years, but now money was so scarce that five years passed before the dome was repaired.

What money the empire could still produce went to the all-important role of defense. There were simply no men to replace those killed by war or decimated by the plague, so Justinian slashed the military, depending more on gold than steel to repel the empire's many enemies. At the start of his reign, the army had numbered more than half a million men; by the end, it was down to a mere 150,000. Since the frontiers had nearly doubled in size, the reduced forces couldn't hope to effectively patrol them all. In 559, the dangerous game Justinian was playing caught up to him when a group of Huns overran the deserted frontier and came within thirty miles of Constantinople.

The city was in no danger thanks to its stout walls, but it was a humiliating experience for the emperor who had humbled the Gothic and Vandal kingdoms to hide behind his walls while a small force of barbarians terrorized the suburbs. Unfortunately for Justinian, there was no army at hand to punish these impudent savages, but there did happen to be a retired general in the city. Summoning the great man before him as he had so many times in the past, the emperor entrusted one last task to Belisarius.

It had been ten years since the general had seen combat, but he had lost none of his brilliance. Improvising an army out of a few hundred guards, veterans, and volunteers, he crippled the Huns with a carefully planned ambush, and even managed to drive the invaders back to the frontier. The sight of his invincible general once more scattering all before him resurrected all the old fears that had lain dormant in Justinian since Theodora's death. With a rather unedifying flash of jealousy, the emperor abruptly dismissed Belisarius and took personal command of the army. The great general, still only in his fifties, faded gracefully into the background, content to watch yet again as another man claimed the victory that should have been his. Justinian's methods were perhaps not nearly as inspiring to his watching subjects, but they were certainly effective. After bribing the Huns to leave, the emperor incited a rival tribe to invade their homeland. It hardly seemed a noble victory, but there was reason to celebrate. The empire at last was at peace.

It remained so for the rest of Justinian's reign. Belisarius was never called on again, but he lived long enough to see Narses smash a Frankish army at Verona, bringing a conclusion to the long and bloody Italian reconquest. Perhaps there was some measure of satisfaction for the general as he saw the final realization of his master's vision. The thought must have occurred to many that though Narses had planted the final standard, it was Belisarius's labor that had brought Justinian's dreams to fruition. Through it all, the general's loyalty had never wavered, and he had suffered his humiliations in silence, preferring to remain the faithful servant of a man he could have overthrown.* Justinian survived him by only eight months, dying in his sleep at the ripe old age of eighty-three on November 14, 565.†

Few emperors had ever worked so hard or devoted so much to the good of the empire. Indeed, the sight of Justinian pacing the labyrinthine halls of the Great Palace deep into the night had been so common that the imperial servants gave him the nickname of "the

---

*He may have been neglected by the emperor, but Belisarius was never forgotten by the common man. Eight hundred years later, the people of Constantinople were still singing songs and writing poems celebrating his life.

†Much that we know about Justinian and Belisarius comes from the pen of the great historian Procopius. By a strange twist of fate, the year 565 saw the death of all three Byzantine giants.

sleepless one." His thirty-eight years on the throne saw vast improvements in the government, the law, and the economy, and left his imprint so firmly stamped on the capital that it has yet to disappear. He added more territory to the empire than any emperor but Trajan or Augustus, and he reconquered every country his armies attempted to take, making the Mediterranean once again a Roman lake. Cities from Antioch to Rome were adorned with breathtaking splendor, and rising at the center of it all stood the golden domes of the Hagia Sophia. Designed to outlast the centuries, it remains the most powerful vision of his reign, capable of momentarily lifting the veil of fifteen hundred years to let us glimpse Byzantium in her most glorious age.

Justinian's human failings may have prevented him from trusting his great general, but that had only slowed the pace of success. The victories had been truly spectacular; nations trembled at his name, and arrogant kings and hostile generals had bowed humbly at his feet. But in the end, his grand dreams were betrayed, not by excessive ambition, but by the arrival of a diseased rat.

As time passed, it became clear that rather than the herald of a new and triumphant order, Justinian was instead the last fleeting glimpse of an old one. Never again would such a visionary rule the empire, nor would a man whose first language was Latin ever sit on its throne again. Despite all of Justinian's energy and daring, the days of the old Roman Empire were gone and wouldn't return. The bubonic plague had seen to that, killing off one-fourth of the population in its disastrous run, making Justinian's reconquest impossible to hold. The new territory should have made the empire far richer and more secure, but instead, with the disease raging, it increased the frontiers at a time when the empire lacked the manpower or money to defend them. To maintain such an expanded empire with diminished resources would have required the ability and energy of both a Justinian and a Belisarius—two luxuries Byzantium would never have again.

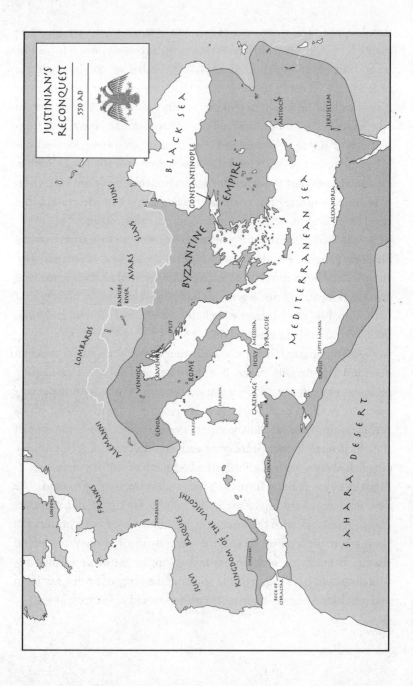

11

A PERSIAN FIRE

As outwardly glorious as Justinian's reign had been, there were few who mourned its passing. The population that gathered silently in the streets to watch the funeral procession blamed him for the miseries of high taxation and the ravages of the plague. The scheming aristocrats packed into the Church of the Holy Apostles to watch the ceremony felt only relief that their oppressor was dead, and the officiating priests gladly buried the man whose meddling wife had added so much division to the church. Even the guard of honor at his massive, porphyry tomb couldn't bring themselves to love the man who had so often delayed the army's pay.

Despite the empire's problems, however, its former emperor had succeeded in making Byzantium a shining beacon of civilization. The architectural triumph of the Hagia Sophia had only been possible by sophisticated advances in mathematics, and it soon spawned a flourishing school dedicated to improving the field. In Byzantium, primary education was available for both genders, and thanks to the stability of Justinian's rule, virtually every level of society was literate. Universities throughout the empire continued the Aristotelian and Platonic traditions that were by now over a millennium old, and the works of the great scientists of antiquity were compiled in both public and private libraries.

The old western provinces under barbarian rule, by contrast, were quickly sinking into the brutish chaos of the Dark Ages, with recollections of advanced urban life a fading memory. Literacy declined precipitously as the struggle to scratch out an existence made education an unaffordable luxury, and it would have disappeared completely without the church. There, writing was still valued, and remote monasteries managed to keep learning dimly alive. But throughout the West, trade slowed to a crawl, cities shrank, and the grand public buildings fell into disrepair.

The East, by contrast, remained a thriving hub of business, an extensive network of prosperous towns linked by the unparalleled Roman road system. Merchants carrying spices, bolts of silk from the Far East, and amber from the distant north crisscrossed busy roads to and from the bustling seaports. Artisans produced stunning works of enamel and gold filigree, jewelry and illuminations. On the coasts of Asia Minor and Greece, skilled workers harvested tiny shellfish to make a luxurious purple dye, and a new state-run industry of silk production sprang up in Constantinople.* In the minor and major cities alike, the professional classes were divided into guilds, students gathered at the universities, and peddlers delivered wares to housewives who didn't want to fight the crowded streets.

Feast days and state holidays provided occasions for lavish parties among the upper class, while those of lower social standing entertained themselves in the pleasant distractions of wine shops, restaurants, and small theaters. Country life continued to hum with the same rhythm it had maintained for centuries. Farmers scattered throughout the countryside cultivated their vineyards and gardens, while villagers worked the communal crop farms. At night, the working class would return from their fields to their wives and children for an evening meal of bread, vegetables, and cereals, usually boiled and combined with omelets and various kinds of cheese. The more affluent could add the meat of hares and birds, salt pork and sausages, or even lamb. For dessert, there were grape leaves stuffed with cinnamon, currants, and pastries filled

---

*Transporting silks from the Far East was both expensive and slow, but fortunately for the empire, two monks had discovered the secrets of the silk moth's life cycle and managed to smuggle several out of China. The delighted Justinian immediately planted mulberry trees in the capital to provide them with food, and Byzantium's most lucrative industry was born.

with nuts and honey or stuffed with jam. Unlike the barbarian custom of smearing bread with animal fat, the Byzantines dipped their food in olive oil, and they filled out the meal with fresh fish, fruits, and various wines. A man's worth could be judged, so they said, by his table.

But as the sixth century drew to a close, there were troubling signs on the horizon. The merchants, industrialists, and small landowners that made up the middle class were diminishing as wars and uprisings began to disrupt trade. Natural disasters and the seizure of their produce by passing troops made life difficult for farmers and frequently led them to borrow money they couldn't hope to repay. Growing numbers of poor tried to flee the land to avoid their creditors, while those who remained sold themselves into serfdom to resolve their debts. Small farms began to disappear, swallowed by the ravenous hunger of the great aristocratic landowners. With a shrinking tax base and powerful landed magnates enjoying considerable tax exemptions, the central government was forced to resort to increasingly severe measures to keep its coffers full, but harsh tactics met with diminishing returns. Always chronically short of funds, the emperors who followed Justinian could spare no time for the relief of their citizens and turned a deaf ear to their complaints.

The growth of arts and sciences, which had reached such a pinnacle during Justinian's reign, also began to slow as the empire's fortunes declined. There was no more time or money for lavish buildings or leisurely inquiry; all resources had to be marshaled for the basic needs of survival. Even that survival, however, must have seemed to ensure only continued misery. Justinian's wars of reconquest had obscured his diplomatic finesse, and the vain emperors who followed him saw war as the first, rather than the last, option. They thought that invincibility came with prestige and all too quickly committed the empire to ruinous conflicts it could ill afford. To the poor farmers building their lives in the countryside, it hardly mattered if the armies that tramped across their land wore Byzantine uniforms or not. The end result was always the same: Their produce was seized, their fields were plundered, and their livestock disappeared. They felt little loyalty to the distant rulers in Constantinople and were perfectly happy to throw their support behind the first pretender to promise them better lives. Revolt became endemic, and emperors found it impossible to hold onto the allegiance of such a diverse and splintering state.

Justinian had boasted that his empire stretched from the Atlantic to the Black Sea, but in the wake of his glory, the empire faced a stunning collapse. The territory added by his reconquest introduced the diverse lands of North Africa, Italy, and Spain to an already volatile mix, and since these new territories were isolated with only tenuous land routes between them, they had little that bound them to the rest of the empire. The great synthesis of the Roman world cracked under the strain of plague, invasion, and religious tension, and its edges drifted steadily away from the center at Constantinople.

To hold itself together, the unwieldy state needed a visionary leader, but the emperors who sat on the Byzantine throne at the end of the fifth century were shortsighted men, neither as wise nor as forceful as Justinian, and they were completely unable to duplicate the delicate balancing act needed to maintain peace with the empire's many enemies. All too often they compounded their problems by trading Justinian's unpopular but necessary policies for the temporary favor of the crowd, and these shortsighted decisions brought the empire to the verge of collapse within a generation. History provides few better examples of the dangers of governing by the interests of the moment.

By the end of the sixth century, the reconquests that had cost so much blood and treasure to gain had been carelessly thrown away, and the empire was retreating on all fronts.* In Constantinople, a demented

---

*After he had completed the conquest of Italy, Justinian's old commander Narses was recalled with an alarming lack of tact. The wife of Justinian's successor mocked the ninety-year-old eunuch by sending him a golden distaff with a letter of dismissal. "Since you are not a man," it supposedly read, "go spin wool with the women." Enraged by the unnecessary insult after a lifetime of service, Narses muttered that "he would tie her such a knot that she would not unravel it in her lifetime." Preparing to go into retirement in Naples, he spitefully invited the *long beards*—Lombards—into Italy. The peninsula was not united again until the risorgimento of the nineteenth century.

usurper without a shred of legitimacy named Phocas seized the throne, and the Balkans disappeared under a flood of Slavic invasion. Armies pushed beyond endurance were demoralized and disorganized, unwilling to fight for an uninspiring and corrupt government. Any wealth that escaped the clutches of the imperial tax collectors disappeared into the bottomless pockets of barbarian hordes that seemed to appear with depressing regularity. Refugees packed the cities, trade slowed to a crawl, and weeds and ruins choked the once-fertile fields. The empire was a spent force, a broken reed, the luster of its past a fading memory.

Virtually the only area of the empire that wasn't collapsing was the prosperous coast of North Africa. There, under the warm sun, merchants continued to ply the waters of its harbors unmolested, and farmers harvested its fertile wheat fields. The province seemed far away from the swirling revolts and chronic unrest that had so thoroughly destroyed imperial prosperity, and some in Constantinople began to see it as the only chance of salvation. Disgusted by their bloody emperor, the Senate wrote secretly to the governor of North Africa, urging him to come at the head of an army and deliver the empire from its present nightmare.

When the letter arrived in Carthage, the governor read it with considerable interest. He was far too comfortable where he was, and, in any case, he felt himself to be too old to go gallivanting around, so he sent his son Heraclius with the African fleet to seize the throne in his stead.

The young man knew he had to act quickly. Each passing day seemed to bring the empire closer to destruction: While the government in Constantinople concentrated on purging itself of suspected dissidents in a horrifying bloodbath, the Persian king Chosroes II took advantage of the distraction to invade. Meeting only token resistance from the demoralized imperial army, the Persians quickly overran Mesopotamia and Armenia, plunging deeply into the Byzantine heartland and even probing into Egypt. Before long, Persian watch fires could be seen from the walls of Constantinople; and as panic rippled through the capital, the plague returned, bringing with it terrified prophecies of the end of the world.

It was at this moment, with the population of the capital at a fever pitch, that Heraclius arrived in the imperial harbor on board his magnificent flagship. At the sight of the vessel, a mob in Constantinople lynched his predecessor, Phocas, dragging the mutilated corpse through the streets. Picking his way through the despoiled palace with care, Heraclius took stock of his shattered empire. It had lost nearly half of its territory, and what was left was demoralized and impoverished, but its roots were deep, and Heraclius was already starting to plan. The empire of the past was gone—of that he was confident. His task was to create something new—an empire that embraced its future. Byzantium would never be the same again.

The crowd milling about outside the imperial palace in the bright October sun of AD 610, waiting to catch a glimpse of their new emperor, didn't quite know what to expect. He'd appeared seemingly out of nowhere like the Athena of their old pagan myths, springing fully grown out of the head of Zeus. There was an aura of success about him, and he was undeniably physically impressive. Barely thirty-six, with a full head of golden hair and impossibly burnished armor, he looked every inch an emperor, like some new Achilles appearing at Byzantium's darkest hour. Energetic and hardworking, the emperor had the rare ability to inspire confidence in even the most desperate circumstances, and he threw himself into the task of rescuing the empire.

The challenges confronting him were enormous. The once-vaunted imperial army was scattered helplessly before its enemies, and Greece was buried beneath a Slavic flood. Refugees crowded into Constantinople, soon bringing with them news too terrible to comprehend. At first, it was only whispered in disbelief, but it spread like wildfire. Jerusalem had fallen to the Persians, and the True Cross was now in the hands of the fire worshippers of Ctesiphon.* All male citi-

---

*The cross had been found in the Holy Land by Constantine the Great's mother, Saint Helena, and was believed to be the very cross on which Christ was crucified.

zens of Jerusalem had been killed, and the women and children had been sold into slavery.

Not since the Visigothic sack of Rome had such a disaster buffeted the empire. The Almighty had obviously withdrawn his hand, allowing pagans to cart off Christendom's holiest relic, and now Byzantium was being punished for its hubris. All resistance to Persian arms collapsed as the terrified citizens scrambled to get out of the way of the terrible army. With nothing to stop him, the Persian king gleefully turned to Egypt and, in 619, managed to sack the province, depriving the empire of its main source of grain. After six centuries, the days of free bread were over. From now on, the citizens of Constantinople had to get their wheat from Thrace—and pay for it like everyone else. The end was clearly at hand, and with the frightening Persian enemy at the gates, Heraclius made the strategically sensible decision to abandon Constantinople and move the capital to his native Carthage, in North Africa. Or at least that's what he announced. When the horrified population begged him to stay, he shrewdly agreed to remain on the condition that they would swear to accept whatever sacrifice he would demand.

Heraclius, it seemed, had learned the lessons of the last fifty years quite well. He had come to power on a wave of popularity but didn't intend to rule with one finger in the wind. The empire was in a dreadful condition, and he knew that the road ahead would be long and difficult. He had little personal military experience, no veteran officers, no disciplined troops, and above all no money. The empire was bankrupt, unable to pay even the reduced salaries of its soldiers, and it couldn't afford to hire costly mercenaries. If there was to be any hope of recovery, Heraclius needed money, and to get it he turned for the first time to the church.

In theory, the patriarch and the emperor were two arms of the same divine will, a spiritual leader and a secular enforcer of God's kingdom here on earth, but all too often their relationship was defined by mild antagonism as each tried to ward off encroachment by the other. The emperor was driven by political necessities and wanted pliable bishops, but the church, always wary of the throne, took great pains to ensure that emperors remembered their place. The imperial role was to implement, not create, church policy, and patriarchs jealously guarded their councils from any hint of imperial interference. Keeping such roles clearly defined obviously needed constant vigilance, but it sometimes made it impossible for church and state to work confidently together.

When Heraclius met with the patriarch, Sergius, and explained the emergency, the patriarch responded immediately, pledging the entire wealth of the church and turning over an immense quantity of gold and silver plate to the emperor. This was especially impressive since Heraclius, violating several commandments (not to mention laws), had recently married his niece, Martina. Tactfully managing to overlook this indiscretion in light of the emergency, the patriarch made his donation, temporarily solving the financial woes of the empire.

Such cooperation would have been impossible in the West, where the pope had lost his emperor and the distinction between sacred and secular power had become hopelessly blurred. Forced to wear both the crown and the papal tiara, the pope entered the political arena, bringing the church into direct competition with the state. The kings of Europe strenuously fought papal interference in their affairs, while the church tried to fight its growing worldliness while maintaining its influence. The struggle between the two would become the defining tension of western history, and make the East— where the original roles hadn't broken down—appear impossibly alien.

The cooperation between church and state may have enriched the emperor, but it failed to cheer the miserable inhabitants of the Eastern Empire. Farms continued to burn, men continued to be killed or enslaved, and still no armies came streaming out of the golden gate to defend the beleaguered citizens. They were left to fend for themselves, to curse the dreaded Persians and the emperor who had seemingly abandoned them, and to survive as best they could.

Heraclius hadn't forgotten about them, however. He simply had his own plans and didn't intend to be rushed. The imperial army was shattered and demoralized, and throwing it in front of the Persians would only destroy it completely. It needed to be carefully rebuilt and reorganized, and only when that task was finished could he lead it to the defense of the empire. For ten long years, Heraclius stubbornly resisted the pleas of his suffering people, the hawks in his government, and the repeated attempts of the Persians to draw him out. The walls of Constantinople would keep him safe, and he wouldn't risk everything in a battle before he was absolutely ready.

By the spring of 622, his preparations were at last finished. It was a testament to Heraclius's power to inspire that during those long years, despite appalling losses to imperial territory, there were no calls for his removal or pretenders rising to usurp him. There was still a nervous sense of disquiet, but the emperor's confidence never wavered, and it proved infectious. The army he finally led out of the golden gate was infused with his charisma and proud in their bright armor to march to the defense of their compatriots.

The great advantage the Byzantines had never lost to the Persians was the control of the sea, and Heraclius used it to its full extent. Landing at Issus—where Alexander the Great had destroyed an earlier Persian Empire nearly a thousand years before—he launched a surprise attack. The battle was a desperate gamble. Heraclius knew that if he should fall the empire was doomed, but he was prepared to risk everything—even bringing along his pregnant wife, Martina. The Persians confronting him were commanded by their most famous general, a man who had conquered Egypt, but it was the inexperienced Heraclius who triumphed. Breaking before the Byzantine charge, the Persians were scattered, according to one source, "like a herd of goats." Morale skyrocketed. The Persians were not invincible after all.

As the army wintered in Cappadocia, Heraclius infused them with his spirit, holding daily training sessions and filling them with confidence. They were honored men, he told them, fighting on the side of truth against the pagans who had burned their crops, killed their sons, and enslaved their wives. That spring they would have their revenge. Marching into modern-day Azerbaijan, the center of Persian Zoroastrian fire worship, the reinvigorated Byzantine army avenged Jerusalem by burning the great fire temple and sacking the birthplace of Zoroaster.

The Persian king Chosroes II was close to panic, but that spring he began to formulate a plan. The Persian Empire was vast, and Heraclius had now penetrated deeper into it than any Roman commander before him. The Byzantines were outnumbered and far from home, unable to maintain a war of attrition, and perhaps the king could use that to his advantage. Gathering an army fifty thousand strong, Chosroes II entrusted it to a general named Shahin, ordering him to destroy Heraclius and warning him that the cost of failure was death. Then, confident that the Byzantines would be tied down, the Persian king contacted the barbarian Avars and offered his support in an attack on Constantinople.

Heraclius was now faced with the most difficult decision of his career. If he rushed back to the defense of the capital, he would lose his best chance of winning the war and undo all the hard work of the past four years. On the other hand, if he stayed, Constantinople might fall for lack of defenders. His solution was to split the army into three parts. The first raced back to defend Constantinople; the second he entrusted to his brother Theodore to deal with Shahin; and the third, and by far the smallest, stayed with him to hold Armenia and the Caucasus Mountains and invade a virtually defenseless Persia.

Heraclius had great faith in the defenses of Constantinople, and in an attempt to bolster its defenders' morale, he sent an avalanche of letters detailing every aspect of a successful defense. Armed with the emperor's letters, and the knowledge that he had not left them to their fate, morale soared despite the rather terrifying presence of eighty thousand barbarians outside the walls. Every citizen of the city cheerfully took his turn manning the defenses or carrying supplies to the soldiers on the walls, and each day the patriarch made a circuit of the land walls while holding high an icon of the Virgin Mary, the protector of the city, who, it was whispered, struck terror into the hearts of the barbarians.*

The city certainly seemed to be under divine protection. Day after day, the siege engines battered uselessly against the walls, and tensions among the attackers began to rise, fraying the alliance between the barbarians and the Persians. When news arrived that the Byzantine army under Heraclius's brother Theodore had met Shahin in a driving hailstorm and completely crushed the Persian army, the frustrated Avars gave up.† Their mighty siege engines had been futile, their Persian allies were useless, and every attempt at subtlety had been effortlessly repulsed. The city was obviously under divine protection after all, and therefore invincible. Dismantling their equipment, the Avar hordes dragged themselves away from the sight of those accursed walls, burning some churches for good measure as they lumbered off.

Everything seemed to be collapsing at once for the Persians. Just a few years before, they had been on the brink of capturing Constantinople, and now their armies were broken and retreating on all fronts. Outside the ancient city of Nineveh, a last, desperate attempt was made to restrain the triumphant Heraclius, but in a bloody, eleven-hour battle, the emperor shattered the Persian army, killing its commander in single combat.

The brutal sacking of Ctesiphon that followed the battle put the finishing touches on the war. So much treasure was captured that Heraclius's army couldn't carry it all, and much of it had to be consigned to the flames. Chosroes II called for women and children to

---

*This was known as the Hodegetria and was the holiest relic in Byzantium. Believed to have been painted by Saint Luke himself, it was brought to Constantinople in the fifth century and installed in a monastery built specifically to house it.

†Shahin committed suicide after the battle to escape the wrath of his vicious overlord, but Chosroes II had the body packed in salt and transported to the capital. When it arrived, he had it whipped until it was no longer recognizable.

defend him, but by now he was widely blamed for the calamity that had overtaken Persia, and no one was willing to fight for him.* Furiously turning on their monarch, the army and people alike rose up in revolt, and their justice was terrible. Chosroes II was flung into the ominously named Tower of Darkness, where he was given only enough food and water to prolong his agony. When he had suffered enough, he was dragged out and forced to watch as his children were executed in front of him. After the last of his offspring had expired, his torment was finally brought to an end when he was shot slowly to death with arrows.

The war had broken Persian strength, and the new king, Shahr-Baraz, immediately sued for peace, surrendering all the conquered land, releasing all prisoners, and returning the True Cross. As a final gesture of submission, he even made the Byzantine emperor the guardian of his son. Heraclius had recovered at a stroke all that had been lost during the long years of decline. The long struggle with Persia was over; never again would they trouble the Byzantine Empire.

The Senate rapturously granted their glorious emperor the title of "Scipio," and when he arrived in sight of the capital, it was to find the entire population streaming out to meet him, waving olive branches and cheering.† Singing hymns, they carried the emperor into the city, following the True Cross through the Golden Gate in a procession complete with the first elephants ever seen in the city. After marching to the Hagia Sophia, they watched as their victorious emperor raised the cross above the high altar. It had been six long years since Heraclius had left the city, but now he sat enthroned in all his glory. He had snatched the empire from the jaws of extinction and overthrown the power of Persia. The True Cross was enshrined, and the Lord's enemies were scattered before it. Surely, this was the dawn of a new age.

---

*Chosroes II certainly didn't help matters with his conduct. After one battle he sent his defeated general a woman's dress, provoking an instant rebellion.

†Scipio Africanus, the greatest of the Roman Republic's military heroes, had defeated the mighty Hannibal and ended the Second Punic War.

Heraclius had restored the empire to its former glory, and, in appearance at least, it still resembled the classical world of antiquity. A Greek or Italian traveler could walk from the Strait of Gibraltar through North Africa and Egypt to Mesopotamia and feel comfortably at home. There were regional differences, but the cities were all reassuringly Roman, the language was Greek, and the culture was Hellenized. Most towns had the same familiar plan, complete with sumptuous baths waiting to wash the dust from tired feet and aqueducts and amphitheaters dotting the landscapes. Life may have been a bit more turbulent and uncertain, but it continued much as it had since the Romans first arrived with their powerful legions and ordered architecture.

But there were important differences, too. Even in educated circles, few men were now bilingual. Latin had always been widely considered an unsatisfactory language for sophisticated discussions, especially theological ones, and over the centuries it had slowly died out. Western officials posted to the East had been able to obtain phrase books with local Greek expressions to assist them, but no one bothered to return the favor. The cultural flow swept relentlessly in one direction only, and though Greek thought still moved west, in the East the Latin classics of Virgil, Horace, and Cicero remained untranslated and widely unknown. By the time of Heraclius, few men could understand the archaic language that the empire's laws were written in, and the emperor, who prized military efficiency above all else, swept away the old trappings of the Latin empire. Greek was made the official language, and even the imperial titles were modified accordingly. Every emperor from Augustus to Heraclius had been hailed as Imperator Caesar and Augustus, but after him they were known only as *Basíleus*—the Greek word for king.* The break with the past was startling but long overdue. The empire was now thoroughly Greek, and within a generation the old imperial language was extinct.

In the spring of 630, Heraclius made the pilgrimage to

---

*After his victory over the Persians Heraclius took their title of "King of Kings," but thought better of it and stuck with the more modest *Basíleus*.

Jerusalem, walking barefoot to Constantine's Church of the Holy Sepulchre to return the True Cross to the Holy City. He was riding high on a wave of popularity, but he soon discovered that his triumph over the Persians brought with it the familiar specter of religious dissension. Syria and Egypt had always been Monophysite, and their reabsorption into the empire ensured that the religious debate was reopened with a vengeance. Such a state of affairs was an ominous weakness for the next invader to exploit, but where faith was involved, not even the conqueror of Persia could force his stubbornly independent inhabitants to fall into line.

The empire had been ravaged by the war with Persia, losing more than two hundred thousand men to the struggle, and now it was ripping itself apart internally as well. Despite the recent victory, the days of prosperity seemed long gone. Too many cities had been sacked and farms burned for the rhythms of everyday life to resume. Perhaps with time and stability the merchants and laborers would be coaxed back to their trades and prosperity would return, but the long, crippling war between Persia and Byzantium had left both empires exhausted. The cost of Heraclius's great victory was a weakened and vulnerable empire, and the only saving grace was that Persia was in an even worse state. In 622, however, the very year Heraclius had set out on his great campaign, a new and infinitely more predatory enemy than Persia had been born.

12

::

THE HOUSE OF WAR

With the Sword will I wash my shame away.
—ABU TAMMAM, ninth-century Arab poet

The hot desert wastes of the Arabian Peninsula seemed neither particularly inviting nor threatening to the Byzantines, and there seemed no reason to suspect that they ever would. Populated by squabbling nomadic tribes, the region hardly seemed likely to pose a serious threat to anyone, much less the huge Byzantine state. In 622, however, the deserts were beginning to stir with a new energy as a man named Muhammad fled from Mecca to Medina and began hammering together the tribes of the interior. Infusing his followers with a burning zeal, Muhammad divided the world between *Dar al-Islam* (the House of Islam) and *Dar al-Harb* (the House of War). Their duty was a holy jihad, to expand the House of Islam at the point of a sword. Within five years, the Muslim armies were unleashed, and they exploded out of the desert with frightening speed. The timing of the invasion could hardly have been better. Hungry for conquest, the Arab armies arrived to find both great empires of the region exhausted and near collapse. The crippled Persians could put up little resistance. Their king Yazdegerd III appealed to both the Byzantines and the Chinese for help, but neither could offer any real assistance, and his fall was swift. Within a year, his tired armies were defeated, and he spent the next decade fleeing from one location to another until a local peasant killed him for his purse.

Muhammad died in 632 of a fever, but nothing seemed able to

slake his army's desire for land. Not even pausing to digest the Persian Empire, by 633 they had crossed the deserted Byzantine frontier, and there they found a land ripe for the picking. Constantinople had never really been able to stamp out the Monophysite heresy, distracted as it was by the war with Persia, and when the Muslims arrived, they found the local populations eager to welcome them in. For the oppressed Monophysites, Islam, with its strict monotheism, was perfectly understandable, and the Arabs were at least Semites like themselves. Better to be ruled by their Arab cousins than the distant heretical emperors in Constantinople, especially since it was always easier to despise a heresy than a different faith. Putting up only token resistance, they watched as the Muslim army poured into Syria, sacked Damascus, and besieged Jerusalem.

In earlier days, the mighty emperor who had broken Persia would have come rushing to Palestine's defense, but Heraclius was no longer the man he had once been. He was already suffering from the disease that was to kill him, his broad shoulders were prematurely stooped, his golden hair was reduced to a few gray strands, and—like his empire—he was near physical and emotional collapse. Having risen to such heights of glory, he now had to endure the agony of watching as his life's work unraveled.

Slipping into Jerusalem, the emperor removed the True Cross from where he had placed it in triumph only six years before and headed for Constantinople, leaving the doomed city to its fate. While the patriarch carried out the odious task of surrendering the Holy City, the emperor made a pathetic last entrance into his capital, tormented by the belief that God had abandoned him. The citizens of Constantinople were inclined to agree with this view and were quick to point out why. The cause of all the imperial misery, they whispered, was Heraclius's incestuous marriage to his niece, Martina. Of the nine children she bore her husband, only three were healthy—the rest either died in infancy or were deformed. Clearly, God had removed his favor, and Martina, never popular, became one of the most hated women in the city. Heraclius, who had delivered the empire in its hour of need, ended his days in misery, deserted by the friends and courtiers who had loudly sung his praises in the years of triumph. A few years after the fall of Jerusalem, he expired, and was interred next to the body of Constantine the Great, in the imperial mausoleum of the Church of the Holy Apostles.

Heraclius's reign had ended on a sour note, and his subjects certainly didn't mourn his passing. Under his watch, the empire had lost huge swaths of its territory to a bewildering new enemy, and the dying emperor had hardly bothered to resist them. The shocked Byzantines had looked to Constantinople for help, terrified by the catastrophe, but had found only an agonized defeatism from their broken emperor.

But as poor as the empire's fortunes were at Heraclius's death, without him they would have been immeasurably worse. If he hadn't arrived to overthrow Phocas, the empire would have fallen easy prey to the Persians; and when the Islamic tide came rushing out of Arabia, there would have been nothing to shield Europe from the flood. Instead, by combining a touch of Justinian's vision with more than a hint of Belisarius's generalship, Heraclius had made Constantinople a bulwark against Islamic aggression, diverting the Muslim advance into the long wastes of North Africa and delaying its entrance into Europe. His early years had seen one glorious victory after another, and had he died after the overthrow of Chosroes II, with the Persian Empire defeated and the True Cross restored to Jerusalem, his subjects would have remembered him as one of the greatest emperors to sit on the Byzantine throne.

His reign saw the great turning point for much of the Middle East. For a thousand years, these lands had been Hellenized, ruled by a Roman Empire at first pagan and then Christian. They had contributed much to classical civilization, providing some of the finest emperors, theologians, saints, and poets of the classical world. After the Arab invasions, however, all that changed. Arabic replaced Greek as the lingua franca, and Islam replaced Christianity. Wrenched out of the Mediterranean orbit, these lands began to look to Damascus, then Baghdad, instead of Rome or Constantinople. A way of life that had lasted for more than a millennium came to a violent and abrupt end. Life in the Middle East would never be the same again.

Of the next five emperors who succeeded Heraclius, only one was older than sixteen when he gained the throne, and all were crippled by the struggles of powerful factions to assert control. Each defeat further diminished their authority and crippled their ability to fight back. Had a stronger ruler than the dying Heraclius been on the throne to confront the Muslims in 633, the subsequent history of the entire Middle East would have been radically different, but he was a sick man, and the imperial teenagers who succeeded him couldn't grab hold of power firmly enough to effectively oppose the Islamic advance. By the middle of the century, the opportunity to contain the threat had passed, and the Arab conquest picked up an irresistible momentum. Frightened Byzantine citizens paraded their holy icons around the walls, invoking divine aid, but still the Muslim tide rolled on, destroying centuries of Roman rule and leaving the empire profoundly shocked in its wake. To many, it must have seemed a terrible divine judgment, and the emotional trauma seemed to paralyze Byzantium.

The unwieldy imperial army was marshaled to defend the long frontier, but the Arabs seemed impossible to contain. The impenetrable desert had always offered a feeling of safety for the Byzantines, but now it was a terrifying weakness. Using the stars to navigate across the featureless landscape, the Arabs slaughtered the camels they rode to consume their water, and emerged unexpectedly behind imperial lines. Whenever the Byzantine army did manage to confront them, the Arabs simply melted back into the desert, only to erupt somewhere else. Only once did an imperial army try to follow them. In 636, it pursued a Muslim army to a tributary of the Jordan River and suffered an appalling defeat. Those who survived the initial fighting tried to surrender but were massacred on the spot. The watching Mediterranean world was put on terrible notice: For those who resisted the Islamic sword, there would be no mercy.

Unnerved by the speed and ferocity of the attack, the East virtually threw away its defenses. Eight years after conquering Jerusalem, the Arabs entered Egypt, and at the sight of the Muslim forces, Alexandria, seat of one of the five great patriarchates of the church, voluntarily surrendered. The dissident Christians who had invited the invaders in soon found their new masters to be considerably less tolerant than the orthodox regime they had swept away, but by then it was too late. A popular uprising ejected the Muslim garrison, but it returned with an army at its back. Battering their way inside, the forces of Islam razed the walls, burned what remained of the library, and moved the capital to Al-Fustat—a small village in the shadow of the pyramids that would later become Cairo.* Only the waters of the Mediterranean seemed to form a barrier capable of checking the desert-dwelling Arabs, but they learned quickly. Navigating at sea was not so different from navigating in the desert, and within a decade, they had constructed a navy and inflicted a crushing defeat of the formerly invincible Byzantine navy.

Faced with the unrelenting attack, the government at Constantinople panicked and moved to Sicily, abandoning the East to its fate. This less-than-inspiring action left most Byzantines feeling bewildered and bitter, but, thankfully, the Arab assault was halted by a civil war.† The Islamic world was further distracted by the conquest of

---

*The great library of Alexandria had been heavily damaged at least twice before—first when Julius Caesar had entered the city, and centuries later when a Christian mob tried to burn the section on necromancy and witchcraft. An impressive repository of the learning of the ancient world, it was probably only a shell of its former self by the time the Arabs arrived. The conquering caliph Omar gave it the coup de grâce, according to an apocryphal story, with the words "if the books of the library don't contain the teachings of the Qur'an, they are useless and should be destroyed; if the books do contain the teachings of the Qur'an, they are superfluous and should be destroyed."

†That war still splits the Islamic world today. An assassin loyal to the fearsome general Muawiyah assassinated the caliph Ali while he was praying in a mosque in central Iraq. Those who rejected Muawiyah and held that only a descendant of Ali could become caliph are known as Shiites, while those who accepted Muawiyah as caliph are called Sunni. Iraq remains largely a Shiite country to this day.

Afghanistan, but by the time a Byzantine emperor cautiously took up his residence in Constantinople again, the Muslim victor of the civil war had announced a pledge to annihilate the Roman Empire, and the conquest resumed. The Sicilian city of Syracuse—so recently the capital of the Roman world—was brutally sacked in 668, and the next year an Arab army virtually annihilated the Byzantine forces in North Africa, leaving the entire province open to invasion.

The Arabs, however, were by now more interested in dealing a knockout blow to the empire than in further conquests of the desolate African coast, and the thrust of their attack was soon directed against Constantinople itself. Moving its capital to Damascus, the Arab caliphate launched yearly strikes at New Rome, probing its defenses. The land walls were virtually impregnable, but the city was vulnerable from the sea, and only the demoralized imperial navy guarded its harbor. The Arab fleet had repeatedly demonstrated its superiority, even managing to seize an island opposite Constantinople while the Byzantines glumly watched, and in 674 they took Rhodes—the proud possessor of one of the Seven Wonders of the Ancient World.* That same year, Tarsus—birthplace of Saint Paul—fell to the Muslims, and it seemed an awful confirmation that God had deserted the Byzantines.

Three Arab fleets converged on the capital, but great moments of crisis have a way of producing heroes from unlikely sources, and a Syrian refugee named Callinicus of Heliopolis saved Constantinople. He invented a devastatingly flammable liquid called "Greek fire," which could be sprayed at enemy ships with terrifying results.† Water

---

*The great Colossus, a magnificent statue of the sun god, lay where it had fallen during an earthquake nine centuries before, and the victorious Arab commander had it broken up and sold for scrap. There was so much bronze that it required nine hundred camels to haul away the pieces.

†The composition of Greek fire was considered a state secret and was guarded so effectively that even today we don't know exactly how it was made. If, as suspected, it was a form of a low-density liquid hydrocarbon, like naphtha, it anticipated modern chemists by a good twelve centuries.

was useless against the horrible conflagration, serving only to spread the flames, and balls of cloth soaked in it could be hurled great distances, immolating anything they touched. The Arab fleet broke against the terrible new weapon, and the waters of the Golden Horn were choked with burning ships.*

Constantinople had been saved, but the rest of the empire was disintegrating fast. The Arab sword now turned against Africa, annihilating Carthage in 697 and using it as a springboard to attack Italy and Sardinia. By 711, Muslim forces had completed the six-hundred-mile trek across Africa, and an invasion force led by a one-eyed warrior named Tariq had crossed to Spain, landing in the shade of the huge rock that still bears his name.†

The Arab empire now had more land, resources, and wealth than the Byzantines, and awaited only the order to begin the final annihilation. In 717, the same year that a Muslim raiding party crossed into France, that order was given, and an immense army set sail in nearly two thousand ships to take Constantinople.

The capital again found an unlikely hero, this time in a Syrian shepherd named Konon. Slipping into the city a month before the Muslim invasion fleet, he adroitly used the political crisis to seize the throne and was crowned as Leo III. Equally fluent in Arabic and Greek, the new emperor had a keen mind and a lifetime of experience fighting the Arabs. Aided by the most ferocious winter in recent memory, Leo easily outmaneuvered the Muslim army while his fireships destroyed the Arab navy and the terrible cold froze livestock and humans alike. Starving and now unable to bury their dead in the frozen ground, the Muslims were reduced to consuming the flesh of their fallen comrades to stay alive. A thaw arrived with the spring, but that merely added the misery of disease to the unsanitary camp, and

---

*The Golden Horn is an inlet of the Bosporus forming the great harbor on Constantinople's northern shore.

†*Jabal al-Tariq* (the mountain of Tariq), better known as Gibraltar.

when Leo persuaded a tribe of Bulgars to attack the hapless Muslims, their commander gave up in despair. The entire campaign had been an unmitigated disaster for the forces of Islam. Less than half of the invading army managed to drag itself back to Damascus, and of the grand fleet, only five ships survived to see their home ports again.*

---

*The rest fell victim to Greek fire and winter storms, and a few met the horrendous fate of being burned by a volcano as they passed the island of Thíra.

13

::

THE IMAGE BREAKERS

Leo III was hailed as a giant from the age of Justinian, a heaven-sent savior of the empire, but his reign would show just how psychologically scarring the Arab invasions had been for the empire. Byzantium's losses had been horrendous. Less than a century before, it had been the dominant power of the Mediterranean, stretching from Spain to the Black Sea, the proud and confident repository of Christian culture and civilization. The divine order of heaven had been mirrored here on earth, with an all-powerful emperor enforcing the Lord's justice. Then, in the blink of an eye, everything had changed. A bewildering enemy had erupted from the desert sands and carried all before them. Two-thirds of the empire's territories had vanished in the flood, and half its population had disappeared. Arab raiders plundered the remaining countryside, and the cities were mere shells of what they had been in happier times. Whole populations fled the uncertainty of urban life and retreated to the more defensible safety of mountaintops, islands, or otherwise inaccessible places. Refugees impoverished and ruined by Muslim attacks roamed Constantinople's streets, and prosperity dried up. The once-powerful empire had shrunk to Asia Minor, and was now poorer, less populated, and far weaker than the neighboring caliphate.

The Byzantine world was left deeply traumatized. The armies of a false prophet had clashed with the Christian empire whose ruler was the sword arm of God, and yet it was the banner of Christ that had fallen back. In only eight years, the Muslims had conquered three of

the five great patriarchates of the Christian Church—Alexandria, Antioch, and Jerusalem—and neither prayers, nor icons, nor steel had
been able to stop them. An arrogant caliph had seized Christendom's
holiest city and built the Dome of the Rock, boasting that Islam had
superseded Christianity. Using Byzantine craftsmen to decorate the
structure, he added an inscription declaring that Jesus was only a
prophet, concluding with an ominous warning for Christians to "re-
frain" from saying otherwise. The Byzantines responded by putting an
image of Christ on their coins—in part to regain God's favor and in
part to annoy the Arabs, who widely used them—but still the imperial
armies suffered defeat after defeat. To an empire which had itself been
Christianized by the convincing argument of victory at the Milvian
Bridge, such calamities shook the very foundations of their belief.
Why, the bewildered citizens asked themselves, had God allowed such
a disaster to happen?

The answer seemed plain enough to Leo III. Christ had withdrawn his hand of protection, and the culprit seemed to be the sacred
icons held in such high regard by so many citizens of the empire. Designed as worship aids for the faithful, the veneration of icons had
grown to the point where the line between honor and outright worship
was blurred. Icons stood in for godparents at baptisms and were offered prayers to intercede for the faithful. People in the streets gave
thanks to an icon of the Virgin Mary for their recent deliverance from
the Muslims, and most icons were treated with a reverence uncomfort-
ably close to the old pagan worship of idols. What had started as a tool
to peel back the veil between the mortal and divine now seemed to
have crossed into a clear violation of the second commandment. The
biblical Israelites had angered God by bowing down to a golden calf,
and now, like the chosen people wandering in the desert for forty years,
the empire was being punished for the sin of idolatry.

The emperor's sacred duty was to end the abuses that were obviously angering God, so in 725 Leo III ascended the pulpit of the
Hagia Sophia and gave a rousing sermon to the packed church, thun-

dering against the worst offenders. The Muslims, he said, with their strict prohibition of all images, had marched from victory to victory, while the Byzantines had been torn by heresy, angering God by praying to paint and wood for deliverance. Few in the congregation could disagree with the emperor's words, and fewer still could argue with the assertion that something was dreadfully wrong with the empire. Leo, however, was just getting started. The time had come to take his reforms beyond mere words.

The main gate to the Great Palace was a magnificent bronze structure, originally built by Justinian after the Nika riots. A series of mosaics celebrating the triumphs of the great emperor and his general Belisarius decorated the interior of its central dome, and rising up directly above the doors was a magnificent golden icon of Christ that dwarfed everything around it. Facing the Hagia Sophia, and visible throughout the great central square, it was the most prominent icon in the city, and with its hand raised in a ubiquitous blessing, it served as a reminder of the duties of a righteous sovereign. To Leo, however, it was the very symbol of all the ills besetting the empire, and he ordered its immediate destruction.

The emperor may have had plenty of support for his sermons, but the sight of Christian soldiers deliberately vandalizing an image of Christ was taking it too far. A group of nearby women were so outraged that they lynched the officer in charge, and a full-scale riot was only prevented by a heavy show of steel from the palace. Riots swept through the countryside, and a pretender rose in Greece who proclaimed that he would hurl the impious emperor from his throne and restore icons to their proper place of veneration.

Fortunately for Leo, his victories had earned him enough respect in the army that he was able to crush the rebels easily; but in the West, he wasn't so fortunate. Shielded from the blows of Arab invasions by the empire, western Europe viewed the whole icon controversy with bewildered horror. Proud of their artistic heritage, they saw no reason to suddenly conclude that painting and sculpture were impediments to faith. The pope in particular was annoyed that the emperor had interfered in matters of doctrine and threw his support behind the outraged population of Italy. The imperial governor of Ravenna was killed as cities throughout the peninsula threw off the Byzantine yoke, and they would have elected another emperor if the pope hadn't balked at the thought of imperial retribution.*

With such a firestorm erupting around him from the destruction of a single icon, Leo could have been expected to pull back from his inflammatory position, but he was firmly convinced that he was right and refused to back down. Issuing a decree condemning images, he ordered *all* holy icons and relics to be immediately destroyed. Setting the example himself, he seized reliquaries, vestments, and church plate throughout the city and destroyed them publicly. When the pope wrote to him, acidly commenting that he should leave church doctrine to those actually qualified to compose it, Leo sent two warships to arrest him. They foundered at sea, sparing the church from the spectacle of the arrest of its most auspicious bishop, but tensions continued to escalate when the pope retaliated by excommunicating anyone who destroyed an icon.

The pope's words had little effect in the East, where thousands of images were smashed or torn apart; but for every one destroyed, there seemed to be a dozen more that escaped. Nearly every household had its share of icons, from simple wooden carvings to more elaborate ones of enamel or etched metal, and these wouldn't be given up easily. Leo, however, was nothing if not thorough, and his soldiers moved through the city, confiscating icons and painting over the mosaics that adorned church walls. The monasteries tried to resist, especially the powerful Saint John of Studius within the city walls, but there was little they could do. Hundreds of monks fled with their precious icons to the wilds of Cappadocia, where they carved secret

---

*On the Venetian lagoon, the horrified citizens rebelled and appointed a local leader as *dux*, or doge, and the Venetian Republic—both an ally and an inveterate enemy of the empire—was born.

churches into the soft rock and waited for popular opinion to sweep their cruel emperor from power.

It was hard, however, for popular opinion to argue with results. Leo had driven the Arabs away from the walls of Constantinople, and when he smashed another Muslim army in 740, it seemed (as Leo himself claimed) that God was pleased and had vindicated the emperor's purge of the idol worshippers. This argument was dented somewhat the next year, when an earthquake—always an ominous sign—rocked the capital, but Leo was already dying, and in the early summer he expired of dropsy, leaving the issue to his son.

He had saved Byzantium from conquest by the Muslims, and he had been the first emperor in half a century to die in his bed, but the empire he left behind was dangerously divided. The iconoclastic controversy (literally, the "smashing of icons") that he had unleashed would rage for the better part of a century and force Christianity to come to terms with a question it had always seen in shades of gray: Where exactly was the line between veneration and idolatry? Did mortal depictions of the divine illuminate faith, by allowing previous generations to speak of their belief, or pollute it, by setting up graven images? For a moment, the fate of Western art hung in the balance.

There was some hope that Leo III's son, Constantine V, would resolve the matter, but he proved even more inflammatory than his father. Steeped in the hatred of icons since birth, he emerged as the most ferocious iconoclast ever to sit on the Byzantine throne. In his view, the church was festering with idol worship, and he demanded that the entire clergy take an oath not to venerate icons. So firm was he in the belief that Christ alone was deserving of worship that the very mention of titles like "saint" or "holy"—even as an expletive—would send him into fits of rage. His hatred of monks who resisted was such that he would on occasion smear their beards with oil and set them on fire. When the patriarch objected to the harsh treatment and refused to take the oath, the emperor had him whipped and incarcerated, then humiliated the man by parading him around the Hippodrome on the back of a mangy donkey. Declaring war on the powerful monasteries in the empire, he forced monks and nuns to marry, confiscated church property, and lodged imperial troops in monastic houses.

The emperor employed theologians to press his case, but he was a highly educated man who was also perfectly capable of defending his beliefs himself. He would often point out that the great fourth-century saint Basil of Caesarea had condemned the veneration of images, when he had written that the worship of a likeness of the emperor was just as bad as worshipping the emperor.* Constantine V, however, wanted more than old quotes to bolster his claims; he wanted official sanction for his war against icons. Church opinion was hopelessly split over the issue and not likely to support the extremist emperor, but there was more than one way to force the issue. Invoking a great council of the entire church, Constantine V packed it with his supporters and refused to let any dissenting opinion be represented. Not surprisingly, the council handed down a ringing endorsement of the emperor's position. Icons, relics, and prayers to the saints were all forms of idolatry and therefore condemned. Even the emperor's most savage purges could now claim the trappings of ecclesiastical support, and public executions took on a momentum of their own. Those who refused to embrace iconoclasm were beaten, mutilated, and even stoned in the streets, all with the tacit encouragement of the throne.

Constantine V was able to prosecute his personal war so ferociously because he—like his father—had the great advantage of being militarily successful and therefore popular. Even the appearance of the plague—the last recorded appearance of the black death in Constantinople until the fourteenth century—couldn't disrupt his success. In nine brilliant campaigns, Constantine V shattered the Bulgars, restoring some control over the impoverished Balkans. Taking advantage of the overextended and internally divided Muslims,

---

*Western Europe went through its own version of iconoclasm during the Protestant Reformation in the sixteenth century. In defense of their destruction of images, the more extreme Protestants quoted the same church fathers that their Byzantine predecessors had.

the emperor chased them from Asia Minor, even managing to restore some semblance of control over the island of Cyprus.*

The unexpected victories were certainly welcome, but even Constantine's most vehement supporters nervously watched the damage that his religious policies were wreaking. Hopelessly split between those who loved icons and those who wanted to destroy them, Byzantium was deeply unsure of itself and breaking apart at the seams. Even worse, Constantine's ferocious war on icons estranged the West at the very moment that Byzantine power depended on loyalty. Abandoned by an emperor who considered him a heretic, the pope could only watch as the Lombards annihilated the imperial government at Ravenna. Byzantine power was reduced to a last bastion in the heel of Italy, and even that seemed vulnerable. After nearly eight centuries, the Caesars had finally been expelled from their ancient capital; never again would a soldier of the Roman Empire set foot in the Eternal City. Casting around for a new protector to shield him from the Lombards, the pope found the perfect candidate in the Frankish king Pépin the Short. Answering the call, Pépin swept into Italy, destroyed the Lombards, and turned over control of what would become the Papal States to the pope.† Constantinople was humiliated by the developments, but worse to the empire than the loss of territory was the spiritual damage.

In Constantine V, the empire at last had a strong, capable emperor on the throne, and if not for his zealotry might have been poised on the edge of a spectacular recovery. As the heir of Constantine the Great, he was in theory the temporal leader of Christendom. Every citizen of the old empire of Rome—even those buried by the shifting

---

*The Greek island had seesawed from Christian to Muslim control since the late seventh century, and Constantine forced the Arabs to recognize joint custody with the empire. This arrangement—oddly foreshadowing the situation today—was eventually resolved in the empire's favor, and Cyprus remained in Byzantine hands until Richard the Lion-Hearted conquered it at the end of the twelfth century.

†The last remaining part of which is still with us today as Vatican City.

barbarian kingdoms of the West—owed him their allegiance and, at least in principle, had always recognized his authority. Political realities may have forced them to acknowledge local petty kings, but there was only one God in heaven and only one emperor on earth. For those in the lost lands that had fallen in the Muslim conquests, the situation was even clearer. The majority of the population was Christian, and they dreamed and prophesied of a time when the emperor would return and deliver them from their bondage. So devoted were they to Constantinople that the Arabs called them the "emperor's church" and lived in fear of a mass uprising. All that was needed was a strong figure who could deliver the counterstroke and satisfy their deep longing to return to an empire that shared the true faith.

But instead of seizing the opportunity, Constantine V threw it away. His harsh persecution cut off Asia Minor from the larger Christian community beyond the imperial borders.* Those in the East turned away, disgusted by an empire that had seemingly lost its mind, while those in the West began to question the imperial claims to universal authority. They didn't yet dare to claim equality with Constantinople, but that day was fast approaching. The chance of a united Christendom, sheltered under a restored empire, slipped away forever. In their anger at icons, Constantine and his father had destroyed their own spiritual claims. Nothing would ever be quite the same again.

---

*Christians in the Muslim-occupied lands of the East vehemently opposed the iconoclasts, and it's fortunate that they did. Some of the most beautiful icons that survived the controversy came from Coptic monasteries that were located safely beyond the borders of the empire in the eighth century.

14

∷∷

THE CRUMBLING EMPIRE

By the time of Constantine V's death on September 14, 775, the Byzantine Empire seemed thoroughly exhausted. The constant disruptions, both within and without, had taken their toll on every level of society. Under pressure from all sides, things were beginning to break down. Records weren't kept as faithfully, family genealogies proudly guarded since the days of the Roman Republic died out, and the old traditions of senatorial rank all but disappeared.* Most cities dwindled to the size of towns, with the shrunken populations huddling amid the ruins of their former grandeur. Civic planning all but vanished, and the wide avenues and lavish public buildings of classical cities were replaced with twisting narrow streets and hastily constructed homes. Buildings were allowed to fall into ruin, and when walls were repaired at all, it was not by a trip to the long-abandoned quarries but by using the masonry of earlier structures. Even the more-important cities showed unmistakable signs of decay. Athens, once the foremost city in Greece, shrank to a provincial town with a few thousand citizens struggling beneath the shadow of the Acropolis, and Constantinople—though it still had its

---

*The old Senate house was gradually absorbed by the Great Palace and used as an audience chamber. The Senate itself, however, did continue to exist and was occasionally used to sit in judgment of high-ranking individuals. Though its prestige and responsibilities were reduced to insignificance by the ninth century, there were still senators present on May 29, 1453, to defend the empire on its last day of existence.

Hippodrome, theaters, and baths—allowed its aqueduct to remain in disrepair for more than a century.

Sea trade remained strong, and the spices of India could still be found along with the silks of China in the markets of the capital, but merchants could no longer afford to cross the dangerous land routes in these insecure times, and much of the interior reverted to the barter system. As the urban populations declined in numbers and attacks came from every side, society became increasingly militarized. State land was turned over to the army in an attempt to reduce the costs of paying it, and political positions were turned over to military officials for greater efficiency. The result was an increasingly powerful political force that interfered in the government with unsettling frequency. In the century after Heraclius's death, no fewer than eight emperors were put on the throne by the army, hopelessly blurring the line between civil and military authority.

Education, like so much else, was a casualty of the troubled times. The capital still had private tutors and primary and secondary schools, and positions in administration and the army were still open to merit, but for most there was no time for extensive study in a century of war and disruption. Literacy dwindled, and with it the quality of civil servants. Faced with the unrelenting pressures of military disasters and social chaos, fields such as philosophy and literature were largely ignored as the luxuries of a more peaceful time. As the value of education declined, Byzantine culture began to wither and die. Each generation was less educated than the one before and less able to appreciate the intrinsic value of learning, and before long the decline had gained its own momentum. At the start of the eighth century, a law had to be passed making it illegal to cut up old texts, throw them away, or boil them into a perfume; by the middle of the century, emperors were complaining that they couldn't find competent officials who could understand the law. With Constantine V adding the ravages of iconoclasm to the decay by declaring war on the monasteries and doing his level best to destroy the works of those who disagreed with him, education was in a deplorable state.

Popular sentiment was turning against the iconoclastic emperor by the time of his death. The aura of military success that surrounded him ensured that he remained popular in the army long after his death, but in the eyes of most Byzantines he was a despicable tyrant, a monster who deserved only to be forgotten. They called him *Copronymos*—name of dung—and a century after his death his reputation was so blackened that a mob broke into his sarcophagus, burned his bones, and threw the ashes into the sea. His son Leo IV, by contrast, was a more mildly tempered man who supported iconoclasm but tried to smooth over his father's worst excesses. Perhaps, had he lived longer, he would have been able to ease the tensions, but, unfortunately for the empire, he died after a reign of only five years. Effective power passed to his formidable spouse, a woman who had dominated him in life, and completely overshadowed him in death.

Constantine V had chosen his son's wife by holding an empire-wide beauty contest and had settled on Irene, a devastatingly attractive orphan from Athens. For the arch iconoclast, it was a remarkably bad choice. Having grown up in the West, Irene was a fervent supporter of icons who had no use for her father-in-law and secretly made it her life's goal to restore icons to veneration. Her husband tried to rein her in, but a month after consigning her to a wing of the palace, he was dead, and Irene was spreading the suspicious rumor that his death was the result of divine retribution. Whether the citizens of Constantinople believed her or not, they grudgingly accepted Irene as regent for her ten-year-old son, Constantine VI, and in doing so gave the throne to one of the most grasping rulers in Byzantium's long history. For those who stood in her way, the young empress had no mercy, and she was determined to cling to power no matter what the cost.

For the next eleven years, the empress ruled with an iron hand, carefully removing iconoclasts from important posts and replacing them with her supporters. Unfortunately for the empire, most of its best officers and soldiers were iconoclasts, and their removal crippled the imperial army. Faced with a massive Muslim invasion two years into her regency, the demoralized and weakened Byzantine army simply defected and joined the Arabs. The humiliating and expensive peace Irene was forced to buy severely damaged her popularity, and insistent voices began calling for her to relinquish the regency.

Military reversals and declining public support, however, meant little to Irene. She was focused on restoring icons to veneration and continued smoothly with her religious program. However powerful the iconoclast emperors had been, they had lacked the full authority of the church, and Constantine V's hollow attempt at an ecumenical council had fooled no one. Irene would put the question of iconoclasm to the whole body of the church, sure that the weight of their one voice would bury the iconoclasts forever. Ambassadors were sent scurrying to the patriarchs of Alexandria, Antioch, Jerusalem, and Rome, inviting them to what would be the eighth and final great ecumenical council of the church.

It convened in the capacious Church of the Holy Wisdom in Nicaea, the scene of the first council 462 years before, and its findings were hardly surprising. Iconoclasm was condemned, but the faithful were admonished to take care that veneration didn't stray into worship. The empire greeted the news with relief, believing that perhaps the long nightmare was over. Iconoclasm had been waning for decades, and had been driven largely by zealous emperors. When it was condemned, not a single voice was raised to defend it.

The religious victory should have provided a high note for Irene to end the regency and turn over effective power to her son. Traditionally, regencies ended when their charges were sixteen, and Constantine VI was now in his twenties. Irene, however, had always been more interested in power than anything else, and she was not about to relinquish it in favor of her pathetic son. Constantine VI was a weak-enough man to be easily manipulated, and all would have been well if Irene could have controlled her ambition, but such restraint wasn't in her nature. Banishing her son's face from the imperial currency, she issued coins that featured only images of herself on both sides.* Not content with this unnecessary insult, she then produced an imperial decree announcing that she was the senior emperor and as such would always take precedence over Constantine VI. When several generals protested, demanding that the rightful emperor be given the throne, Irene angrily executed them and had her bewildered son savagely beaten and thrown into a dungeon.

The empress could hardly have handled the situation more poorly. Even a successful emperor would have thought twice before antagonizing the army, and militarily Irene had been nothing short of a disaster. Thanks to her endless purges, the army had been performing poorly throughout her reign, and its loyalty to her was correspondingly weak. The last two years had seen major imperial defeats against the Arabs, the Bulgars, and the Franks, and there was a lingering suspicion that perhaps the iconoclasts had been right after all. Revolt swept through the ranks of the army. Soon angry mobs were swarming the streets of Constantinople, calling for Irene to step down in favor of her son. Transformed overnight from a prisoner to a folk hero, Constantine VI was swept from his jail cell to the throne, and Irene was placed under house arrest in one of her many palaces.

But Constantine VI had taken no active role in events before he had been thrown into prison, and he would take none on the throne. Lacking a single shred of ambition, the young prince was content to let life happen and would soon prove to be hopelessly incompetent. When an Arab army invaded imperial territory, he was immediately frightened into negotiating a peace that managed to be both humiliating and prohibitively expensive. The resulting accusations of cowardice provoked him to take the field himself, but his first sight of the enemy caused him to lose his nerve and panic, further tarnishing his

---

*Just before the iconoclastic controversy broke out, imperial tradition had been to put images of Christ on the coins. Since Irene had just restored icons to favor, she was expected to celebrate it with her coins, but ambition appears to have trumped piety.

reputation. The disaster convinced him to restore his mother to power; then, having made this awful decision, he marched off to yet another disastrous defeat at the hands of the Bulgars. The disgusted imperial guards in Constantinople hatched a plot to get rid of both Irene and her incompetent son, but news of it somehow leaked out. The badly frightened emperor acted with all the vigor of a bully, ordering the tongues cut out of the offending men.

Such mindless cruelty cost Constantine VI any remaining support in the army, and Irene decided to get rid of her pathetic son once and for all. Constantine was already blaming his Bulgar debacle on his soldiers, and it was easy for her to convince him to punish the frustrated troops by tattooing the word "traitor" on the faces of a thousand of them. As Irene had forseen, this act made him the most reviled man in the city. Stripped of any friends or allies, Constantine VI was now helpless before his most formidable enemy.

In May 797, Constantine's infant son died, and while the emperor was distracted in mourning, Irene struck. As he was riding home from the Hippodrome, some of her palace guard burst out of the underbrush and tried to seize him. He managed to escape to the docks but was soon caught and dragged to the Great Palace. There, in the very room where he had been born twenty-six years before, Irene had him blinded so brutally that he died.

She had never really been a mother to him, busy as she was with the affairs of state, and like all imperial heirs he had been raised by a swarm of nursemaids and tutors with little time to grow close to either of his parents. Even so, the vile murder deeply shocked the empire. Irene had violated the maternal bonds that every member of society, from the highest patrician to the lowest stable hand, held sacred. She had lost a part of her humanity, and though her subjects tolerated her continued rule, they could never respect her. She was the first woman to rule the Roman Empire, not as a regent or an empress but as an emperor, but she wasn't to enjoy it for long. Guilt robbed her of her energy, and when the Arabs sensed weakness and invaded, she immediately offered an immense tribute the empire couldn't afford. Trying to bolster her flagging popularity, she took to riding around on a golden chariot pulled by the finest white horses and sprinkling gold coins to the crowd. The assembled populace took the money, but their love couldn't be so easily bought. They were well aware that thanks to her promises of tribute to the Saracens, the treasury was quite empty, and flinging what was left into the crowds brought her only increased scorn. The only surprise was that the revolt, when it came, was sparked not by a disaffected Byzantine but by a barbarian in the far west.

The trouble started in Rome, where Pope Leo III was growing more unpopular with each passing day. He had risen from peasant stock and as such was hated by the powerful Roman senatorial families who believed that the papacy should be reserved for members of the nobility. Their hatred was so intense that in 799 they sent a gang to ambush the pope as he was walking in the streets, ordering their henchmen to gouge out his eyes and rip out his tongue. Thankfully for the pontiff, in the excitement of the attack, the mob merely left him unconscious with his vision and speech intact. Smuggled out of the city before his assailants could correct their mistake, Leo fled to the court of the Frankish king and waited for tempers to cool. The moment he was gone, his enemies tried to depose him, charging him with everything from public drunkenness to adultery. Leo angrily denied the charges from the safety of his shelter, but it was clear that the two sides had reached an impasse. Some sort of trial would have to be held, but that involved damaging complications. Who was qualified to sit in judgment of the Vicar of Christ?

The answer, of course, was the emperor of Constantinople, the temporal head of Christendom, but not only had she disgraced herself by killing her own son, she was also a woman and therefore in western eyes disbarred from ruling. Leo needed a champion, and he turned not to the East but to the far more immediate power of the Franks.

Though it was not yet a century old, the Frankish kingdom already had an illustrious history. Its founder, Charles "the Hammer"

Martel, had stopped the Muslims at the battle of Tours, permanently turning the tide of the formerly irresistible Islamic advance into western Europe. His son Pépin the Short had come to the rescue of the pope while the Byzantines had been busy fighting over iconoclasm and was personally crowned and rewarded with the rank of patrician by the grateful pontiff. It was with Pépin's illustrious son, however, that the kingdom of the Franks really came into its own.

For someone who was known to history by the nickname "the Short," Pépin had a remarkably tall son. Named Charles like his grandfather, he stood nearly six-foot-four, and he had a personality as large and dominating as his frame. By the year 800, he had transformed the relatively minor kingdom he inherited into the most powerful state of western Europe, an empire unparalleled in the West since the days of ancient Rome. After crossing the Alps at the pope's request, Charles the Great—or Charlemagne, as he was soon to be known—descended on Italy in December of the year 800 and testified on Leo's behalf. The pope swore on the Gospels that he was innocent, and with the looming figure of the Frankish king behind him, the assembled clergy accepted his word. Two days later, while Charlemagne was kneeling at the Christmas Mass, Leo lifted a jeweled crown from the altar and placed it on his head, declaring to the startled assembly that Charlemagne was now a "Holy Roman Emperor"—adding for good measure that he was descended from the biblical kings of Israel. Shock waves rippled through the electrified crowd. After four hundred years in abeyance, an emperor had returned to the West.

Life in Dark Ages Europe was all too often brutish and short, but the inheritors of the wreckage of the Western Roman Empire were fully conscious that it hadn't always been so. The white marble ruins of ancient Rome were sprinkled from Britain to Sicily, constant reminders of a time before the light of learning had given way to darkness. They longed for the day that the empire would rise again, phoenixlike, from its own ashes and restore the proper order to the world. Now, on Christmas day at the dawn of the ninth century, Pope Leo had declared that that day had come.

The coronation was breathtaking in its presumption. By placing the crown on Charlemagne's head, Leo was implying that the true crown of the Roman Empire was his alone to give—and what he could make, he could unmake as well.* The church, Pope Leo was firmly declaring, was a higher authority than the state. Such statements struck at the very heart of Byzantine authority, for if Charlemagne was the true Roman emperor, than obviously Irene—or anyone else on the Byzantine throne—was not. At a stroke, Leo had created a rival empire that not only dared to claim equality with the ancient line of the Caesars, but also declared Constantinople's throne to be full of impostors, mere pretenders to the throne of Augustus.

Leo, of course, didn't have the slightest authority to create a new emperor, but to bolster his position he trotted out what was surely the most shameful forgery of the Middle Ages—the "Donation of Constantine."† According to this document, Pope Sylvester had miraculously cured the emperor Constantine of leprosy, and the grateful emperor had "retired" to Byzantium and given the pope authority over the Western Empire and the ability to bestow the crown on whomever he chose. The Latin it was composed in was anachronistic and referred to events that had taken place after it was supposedly written, but education in the West had sunk so low that it was used to bolster papal claims for the next six hundred years.

The news of the coronation was greeted with horror in Constantinople. Just as there was one God in heaven, there was only one Roman Empire and only one emperor here on earth. Irene may not

---

*This lesson wasn't lost on the shrewd Charlemagne, but the deed was done and there was nothing for the irate monarch to do. A thousand years later, when it came time for his own coronation, Napoléon made sure he crowned himself.

†It was probably written a few decades before Leo used it, and it remained a standard weapon in the papal arsenal until the humanist Lorenzo Valla conclusively proved it a fake in 1440.

have been a satisfactory ruler, but that didn't mean an illiterate barbarian could claim equality with her throne. The blasphemous coronation was an affront to the correct world order, and that the pope had performed the ceremony made the betrayal that much worse.

Tempers were not improved when early the next year the ambassadors of this boorish Frank arrived in Constantinople with a startling marriage proposal, offering their monarch's hand to Irene. The empire would again be united under a single hand, they said, and Irene could rule like a new Theodora over both the East and the West. To the shocked Byzantine courtiers, the only thing more insulting than the arrogance of the barbarian envoys was the fact that Irene actually appeared to be seriously considering their proposal. Now almost universally hated in her own domains, she felt the walls closing in, and this seemed like the perfect escape.

Her subjects, however, had no intention of letting Irene turn over their empire to this barbarian pretender, and they moved quickly to get rid of their discredited monarch. Irene hardly bothered to resist. After a lifetime spent tenaciously gripping power, she was a spent force and was overthrown by a group of patricians with barely an effort. Imprisoned tamely in the palace that she had so recently commanded, she waited quietly while the assembled populace in the Hippodrome acclaimed one of her ministers of finance as emperor, and then obligingly headed into exile on the Aegean island of Lesbos.

Irene's fall brought an end to more than just a tired regime. Her reign marked the last time Christendom had a single, undisputed temporal head and saw the final collapse of the old Roman world. Her empire bore little resemblance to the proud state of Augustus, and the differences were more profound than the empty treasury and ruined economy that her shortsighted attempts to buy popularity had brought. The old order had lingered in the East long after its light had gone out in the West, but raids and plagues had taken a heavy toll even as the unrelenting attacks of Islamic armies had robbed the empire of Spain, Syria, Palestine, Egypt, and North Africa.

What had begun with the shattering advance of Islam had been completed with the coronation of Charlemagne. Byzantium had been subjected to tremendous pressures, both spiritual and physical, and every level of society had been transformed. No longer was it the confident master of the Mediterranean, straddling the warm shores that had given it birth. The last traces of that classical empire of Constantine and Justinian had disappeared in the wreckage of Irene's rule, and the enemies pressing in on every side threatened its very existence. It was too late to try to undo the damage. Byzantium would either adapt or be extinguished.

15

∷∷

THE TURNING TIDE

As if to underscore the empire's peril, a new and deadly threat arrived at the dawn of the ninth century. A great warlord crossed the Carpathians and hammered together the Bulgars from Transylvania to the Danube, forging the first great Bulgarian empire. Known only as Krum, the terrible khan swatted aside the Byzantine armies sent against him, killing one emperor and managing to cause the overthrow of another.* Meeting scarcely any resistance, his soldiers fell on the rich cities of the Black Sea, carrying off entire populations into captivity and threatening to completely overrun the Balkans. Even Constantinople seemed poised to fall to the all-conquering khan, but its walls proved to be too stout, and the disappointed Bulgarian had to satisfy himself with leveling the suburbs and killing every living thing that wasn't quick enough to get out of the way.

Fortunately for the empire, the menace of Krum, like that of Attila before and Genghis Khan after, was based more on personal charisma than underlying strength, and after the khan's death it evaporated as quickly as it had appeared. The humiliations suffered from such an unexpected direction, however, impressed themselves deeply

---

*The emperor Nicephorus I's body was identified by its purple boots and dragged to Krum's tent, where the khan gleefully had the head cut off and impaled as a testament to his victory. After several days of public ridicule, he had the rotting skull lined with silver. In true barbaric fashion, he used it as a drinking cup and would force visiting Byzantine diplomats to drink from it.

on the frightened citizens of the empire and led to a second flirtation with iconoclasm. Whatever else could be said about the iconoclastic emperors, they had been remarkably effective militarily, and that prowess now seemed sorely needed. Less than a decade after Irene's death, a mob interrupted a service in the Church of the Holy Apostles by breaking into the ornate marble tomb of Constantine V and begging the great iconoclast to rise from the dead and lead the Byzantine armies to victory again.

Unfortunately for the empire, however, consigning its works of art to the flames did little to strengthen its military. After several decades of relative quiet, the caliphate resumed the offensive, and the imperial army proved just as incapable of stopping them. In 826, a Muslim force landed on Crete, imposing Islam on the reluctant population and turning the capital of Candia into the busiest slave market in the world. By 838, the Muslims had burst into Asia Minor, sacking the city of Amorium and burning most of its citizens alive in the city's church, where they were trapped.* The next year, most of western Sicily fell and the Arabs crossed into Italy, conquering Taranto and using the heel of the Italian boot as a base from which to launch attacks against what is now the Croatian coast. The imperial government was so alarmed that it sent envoys begging the western emperor Louis the Pious for help, but the crusading spirit was still more than two hundred years in the future, and the talks came to nothing.

Ignoring the mounting evidence to the contrary, emperors continued to stubbornly insist that iconoclasm was the only way to restore divine favor to the imperial armies. One emperor even personally administered beatings to two Palestinian monks who refused to destroy their icons, and when a week of such treatment failed to induce them to change their minds, he had insulting verses tattooed on their faces and exiled them to Anatolia. Such ham-fisted measures have never been particularly successful where religion is concerned, and without

---

*In addition to the honor of being the origin city of the current dynasty, Amorium was famous as the birthplace of the Greek fable writer Aesop.

the argument of victory to bolster it, iconoclasm was a spent force. Most Byzantines realized that they had destroyed their icons and starved their artistic senses in vain. In 843, after less than three decades, iconoclasm disappeared again with barely a whimper. On the first Sunday of Lent that year, the beautiful and brilliant empress Theodora officially ended Byzantium's last major religious controversy by holding a general church council and a service of thanksgiving in the Hagia Sophia.* Artists once again picked up their brushes, hammers, and chisels and resumed their attempt to portray the divine in paint, wood, and stone. Several years passed before the first icon appeared in the great church of the Hagia Sophia, but its unveiling clearly demonstrated that the years in exile had done nothing to diminish the power of Byzantine art.†

Military reverses aside, there were encouraging signs in the ninth century that the empire was slowly regaining its strength. Shrunken by the losses of war, it had been reduced to a core in Asia Minor, Thrace, and Greece, but these territories were strong and united. Religious dissent had largely disappeared with the turbulent territories of Syria and Egypt, and the smaller imperial government was reasonably efficient regardless of who sat on the throne. New gold mines were uncovered, overflowing the impoverished treasury, and a rich merchant class sprang up in the wake of such unexpected wealth.

Even more encouraging was a great revival of learning sparked, ironically enough, by the dying embers of iconoclasm. Attempts to justify one side of the argument or the other by quoting obscure references to earlier church fathers led to further study to rebut them. Private schools began to appear throughout the empire as interest in education spread, and literacy began to pick up a momentum of its own. Under the emperor Theophilus in the mid-ninth century,

---

*An event that is still commemorated each year by the Eastern Church as the "Sunday of Orthodoxy."
†It can still be seen today—the haunting image of the Virgin Mary with the child Christ, seated on the throne of heaven and gazing sadly down toward where the great altar once stood.

teachers were endowed at the public expense, scriptoria were opened, and the University of Constantinople was endowed with new faculties of law and philosophy.*

This was in marked contrast with the West, where the church was slowly spreading the fragments of learning that it had preserved. Western medieval thought, though quite vital, had been cut off from its rich classical heritage and would have to wait for the Renaissance to build on the learning of antiquity. Eastern schools, however, could draw on their undiminished philosophical and literary traditions. Within a few years, Byzantium's renewed intellectual fame was so great that a caliph even asked for a specialist to be sent to Baghdad. Perhaps wisely, the emperor refused to let him go, choosing instead to set the scholar up in the capital to continue the ferment. Encouraged by the new air of curiosity, court historians once again took up their pens, young nobles returned to their study of the classics, and Byzantine scholarship, which had been nearly dormant since the reign of Irene, sprang once again into bloom. His armies may have been scattered in Asia Minor, but Theophilus presided over a cultural renaissance, winning the hearts of his subjects with his concern for justice.†

In an age in which the emperor was seen as an unapproachable figure—the human representation of God on earth—Theophilus was remarkably visible to his subjects. A devoted fan of chariot races, he once entered the competition under the banner of the Blues and delighted the crowd with his skill.‡ Most astonishing of all to the citizens of Constantinople, however, was the emperor's habit of wandering in

---

*The rigorous Byzantine curriculum remained virtually unchanged from the fifth century to the fifteenth. It usually included rhetoric, mathematical studies, and philosophy, and it wasn't uncommon for advanced students to commit the entire *Iliad* to memory.

†When his troops proved ineffective, Theophilus sent an ambassador to scatter thousands of gold coins among the citizens of Baghdad in an attempt to impress the caliph. Unfortunately, the emperor's gold was as unsuccessful as his armies.

‡Of course, the gesture was spoiled somewhat since the factions were carefully instructed to let him win.

disguise through the streets of the capital, questioning those he met about their concerns and ensuring that merchants were charging fair prices for their wares. Once a week, accompanied by the blare of trumpets, he would ride from one end of the city to the other, encouraging any who had complaints to seek him out. Those who stopped him could be certain of a sympathetic ear no matter how powerful their opponent. One story tells of a widow who approached the emperor and made the startling claim that the very horse he was riding had been stolen from her by a senior magistrate of the city. Theophilus dutifully looked into the matter, and when he discovered that the widow was correct, he had the magistrate flogged and told his watching subjects that justice was the greatest virtue of a ruler.*

To be accessible, however, didn't mean that the emperor intended to be an inch less regal, and he poured gold into a building program unlike anything seen since the days of Justinian.† All emperors have expensive tastes, but Theophilus put most of his predecessors to shame. With a flurry of activity, the walls along the Golden Horn were strengthened, a magnificent new summer palace was built, and the Great Palace was completely renovated for the first time in nearly three hundred years.‡ This last accomplishment caught the imagination of contemporary historians, who left breathless accounts of the

---

*This passion for justice made Theophilus a legend in his own lifetime, and numerous apocryphal stories (possibly including this one) were soon being circulated. Three hundred years later, his reputation was still such that the Byzantine writer of the satirical *Timarion* portrayed him as one of the judges of the underworld.

†There were few things that Theophilus didn't do extravagantly. When it came time for him to choose a wife, he held a huge bride show, presenting the winner with a typically elaborate golden apple in a scene meant to be reminiscent of the judgment of Paris.

‡Not surprisingly, the last emperor to significantly enlarge the palace had been Justinian. A glimpse of this original work still remains today in the remnants of a vast floor mosaic that was uncovered early in the twentieth century. Filled with a strange mix of pagan and Christian symbols, violent hunting scenes, and whimsical vignettes, the mosaic remains one of the finest surviving works of art from the ancient world.

work. Before their watching eyes, Theophilus transformed the sprawling, somewhat stuffy collection of buildings that made up the Great
Palace into a residence fit for a ninth-century emperor.* Such a reno-
vation was long overdue. Originally built by Septimus Severus in the
second century, the palace had been haphazardly added to by successive emperors, who had built reception halls, living quarters, churches,
baths, and administrative buildings, until the rambling structures
threatened to cover the entire southeastern tip of the city.

Theophilus imposed a welcome order on the Great Palace, clearing out cluttered walls and unused rooms and linking its buildings
with clean corridors. The polo grounds that had been built by Theodosius II four centuries earlier, when that emperor had imported the
royal sport from Persia, were enlarged, and fountains fed by underground cisterns soon adorned graceful walkways and terraced gardens. Creamy white marble steps led up to breezy chambers, forests of
rose and porphyry columns supported delicate apses, and silver doors
led to rooms filled with glittering mosaics. The true luxury, however,
was saved for Theophilus's unparalleled throne room. No other place
in the empire—or perhaps the world—dripped so extravagantly in
gold or boasted so magnificent a display of wealth. Behind the massive
golden throne were trees made of hammered gold and silver, complete
with jewel-encrusted mechanical birds that would burst into song at
the touch of a lever. Wound around the base of the tree were golden
lions and griffins staring menacingly from beside each armrest, looking as if they could spring up at any moment. In what must have been
a terrifying experience for unsuspecting ambassadors, the emperor
would give a signal and a golden organ would play a deafening tune,
the birds would sing, and the lions would twitch their tails and roar.
Rare indeed was a visitor who wasn't awed by such a display.

Nowhere was the growing confidence of the empire more apparent, however, than in the religious realm. There were few things more

---

*The buildings covered more than four and a half acres.

galling to the Byzantine religious mind-set than the increasingly insistent papal claim that the Bishop of Rome's voice was the only one that really mattered in deciding church policy. The four other patriarchs of the Christian world had traditionally deferred to the successor of Saint Peter, but great questions of faith had always been decided by consensus, in contrast with the growing authoritarianism of the western capital. In the past, the East and the West had managed to mask their increasing divisions beneath polite, distant relations, but a new combative spirit was in the air. When the pope sent Frankish missionaries to convert the Slavs, the patriarch Photius responded by sending his own contingent, the brilliant brother monks Cyril and Methodius.

The pope's men had a head start, but they alienated the Slavs by insisting that all services be conducted in Latin, even though their new converts didn't understand a word of it. Cyril and Methodius, by contrast, set to work immediately learning Slavic, and when they found it had no written alphabet, Cyril provided one.* Western bishops angrily complained that Hebrew, Greek, and Latin were the only tongues worthy of a sacred liturgy, but Cyril countered by saying that since God's rain fell on all equally, then all tongues were fit to praise him.† The Bulgarian khan, impressed by the new freedoms promised by Photius (and in any case unwilling to subordinate himself to Rome), traveled to Constantinople to be baptized in the Hagia Sophia, and Bulgaria entered the Byzantine cultural orbit, in which it remains to this day. By allowing Byzantine culture to be separated from the Greek language, Photius had spread the empire's influence far beyond its borders and immeasurably strengthened the bonds that held the diverse Byzantine world together. It would be more than six centuries before Latin was similarly dethroned in the West.

---

*The Cyrillic alphabet used by most of the Slavic world today was named so in his honor.

†Pope Adrian II got the point and allowed the brothers to work unmolested, requesting only that the Mass be read in Latin first and the vernacular second.

Adding the Slavs to the imperial cultural orbit had increased imperial prestige, but it had also sounded an ominous note. By openly contesting with Rome for the Balkans, Constantinople had brought tensions between the East and the West to the surface, and relations with the pope were always easier to rupture than repair. Memories were long on both sides of the cultural divide, and when the mutual suspicions and hatreds eventually bore fruit, it would be a bitter harvest indeed.

That, however, lay centuries in the future. The empire was newly confident and seemingly poised for a spectacular recovery. The only thing missing was an effective emperor. The men who sat on the throne in the ninth century, though they led colorful lives, were largely militarily incompetent.* Despite their cultural and religious accomplishments, they could never quite lift the empire out of its military slump. As unlikely as it seemed, the first stumbling steps toward recovery were taken under the auspices of an emperor named Michael the Drunkard.

As his name implies, Michael was hardly an inspiring figure, but he had the great advantage of having a visionary uncle. While the emperor absorbed himself in earning his nickname in the taverns of the capital, his uncle Bardas led the empire to its first significant victories against the armies of Islam. Under his leadership, a Byzantine army crossed the Euphrates for the first time since the seventh century, and the navy conducted a daring raid on Egypt. When the emirs of Meso-

---

*On Christmas Eve of 820, the emperor Leo V condemned the pretender Michael II to death by the rather bizarre method of having him tied to an ape and thrown into the furnaces that heated the imperial baths. Before the execution could take place, Michael's supporters dressed up as monks and crept into the imperial palace to attack the emperor. Leo reportedly defended himself for more than an hour armed with nothing but a heavy metal cross that he swung around wildly before succumbing to the blades of his assailants. In what was surely the most undignified coronation in Byzantine history, Michael II was hastily brought up from the dungeons and crowned with the chains of his captivity still around his legs.

potamia and Armenia responded by invading imperial territory, Bardas ambushed them, killing the emirs and most of their men.

The victories gave a welcome boost to Bardas's reputation, and since there was no telling how long the royal liver would hold out, most assumed that when Michael eventually expired, his capable uncle would succeed him. There was still, of course, the outside chance that the emperor would nominate another man as his successor, but though Michael had many favorites, most of them were chosen for their conviviality, not their governing abilities. Bardas, meanwhile, was perfectly happy to let his pathetic nephew have his fun, content to rule the empire in fact if not in name.

The trouble with weak emperors, however, is that they're swayed by every passing breeze, and Michael the Drunkard was soon under the spell of a rough Armenian peasant named Basil the Macedonian.* Basil had originally attracted the emperor's attention with an especially impressive display of strength in a wrestling match, and since this was as good a reason for advancement as any other in Michael's eyes, the young Armenian had been taken into the imperial service. For the capricious emperor, it was a terrible mistake. Basil was intelligent and ambitious with a terrifying ruthless streak. Bardas warned his nephew that Basil was a "lion who would devour them all," but the emperor paid him no heed. Within a year, Basil had personally assassinated Bardas, and Michael, flush with the excitement of being free from his powerful uncle, rewarded his brutal favorite with the title of coemperor. A few months later, Michael was dead as well, viciously murdered after his usual long night of drinking. After throwing a horse blanket over the emperor's body to conceal the spreading blood, Basil raced to the Great Palace, hoping to capture it before anyone could

---

*Despite his name, Basil (or anyone in his family for that matter) never—as far as we know—set so much as a foot inside Macedonia. Captured as a young man by the Bulgarian king, Krum, he had been relocated to an area filled with "Macedonian" prisoners, thus acquiring his nickname. For this and many other reasons, the dynasty he founded had no business calling itself Macedonian.

object. He need hardly have worried. Michael the Drunkard had long ago squandered whatever dignity he possessed, and not a single voice was raised against his murderer. When the sun rose the next morning over the quiet capital, it found a former peasant as the sole ruler of the Roman Empire. As unlikely as it seemed, a golden age had begun.

16

THE GLORIOUS HOUSE
OF MACEDON

Having come to the throne with enough blood on his hands to make Macbeth blush, Basil seemed destined to have an insecure reign. The murderous swath he had cut to the crown was flagrantly illegal, and it proved to be a source of considerable embarrassment to future members of his dynasty. But the medieval world was a remarkably volatile place, and most Byzantines were quite willing to forgive a questionable path to power if it resulted in effective rule. Great good, after all, can sometimes come from evil men. Michael had disgraced the office and would have drunk himself to an early death if Basil hadn't intervened. By contrast, the new emperor—murderer though he might be—would prove to be a beacon of good stewardship. Almost two centuries later, a member of his family was still sitting on the imperial throne.

Basil was uneducated by eastern standards, but he was astute enough to recognize the possibilities of a Byzantine recovery. Byzantium was no longer the sprawling empire of antiquity, but what had emerged from the wreckage of the Arab conquests was a vastly smaller, compact state with considerably more defensible borders. Its deep foundations had seen it through the years of turmoil, and now it had emerged from the darkness with its internal strength intact. While there was no need—or desire—to return to the vast territory of Justinian, Basil wanted to reclaim the empire's place in the sun.

Clearly, nothing could be achieved without a strong military, but while the army was sturdy enough, the fleet was in an appalling condition—a fact made obvious a few months after he took power, when Arab raiders easily brushed it aside and captured the island of Malta. As a Mediterranean power, the empire's strength depended on a strong navy, and leaving it in such a decrepit state was an invitation to disaster. Opening up the treasury, Basil poured money into rebuilding the fleet from the ground up, constructing top-of-the-line ships and scouring the empire to find men to fill their crews.

The refurbished sea power was to be the tip of the spear for Basil's grand offensive. The past century had seen only sporadic campaigns against the Muslims, and the time was ripe for a concerted attack. After years of aggressive expansion, the caliphate was divided and crumbling, unable to keep up the pressure against Byzantium. Now was the time for a campaign. The Arabs were on their heels, and such an opportunity wasn't to be missed. Sailing proudly out into the Saronic Gulf, the new navy proved its worth immediately when it got word that Cretan pirates were raiding in the Gulf of Corinth. Not wanting to waste his time sailing around the Peloponnese, the ingenious Byzantine admiral Nicetas Oöryphas dragged his ships across the four-mile width of the isthmus, dropping them safely into the gulf in time to send the pirates to the bottom.

Flushed with victory, Basil launched his great offensive. The fleet swept toward Cyprus, soon reconquering the island for the empire, and the imperial armies battered their way into northern Mesopotamia, annihilating the hapless Arab army that wandered into their path. The next year, Basil turned west, clearing the Muslims out of Dalmatia and capturing the Italian city of Bari. By 876, he had extended Byzantine influence into Lombardy, laying the groundwork for the recovery of all of southern Italy.

While his armies marched from one victory to the next, Basil turned his prodigious energies to the domestic front. In his mind, there was no greater testament to the decline of Byzantium than the lack of building in the capital. Old churches had fallen into shameful disrepair, and public monuments were beginning to have a distinct atmosphere of decay. Sending his workmen throughout the capital, he began a massive program to refurbish the queen of cities. Timber roofs were replaced by stone, walls were patched, and glittering mosaics restored numerous churches to their former glory. The most effort of all, however, was saved for his personal residence in the imperial palace. Heavily carved columns of green marble with rich veins of yellow supported a ceiling covered in gold, and huge portraits of the emperor and his family were arrayed in sumptuous mosaics. Massive imperial eagles decorated the floor, and glass tesserae filled with gold sparkled above them. Just to the east of these apartments rose his magnificent new church, officially dedicated to four saints but more commonly known by the rather uninspired name of Nea Ekklesia—"new church." Not since Justinian had finished construction on the Hagia Sophia had such a bold new church graced the imperial skyline. Countless angels and archangels looked down from its cascading domes, and priceless jewels studded its interior. This was to be Basil's supreme architectural triumph, a perpetual reminder of the splendor of the house of Macedon. So intent was the emperor on finishing it that when he heard the Arabs were besieging Syracuse—the last major Byzantine stronghold in Sicily—he refused to dispatch the fleet to help, preferring to use the navy to transport marble for his church instead. Syracuse fell, but the Nea was completed.*

Byzantium had clearly found its footing again, and in addition to a resurgence of power and prestige, the empire now entered a startling cultural renaissance. It started with the brilliant patriarch Photius, who virtually single-handedly reawoke a love of classical Roman and Greek literature in the empire.† A flurry of intellectual activity

---

*Sadly, the written accounts are all that is left of the splendid church. After the fall of the city in 1453, the Turks used it to store gunpowder, and not too surprisingly it exploded.

†An avid reader, Photius took copious notes of the manuscripts in his possession, and in what amounts to the first real book reviews in history, he left us a wonderful account of what he thought of them. Unfortunately, most of the works he

followed, and Basil began an ambitious new project to translate Justinian's law codes into Greek. It would have been a remarkable achievement for an emperor whose own education was lacking, but he never had the chance to complete the project. His beloved eldest son Constantine, who had been groomed for the throne, suddenly died, and Basil was thrown into a deep depression from which he never recovered.

Basil's melancholy was made much worse by the fact that the death left his second son, Leo VI, as the heir apparent. Thanks to a rather complicated arrangement, Basil had married his predecessor's mistress, and Leo was widely believed (especially by Basil, who presumably would have known) to be the child of Michael the Drunkard. The thought that this boy would soon inherit the throne that should have gone to Constantine nearly pushed Basil over the edge. When the emperor discovered that the fifteen-year-old Leo had taken a mistress named Zöe, he beat the boy severely with his own hands, restricting the prince to a wing of the palace and marrying off Zöe to someone else. This failed to stop the affair, however, and the moment Leo was released, he resumed relations with Zöe. The enraged emperor threw Leo into prison and, in a scene that shocked his courtiers, threatened to put out the boy's eyes.

Zöe's father finally managed to talk the emperor into releasing Leo by pointing out that since he was in his mid-seventies, keeping the heir to the throne disgraced was an invitation to all the horrors of a disputed succession. Reluctantly, Basil relented and the two were reconciled, but few believed it would last for long. The emperor was increasingly unpredictable, burdened down by the weight of his depression and frequently subject to bouts of insanity. He had never shown even the remotest scruple about murder, and Leo was perfectly aware that the odds were against his continued survival if the emperor lasted much longer. Basil, however, had always been renowned for his

referred to have long since disappeared, but it gives us a rare glimpse at some of the glittering, lost Byzantine masterpieces.

physical prowess, and at seventy-four didn't show many signs of slowing down. Perhaps nature needed to be nudged along.

A month after his reconciliation with Leo, the emperor was dead. The official story was that he had been killed during a hunting accident, a wildly improbable tale involving an enormous stag that dragged him sixteen miles through the woods. Even more suspicious was the fact that Zöe's father—a man who certainly wasn't enjoying the imperial favor—led the rescue party. The full extent of Leo's involvement has, of course, been long buried by the intervening years, but whatever the truth, most citizens were willing to turn a blind eye toward the cloudy circumstances in favor of the bright promise of the nineteen-year-old heir. A few days later, Leo VI took possession of the empire, and his first action was to exhume Michael the Drunkard's body from its shabby tomb and have it reburied in a magnificent sarcophagus in the Church of the Holy Apostles. At last the murdered emperor could sleep in peace—his death had been avenged. As for Basil, his reign had begun with the dark stain of a murder, and perhaps it's fitting that it ended the same way. For all the violence, however, he left the empire immeasurably strengthened both militarily and culturally, and it had good cause to mourn him.

Teenagers had been cast to the forefront of Byzantium before, but none had ever been as superbly prepared for the role as Leo VI. Easygoing and charming, the emperor could boast an education more extensive than any ruler since the days of Julian the Apostate, and an intellect to match it. His reign saw the return of classical architecture, a burst of literary activity, and a new spirit of humanism. Within weeks of his inauguration, he had talked the church into appointing his youngest brother, Stephen, as patriarch, a move that united the offices of the sacred and the secular under a single family and let the emperor exercise a control over church and state unrivaled in imperial history. Presiding over an astonishing period of domestic peace and prosperity, Leo was able to concentrate on Basil's great unfinished work—the recodification of Roman law.

More than three and a half centuries had passed since Justinian had brought order to the chaotic Roman judicial system, and the law books were in desperate need of review. The passing years had piled on thousands of new legal decisions, adding volumes to a legal code that already had the disadvantage of being written in Latin—an impenetrably dead language now accessible only to a few antiquarians. In just two short years, the emperor managed the monumental task of translating the entire mess, systematically arranging it, and publishing the first of six condensed volumes. The unveiling of the finished work earned the emperor the nickname "Leo the Wise" and saw him hailed as the greatest lawgiver since Justinian (a fact that would have severely irked his predecessor). Those who expected him to lead the armies to equal glory, however, were soon to be disappointed. The young emperor was more of a lover than a fighter, and perhaps inevitably he proved a good deal less successful in his foreign policy than in his domestic pursuits.

Byzantium never wanted for hostile neighbors, but, at the start of Leo's reign, it seemed as if at least the northwestern border was somewhat safe. There the Bulgar khan Boris had adopted Christianity, and many in Constantinople began to hope that the awful specter of Krum had been banished once and for all. This feeling was strengthened when Boris abdicated in favor of his youngest son, Vladimir, and retired meekly to a monastery, but no sooner had he gone than Vladimir tried to resurrect paganism, threatening to undo all of his father's hard work. Displaying a certain lack of monastic tranquillity, the enraged Boris blinded Vladimir and put his younger sibling, Simeon, on the throne instead. The watching dignitaries of Byzantium were relieved to have a friendlier candidate in power. It was widely known that Simeon had grown up in Constantinople and was a firm Christian to boot. Here, surely, was a man who understood the civilized world and could recognize the advantages of remaining on good terms with the empire.

Perhaps that would have been the case if Leo had lived up to his nickname, but he foolishly decided to raise the import taxes on Bulgarian goods, completely ignoring Simeon's protests. The annoyed Bulgarians immediately invaded, catching the empire by surprise, and within a matter of weeks they had swept into Thrace and had started plundering. Unfortunately for Leo, all of his armies were busy fighting in the East, so he resorted to the tried-and-true method of calling in allies to do his fighting for him. Byzantine messengers sped to the Magyars, a hostile tribe to the east of Bulgaria, inviting them to fall on the Bulgar rear. Caught in the pincer, Simeon had no choice but to withdraw and ask for peace. Leo sent his ambassadors to hammer out the details of the treaty and withdrew to deal with some Arab raiders, convinced that the chastened Bulgars had learned their lesson.

Leo may have been satisfied with himself, but Simeon had no intention of letting the matter drop. He had been outmaneuvered by the emperor, but the Bulgarian khan was a fast learner who was fully capable of employing Byzantine tactics. The moment the last imperial troop had disappeared down the road to Constantinople, he called in his own proxies, the Pechenegs—a Turkish tribe that was the natural enemy of the Magyars. Attacked from all sides, the Magyars were forced to flee, leaving Simeon free to invade Thrace once again.* A Byzantine army tried vainly to contain the damage, but it was easily crushed, and Leo was forced to conclude a humiliating and expensive peace.

The emperor had badly mishandled the situation, and when Taormina—the last Byzantine outpost in Sicily—fell to the Muslims in 902, it seemed as if the empire was once again going to slip back into weakness and enervation. Fortunately for Leo, his generals saved his military reputation in the East, where they were keeping up a steady pressure against the disintegrating caliphate. The next decade saw a surge of activity as Byzantine armies expelled the Muslims from western Armenia, destroyed the Arab navy, and raided as far as the Euphrates. There were, of course, the occasional setbacks. A major

---

*Blocked from returning to their homes by the Pechenegs, the Magyars ended up in the fertile plains of central Hungary, where they still remain today.

naval expedition failed to reconquer Crete, and in 904 an earthquake leveled the seawalls of Thessalonica—the second most important city of the empire. Its citizens hurried to repair the walls, but before the work was completed, an Arab fleet appeared, and the Saracens managed to batter their way inside. For an entire week, the Muslims plundered the city, butchering the old and weak before carting the rest off to their busy slave markets. The insult of Thessalonica was avenged the next year as Byzantine armies left the Arab port of Tarsus a heap of smoking ruins, but not many people were paying attention. The entire capital was gripped in the very public spectacle of the emperor's love life.

Leo had never really been happy with the woman Basil had forced him to marry as a teenager, and he had found comfort instead in the arms of his longtime mistress, Zöe. Not surprisingly, the imperial couple failed to produce an heir, and when the empress died in 898, Leo had happily summoned Zöe to the capital. There was the small obstacle of Zöe's husband, but he rather conveniently died, and the two lovers were hastily married. Their idyll, however, proved to be short-lived. After presenting her husband with a daughter, Zöe died of a fever only two years into the marriage. Leo was devastated with grief. Not only was his love gone, but he still hadn't managed to produce an heir, and the ramifications of that were terrible indeed. His brother Alexander was a hopeless reprobate by now, thoroughly incapable of progeny, and if Leo died it would be the end of the dynasty. The empire seemed destined to be subjected to all the horrors of a civil war.

Third marriages—at least in the East—were strictly forbidden by the church, but since the future of the empire was at stake, the patriarch reluctantly decided to allow Leo to choose another wife.* A stun-

---

*Divorce was generally not tolerated, but there were some examples in which a special dispensation was given. In one case in particular, an unhappy couple was locked in a house for a week, and when that failed to lead to a consummation of the marriage, they were granted a divorce on the grounds of mutual hatred.

ningly beautiful woman by the name of Eudocia was selected, and within a year she was pregnant. The court astrologers assured the emperor that it was a boy, and he was overjoyed when they proved to be correct. Leo VI, however, seemed destined for tragedy, and his uneasy subjects could only shake their heads when Eudocia died in childbirth and the baby expired a few days later. Canon law, it seemed, could not be flouted so easily.

Leo was now in an awkward position. He was desperate to have a son, but he himself had written the law forbidding multiple marriages. Now deeply regretting the thundering sermons he had given against those who "wallowed in the filth" of a fourth union, he gingerly sounded out the new patriarch, Nicholas, but was sternly informed that a fourth marriage would be "worse than fornication." Deciding that if this was the case he might as well enjoy some fornication, he found a devastatingly beautiful mistress named Zoë Carbonopsina.* Leo was a resourceful man, and he knew that with a bit of arm-twisting he could probably arrange for another marriage, but since this would unquestionably be his last chance, there was no reason to try unless she produced a son. That fall Zoë became pregnant with a son, and the overjoyed emperor had her moved into a special room in the palace. Decorated with porphyry columns and hung with purple silks—a color specifically reserved for emperors—it was known as the *Porphyra,* or Purple Room. Only imperial children could be born there, and from that day on Leo's son would bear the proud nickname "Porphyrogenitus," the Purple-born. Leo clearly intended to have the boy follow him on the throne, and just in case anyone missed the point, he named him Constantine VII to further strengthen his prestige.†

Leo finally had his heir, but since he wasn't married, the boy was

---

*The name Carbonopsina means "of the coal-black eyes" and it seems to have been this feature that struck most of Zoë's contemporaries. She was by all accounts one of the most beautiful women who ever lived in Byzantium.
†The normal custom would have been to name the boy after his grandfather, which in this case would be Basil, but Constantine was a more prestigious name— and, more important, an imperial one.

illegitimate, and no amount of clever naming could change that. For all the purple draped around him, Constantine VII was unbaptized, and, ironically enough, the very laws that Leo had written specifically forbade baptism for any child of a fourth marriage. If the emperor couldn't get Constantine recognized in his lifetime, then it would all be for nothing, and the empire would be doomed to a disputed succession. Summoning Patriarch Nicholas, Leo pulled out all the stops, and with a good deal of begging and a dash of blackmail he managed to force an agreement. He would eject Zoë from the palace and submit to never seeing her again, and in return Nicholas would baptize Constantine in the Hagia Sophia. Zoë had her bags hastily packed and the ceremony was duly carried out, but Leo had no intention of keeping his side of the bargain. Three days after the baptism, Zoë was smuggled back into the palace, and an obliging parish priest married her to the emperor.

The church exploded in controversy when word of Leo's actions became public. The furious patriarch refused to recognize the marriage and barred the doors when the emperor tried to enter the Hagia Sophia. Once again, however, Leo outmaneuvered his opponents. When the church doors were slammed in his face, he calmly returned to the palace and wrote an appeal to the pope. He was well aware that in the barbarian West, where death was an all-too-common event, church fathers took a more pragmatic view of widowers and remarriage. Moreover, by cleverly submitting the question to the pope when his own patriarch had vocally made his position known, Leo was giving the pontiff a golden opportunity to reinforce papal supremacy. The pope, he rightly guessed, wouldn't miss such a chance.

Once armed with the pope's muted approval, Leo acted quickly. The patriarch was arrested on charges of conspiracy and forced to sign an act of abdication. To replace him, Leo chose a mild man who was opposed in principle to the marriage but was willing to allow it for the appropriate concessions. Leo would have to make a public statement condemning fourth marriages and for the rest of his life would have to enter the church as a penitent—enduring the humiliation of remaining standing throughout any service he attended. The emperor was only too happy to accept these terms. This time he was as good as his word, and the church grudgingly accepted his marriage. His son, Constantine VII, was now legitimate and recognized as such throughout the empire. Two years later, the little boy was crowned coemperor, and his face appeared on his father's coins. Leo could do no more to guarantee a peaceful succession.

The emperor lived for four more years, and after one last attempt to reconquer Crete, he died in his bed on May 11, 912. He hadn't been a great military leader—in fact, he had never even led an army into battle—but through his law codes he left the empire far stronger internally than he had found it. Through sheer force of will, he had provided the empire with an heir—truly a gift of inestimable value—and it's fitting that the most enduring image we have of him is from a mosaic above the great imperial door of the Hagia Sophia. There, in a lunette above the entrance that was denied to him in life, the emperor bows humbly before the throne of God while the Virgin Mary intercedes on his behalf. He had ruled wisely and well for nearly a quarter of a century, and, as far as most of his citizens were concerned, he was worthy of a little forgiveness.

17

THE BRILLIANT PRETENDER

Ironically enough, considering the tremendous effort that his father had spent legitimizing him, there was little chance that Constantine VII would ever really rule. Only six at the time of Leo's death, Constantine was so sickly that most privately doubted he would live to reach maturity. As Leo had feared, effective power was held by the royal uncle, Alexander III, a man already famous for his lecherous behavior. Sullen from years spent under his more able brother's shadow, the new emperor took every opportunity to undo Leo's work. The deposed Nicholas, who had vehemently protested Leo's fourth marriage, was restored as patriarch, and Zoë Carbonopsina was unceremoniously expelled from the palace. The young prince, Constantine, was left to wander pathetically from room to room of the Great Palace, weeping for his mother, and rumor had it that the spiteful Alexander intended to castrate him to prevent his accession.

Mercifully, after a reign of only thirteen months, Alexander expired from exhaustion as he was returning from a polo game on the palace grounds. He had not gotten around to harming his nephew—if such had ever been his intention—but he did leave him with a hostile patriarch as regent as well as a disastrous war. When Bulgarian ambassadors had appeared at his court expecting the usual tribute, Alexander had chased them out of the room, shouting that they wouldn't see a single piece of gold from him. The insulted Bulgar khan immediately mobilized his army and headed for Constantinople, meeting virtually no resistance as he crossed the frontier.

The patriarch Nicholas, acting as regent after Alexander's death, managed to bribe the Bulgars to go away by promising to marry off Constantine VII to Simeon's daughter. Unfortunately, the patriarch neglected to inform anyone of his plan, and he was nearly lynched when the outraged population found out. The humiliated patriarch was obviously no longer capable of acting as regent, and someone else had to be found who would have the young emperor's best interests at heart. Fortunately for the empire, the perfect candidate was near at hand. Zoë was triumphantly brought back from exile and immediately took a tougher stance. She categorically refused to allow her son to marry the progeny of a man whose great-grandfather had used an emperor's skull as his drinking cup—and since that meant war, she was determined to fight.

Zoë bribed the Pechenegs to invade Bulgaria and dispatched a fleet to ferry them across the Danube, while a patrician named Leo Phocas led the Byzantine army down the Black Sea coast. Everything went smoothly enough until the Pechenegs arrived to be transported across. The Byzantine admiral, Romanus Lecapenus, got into a furious shouting match with the Pecheneg commander and refused to have anything more to do with them, sailing back to Constantinople without ferrying a single soldier across the river. This petulant display left the Byzantine army dangerously exposed, and Simeon easily wiped it out.

The disaster ruined Zoë's credibility, but since Constantine was still only thirteen, she had to find some way to remain in power to protect him. Deciding that a marriage was the only possible solution, she settled on the dashing Leo Phocas, whose recent defeat had only slightly dented his military reputation. It was not by any means a universally popular choice. The Phocas family was well known for its ambition, and the young prince would be easy prey for the unscrupulous Leo. For the worried friends of Constantine VII, there was only one alternative. Gathering together in secret before the marriage could take place, they wrote a hasty letter to the only man with enough prestige to save the young prince.

Admiral Romanus Lecapenus was enjoying the popularity of being the highest-ranking military official without the stain of a Bulgarian defeat (although that wasn't saying much since the Bulgarians lacked a navy), and when he got the letter he immediately agreed to become young Constantine's protector. Upon entering the city, he appointed himself head of the imperial bodyguard; a month later, he had the emperor marry his daughter. The outmaneuvered Leo Phocas furiously started a civil war, but Romanus—now calling himself *basileopater* (father of the emperor)—had control of Constantine VII and easily won the propaganda war.* Leo's men deserted him en masse and the hapless rebel was captured and blinded.

Having dispatched his rivals, Romanus now moved to secure his own power. Within days of Constantine VII's fifteenth birthday, he was appointed Caesar, and just three months later he was crowned co-emperor. Those watching could reflect that it had been a remarkably gentle rise—Romanus I Lecapenus had reached the throne without a single murder—but they couldn't help but wonder how long Constantine VII would survive the new emperor's "protection."

They were right to be worried. Romanus had at least eight children and was determined to start a dynasty. After all, the current imperial family had gained the throne by usurpation, so Romanus was only following the example of Basil the Macedonian. Within a year, he elbowed Constantine aside, declaring himself the senior emperor, and crowned his eldest son, Christopher, as heir—relegating Constantine VII to a distant third place. There were limits to the usurper's ambition, however. Romanus wasn't a violent man by nature, and he lacked Basil's ruthlessness. Constantine VII could be ignored and pushed around, but Romanus would never raise a hand against him.

---

*Romanus had Constantine write an announcement saying that he completely trusted his "father" and smuggled copies of it to Leo's army by means of both a priest and a prostitute. Perhaps not altogether unsurprisingly for an army camp, the prostitute proved the more successful of the two, and within a short time Leo's troops became convinced that they were fighting against the legitimate emperor.

In Bulgaria, Simeon was still fuming at his change in fortunes. As long as Constantine VII had remained unmarried there was a chance he could get close to the throne, but with the prolific Lecapeni brood firmly installed in the great palace, any hope of that had been rudely snatched away. Vowing to pull down the walls of Constantinople if necessary, he gathered a massive army and swept down onto the European side of the Bosporus. Finding the delightful little church of the Pege—a particular favorite of Romanus—he burned it to the ground, fouling its healing waters with the blood of those monks not spry enough to get away. He rampaged his way through the houses clustered outside Constantinople's land walls, hoping to lure the emperor out of the city, but Romanus looked out impassively. He was well aware that he was perfectly safe behind the walls—and after a few weeks, Simeon realized it too.

The emperor was willing to negotiate—he had always preferred diplomacy to fighting—and a meeting was soon arranged between the two monarchs. Simeon arrived dressed in his finest armor, attended by soldiers bearing golden and silver shields, proclaiming him emperor loudly enough to be heard by the senators watching from the walls. Romanus, by contrast, came on foot, dressed simply and clutching a relic, every inch seeming to say that the glory of the Roman Empire was splendid enough attire to put his opponent's garish display to shame. Addressing Simeon, he spoke with a subtle dignity: "I have heard you are a pious man and a true Christian, but I see deeds which do not match those words. For it is the nature of the pious man and a Christian to embrace peace and love since God is love. . . . Mankind is awaiting death and resurrection and judgment. . . . Today you are alive, but tomorrow you will be dissolved into dust. . . . What reason will you give to God for the unjust slaughters? If you do these things for love of wealth I will sate you excessively in your desire. . . . Embrace peace, so that you may live an untroubled life . . . "*

---

*I. Bozhilov, "L'idéologie politique du Tsar Syméon: Pax Symeonica," *Byzantinobulgarica* 8 (1986).

Simeon didn't miss the emperor's offer of tribute—cleverly disguised as it was as an appeal to his better nature—and after a show of acceptance and a small gift exchange, he turned around and headed for Bulgaria. The next year, in a fit of pique, he took the impressively empty title of Emperor of the Romans and Bulgarians (at which Romanus merely laughed), but he never crossed the imperial frontier again. A year later, his armies suffered a bloody defeat trying to annex Croatia, and Simeon died a broken man, leaving his crippled empire to his uninspired son Peter. A marriage alliance was hastily arranged with one of Romanus's granddaughters, and a welcome peace descended between the formerly bitter opponents. The Bulgarian menace had been the most frightening danger to the empire since the Arabs had besieged Constantinople, but under Romanus's deft guidance, the threat had dissolved with barely a whimper.

At last freed from the specter of a barbarian horde sweeping down on his back, Romanus could turn to administration. His central concern was the alarming growth of aristocratic power, and he feared with good reason what would happen if the rich kept expanding at the expense of the poor. Imperial defense depended on the peasant farmer who made up the backbone of the militia, but large areas of the frontier were now being converted to wealthy estates as nobles gobbled up land at a frightening rate. Determined to put an end to such sharp practices, Romanus passed various land laws designed to protect the impoverished farmers. These measures inevitably earned the emperor the undying hatred of the nobility, who continued to try to undercut him, but for the rest of his reign he refused to back down. The damage to the militia system could hardly be undone, but he was determined to at least put a halt to its spread.

While the domestic war against aristocratic growth rumbled in Constantinople, Romanus launched his armies in the East. There was no hope of a similar diplomatic triumph on the Arab frontier. The coming of Islam had brought three centuries of unending war, retreat, and disaster, and only force was understood. The Macedonian dynasty had stopped the bleeding and begun to turn the tide, but it had been too distracted by the Bulgarians to make any real gains. Now, however, the empire could afford to throw its entire weight against the Arabs. John Curcuas, the empire's most gifted general, was given command of the eastern field armies and ordered to march toward Armenia—the ancestral homeland of the Lecapeni family.

Squeezed between the great powers of the caliphate and Byzantium, the Kingdom of Armenia had passed back and forth between them more times than any Armenian cared to remember. With Christian power in the area seemingly broken, the kingdom had once again fallen under the sway of the Abbasid caliphate, but Curcuas swept in and expelled the Muslims, frightening the local emir so badly that he agreed to provide troops for the imperial army. The next year, the general plunged south, spreading a ripple of fear along the entire length of the Arab frontier. Marching to the foot of the Anti-Taurus Mountains—the craggy range that separated Asia Minor from Asia proper, that had long been the border between Christianity and Islam—Curcuas captured the pleasant city of Melitene, the first major city to be recovered from the Muslims. Leaving its pleasant apricot orchards, the general led a quick raid into northern Mesopotamia, but was recalled to the capital in 941 to chase away a huge Russian fleet that suddenly appeared in the Black Sea.* Thanks to a copious amount of Greek fire that seemed to light the very waves on fire, the Russians were soon in full retreat, but when they fled to the shore, Curcuas appeared out of nowhere, forcing the panicked Russians to leap back into the burning waters.

The triumphant general didn't stay long in Constantinople to celebrate his victory. That autumn, as a Byzantine fleet annihilated an

---

*These were the descendants of Viking warriors who had as yet to be absorbed into their Slavic surroundings. Elsewhere in Europe, they had already ripped apart Charlemagne's empire, and for centuries Western prayer books would include the plea "O Lord, spare us from the fury of the Northmen." This encounter with the Byzantines was the first time the Viking "Sea Wolves" had met a state capable of mustering a formidable navy, and the experience deeply impressed them. Forty years later, they would gain entrance to the city by joining the elite imperial guard, and they remained its backbone until the empire itself collapsed.

Arab navy off the coast of Provence, he stormed through northern Mesopotamia, sacking the ancient Assyrian city of Nisibis, which had slipped from the imperial grasp under the reign of Jovian almost six hundred years before. Returning home along the Mediterranean coast, his army stopped at the city of Edessa, sparing its largely Christian population the horrors of a siege in exchange for its most priceless relic.*

When Curcuas returned to Constantinople, he found the emperor a pale shadow of his former self. After more than a decade on the throne, Romanus was now in his seventies and seemingly a spent force. Most of his energy had been expended fighting domestic and foreign wars, and each new struggle further taxed his diminishing resources. The nobility was as grasping as ever, always clawing around the limits he tried to impose on them, and his land laws were proving nearly impossible to enforce. Perhaps some final reserve of strength might still have been found, but in the spring of 944 his favorite son died, and Romanus was plunged into despair.

The emperor had never really been comfortable with the humiliations he had inflicted on the legitimate Constantine VII, and now he was crippled with guilt. There were other sons, of course, but Romanus was painfully aware of how worthless they were. Brought up in the splendor of the imperial palaces among power and privilege, they were spoiled, entitled, and already famously corrupt. When the gifted John Curcuas arrived in Constantinople, they badgered their weary father into replacing him with a relative named Pantherius—a man whose name was unfortunately more impressive than his abilities. As a younger man, Romanus would never have allowed such a thing to happen, and after several military reversals, he realized that his

---

*The relic in question was the Holy Mandylion, widely believed to have been the first icon ever created. According to legend, the dying king of Edessa had written to Jesus asking to be cured of a crippling illness. Christ had responded by pressing a piece of cloth to his face and sending the miraculous image back. The relic somehow survived the Fourth Crusade intact, eventually ending up in France, where it was destroyed during the French Revolution.

spoiled sons couldn't be allowed to follow him on the throne. Finding some last reserve of energy, the aging emperor composed a new will, officially naming the half-forgotten Constantine VII as his heir.

The decision to disinherit his own family shocked his contemporaries, but Romanus was tormented by his sins and could find no peace in his last years. With his body failing and death approaching, the fleeting glories of temporal power now seemed a poor exchange for the stains on his conscience. He had brushed aside the legitimate dynasty and forced his own grasping brood on the empire. Perhaps now, by setting things right, he could find some salve for a troubled conscience.

When the will was made public five days before Christmas of 944, the sons of Romanus were horrified. They had been mistreating Constantine VII for years, and the thought of him actually having power was too terrible to contemplate. This bitter betrayal convinced them that they had to act quickly to avoid their impending irrelevancy. Romanus was quickly seized and (somewhat willingly, one suspects) sent off to a monastery on the Princes Islands in the Marmara. The people of Constantinople, however, had no intention of being ruled any longer by the Lecapeni. Romanus had been acceptable enough—his combination of quiet diplomacy and military power had arrived just in time to guide the empire past the threat of Bulgaria—but no matter how able, he was still a usurper, and his squabbling sons had no right to follow him.

During Romanus's reign, Constantine VII—driven by a survival instinct—had never made the slightest effort to assert himself, quietly allowing Romanus to push him ever further into the background. Whenever his name was needed to give something additional weight, he was willingly trotted out to wave to the crowds or add his signature to a document, and he hadn't shown even the slightest whiff of ambition. During those long years in the shadows, however, something unexpected had happened. No one remembered—or cared any longer—that he had been born an illegitimate son to a father whose own paternity was in doubt. There was a certain sympathetic charm about the serious little boy who had been orphaned in the palace, surrounded and humiliated by a large and hostile family for so many years without complaint. Constantine VII had been "born in the purple"—a distinction that none of the arrogant Lecapeni could claim—and in his veins ran the true blood of the house of Macedon. The despised sons of Romanus had abused the rightful heir for long enough, and the people of the capital were no longer willing to tolerate that. When the elderly Romanus fell from power, Constantine VII suddenly found that he was wildly popular. Within days, a rumor started flying that his life was in danger, and an angry mob forced the unwilling Lecapeni brothers to recognize him as the senior emperor.

The thirty-nine-year-old Constantine VII, though he had given no indication of it before, proved capable of decisive action. When the desperate Lecapeni brothers plotted to overthrow him just days after hailing him as senior emperor, he struck first, surprising them at a dinner party and sending them off to join their father in exile. Some of the remaining relatives were rounded up and castrated, but the emperor didn't indulge himself in any bloodbaths or vicious recriminations against the family that had held him down for so long. Romanus had ruled well, and Constantine VII was intelligent enough not to let his bitterness blind him from following his example. The agrarian policies were continued, the aristocracy was checked, and Romanus's laws were kept in place. Where Constantine VII differed with his predecessor at all it was to favor the Phocas family—longtime enemies of the Lecapeni.

To replace the long departed John Curcuas as commander of the empire's eastern armies, Constantine VII chose the even more brilliant Nicephorus Phocas—the young nephew of the man from whom Romanus Lecapenus had snatched the throne years before. Nicephorus was a boorish man who lacked even the rudiments of tact or taste, but the empire hadn't seen a general of such ability since Belisarius was hurled against the barbarians more than four hundred years before. In four years of campaigning, Nicephorus and his gifted nephew John Tzimisces broke the mighty Syrian emir Sayf al-Dawlah, capturing cities on the Euphrates and even reaching Antioch.* To the terrified Muslim armies on the Syrian frontier, he was soon known as the "Pale Death of the Saracens," and Arab forces would flee the field at the rumor that he was on the march.

Propelled by its newfound power, the empire was reinvigorated and optimistic. When the Magyars raided Thrace, hoping that Byzantium would be too distracted with the collapsing Syrian frontier, an imperial army inflicted a crushing defeat, completely annihilating the hapless raiders. Dignitaries and ambassadors from the caliph of Córdoba to the crowned heads of Europe came flocking to Constantinople, where they were dazzled with the breadth of the emperor's knowledge and the splendor of his court. Entertained in the sumptuous palace known as the Hall of the Nineteen Couches, visiting guests would recline to eat in the ancient Roman fashion, clapping in wonder as golden plates laden with fruit would be unexpectedly lowered from the ceiling. Cleverly concealed cisterns would make wine splash from fountains or cascade down carved statues and columns, and an automatic clock in the city's main forum would complete the imperial tour de force. Most impressive of all, however, was the emperor himself. An accomplished artist and writer, Constantine VII so overwhelmed the Russian regent princess Olga that she converted to Christianity, planting the seeds of Orthodoxy in the land that would one day call itself the third Rome.

The only concern that troubled the emperor's mind was his son Romanus II. In 949, the young man had most inappropriately fallen in love with an innkeeper's daughter, a devastatingly beautiful Spartan woman named Theophano. The match wasn't suitable by any stretch of the imagination, but perhaps a lifetime spent as a pawn in Romanus Lecapenus's hands convinced Constantine VII not to inflict the same treatment on his own son. Making a solemn vow not to interfere, he

---

*Interestingly enough, John Tzimisces was also the grandnephew of John Curcuas. "Tzimisces" comes from an Armenian word referring to his short stature (an attribute shared with Nicephorus Phocas). His real family name was Curcuas.

sat back stoically as the two were married, gracefully maintaining the fiction that she belonged to a worthy and ancient family. Nine years later, Theophano presented her husband with a son, and the happy couple named him Basil, after the founder of their dynasty. As much as it could be in those uncertain times, the future of the imperial family seemed secured. A year later, Constantine VII was dead of a fever that neither the healing waters of a local spring nor the purifying cold of a mountaintop monastery could cure, and the genuinely mourning empire passed smoothly to his son Romanus II.

Though the dashing new emperor was more interested in hunting than administration—and was besides completely under the thumb of his wife—he was smart enough to stay out of his general's way, and the empire's recovery continued unabated. As Romanus II enjoyed himself, domestic policy was run by his closest adviser, a gifted eunuch named Joseph Bringas. Under the chamberlain's able hand, the arts flourished, the University of Constantinople was chaired with new faculty, and the economy boomed. The land laws of Romanus's grandfather had given peasants more protection than they had seen in centuries, and merchants carrying the wealth of India and China flooded into Constantinople's busy markets. The empire was prosperous and peaceful, and Romanus II—or more likely his wife—decided the time had come to flex the imperial muscle.

The surest reminder of the empire's dark days was the island of Crete. During the empire's weakest moments a hundred years before, the island had fallen to a group of Arab pirates who had been kicked out of Egypt by an annoyed caliph in 826. The embarrassment of having this important island—one that had been in Roman hands since 69 BC—snatched away by a band of freebooters was more than the imperial dignity could bear. The once-prosperous island was now a nest of pirates that had infested the entire eastern Mediterranean, but every attempt to retake it had only produced spectacular failures. Constantine VII had prepared yet another offensive before he died, and all Romanus II had to do was to pick a general to lead it. His choice couldn't have been easier, as throughout the city there was only one name on everyone's lips. Looking down at the imperial harbor where an immense fleet of 307 warships and nearly eighty thousand men waited, the emperor summoned Nicephorus Phocas and entrusted him with upholding the honor of Byzantium.

Crete was heavily fortified, but Nicephorus brushed aside the waiting Arab army by sending in his marines—terrifying Norse warriors whose terrible double-bladed axes could smash through armor and bone alike. After marching up the coast in pursuit of his fleeing enemies, Nicephorus pulled up outside of the island's main city of Candia and settled down to a nine-month siege. Autumn gave way to the severest winter in living memory, and while it was hard on the citizens of Candia, it was far worse in the flimsy tents of an army camp. Serious food shortages added to the misery of brutal conditions that would have broken most men, but somehow Nicephorus was able to keep up morale by daily making his rounds, infusing his troops with his unflagging charisma. Arab spirits, meanwhile, were depressed by the ambushes they fell into every time they tried to forage outside the walls, and they were weakened further when Nicephorus started lobbing the severed heads of their compatriots into the city.

When spring arrived, the exhausted defenders could take no more, and the Byzantines managed to batter their way inside, capturing a century's worth of pirate loot. The triumphant general sailed back to Constantinople to receive a much-deserved ovation in the Hippodrome, and the gratitude of an empire.* Byzantium's honor had been avenged. After 135 years under the Arab yoke, Crete returned to the imperial fold.

The Byzantine armies of the East had also won an important victory. The moment the bulk of imperial soldiers had left for Crete, the Syrian emir Sayf al-Dawlah had tried one last time to restore the bal-

---

*An ovation was a slightly less prestigious award than a triumph. Nicephorus had accomplished what no Byzantine had managed for centuries and certainly deserved the latter, but like Justinian with Belisarius, Romanus II was somewhat wary of his successful general.

ance in his favor by raiding Asia Minor. Leo Phocas—the brother of Nicephorus, who was charged with the eastern defenses—decided to let him plunder unmolested and hid in the Taurus Mountains, hoping to ambush the emir on his return. Early that November, Sayf dutifully appeared at the head of his army trailed by a long train of Christian prisoners. Though Sayf managed to escape the ambush, his army was cut to pieces, and the same chains that had held the Christians only moments before now bound the survivors.*

By the time the fleeing emir reached his sumptuous palace in Aleppo, Nicephorus had returned from Crete and together with his brother Leo and nephew John Tzimisces had started a new offensive. Racing through Syria and northern Mesopotamia, they captured an astonishing fifty-five fortresses before appearing in front of the gates of Aleppo. Sayf desperately tried to defend the city with a makeshift army, but while John Tzimisces chased him away, Nicephorus burned the palace and besieged the city. After a siege of only three days, it fell, and Byzantine troops entered a city they hadn't seen since the days of Heraclius. The Pale Death of the Saracens, however, hadn't come to reabsorb lost territory into the empire. His intention was simply to exhaust his opponents. After ransacking Aleppo, he made his slow way back to Cappadocia, bringing with him two thousand camels and fifteen hundred mules burdened with the weight of the tremendous loot. When he arrived, he was greeted with stunning news. The twenty-four-year-old Romanus II was dead, and rumor had it that his wife Theophano had murdered him.†

---

*He did so by scattering gold coins behind him as he galloped away. The pursuing Byzantine troops were too busy picking up coins to continue the chase.

†Romanus had in fact been injured while hunting—a scandalous event, since it was the middle of Lent and hunting was strictly forbidden.

18

DEATH AND HIS NEPHEW

Poisonings were nothing new in Byzantium, and the empress Theophano was well known for her grasping ambition, but to have killed her husband would have been an act of sheer folly for such an intelligent woman.* Romanus's death (as she must surely have known it would be) was a disaster for her. Their son Basil II had been crowned, but he wasn't yet six years old, and, as recent imperial history so strongly demonstrated, it was all too easy for an ambitious man to displace a rightful young heir.

With her husband gone, Theophano desperately needed a protector for Basil II, and she secretly wrote to Nicephorus Phocas, begging him to return to Constantinople. The great general was by now the most popular man in the empire by a comfortable margin, and his military reputation was unparalleled. The book he had written on tactics and strategy was already viewed as a classic among the ranks of the army and would, in fact, be quoted for centuries as the authority on countering Arab attacks. The imperial court, however, sniffed at his origins and uncouth manner, and was horrified that the empress would consider relying on such a man. Opposition soon crystallized around the powerful figure of the head chamberlain, Joseph Bringas, who had effectively been wielding power behind the scenes during Romanus's reign and didn't intend to let some provincial general

---

*It would also have been quite an accomplishment, since she had given birth two days previously and was still in bed recovering.

displace him. Determined to prevent Nicephorus from entering Constantinople, Bringas issued a decree banning him from the city and ordered the gates shut.

It soon became apparent that Bringas had overplayed his hand. Nicephorus was a popular general who had spent his career in service to Byzantium, and no amount of proclamations from a scheming court could convince the populace otherwise. Mobs took to the streets loudly demanding that the general be admitted to the city, and the panicked chamberlain was forced to back down. Desperate to get rid of Nicephorus, Bringas tried to assassinate him, but once again the general's popularity saved him. Marching into the Hagia Sophia the moment he caught wind of the threat, Nicephorus loudly announced that his life was in danger. The patriarch hastily summoned the Senate, and its members took oaths before the packed congregation to make no major decision without him. Bringas had no choice but to sullenly add his consent. At last satisfied that he was secure, Nicephorus left to make arrangements with his army in Anatolia.

Joseph Bringas was now a desperate man. He had made no secret of his disgust for the swarthy general, and he knew that the moment Nicephorus returned to claim the throne, his days were numbered. Resorting to the only thing he could think of, the chamberlain wrote to John Tzimisces, offering to make him emperor if he would only betray his uncle. A fall from power might be inevitable for Joseph Bringas, but at least he could bring Nicephorus Phocas down with him.

Unfortunately for the eunuch, Tzimisces brought the treacherous letter directly to his uncle. There was no longer any reason for the general to hesitate. At dawn the next day, in a ceremony that stretched back to the half-forgotten glory days of imperial Rome, his soldiers raised him on a great shield under the open sky and proclaimed him emperor. They then struck camp and marched on Constantinople, but when the army arrived at the Asian side of the Bosporus, they found two unpleasant surprises waiting for them. The first was that Bringas, in a fit of spite, had thrown Nicephorus's family—including his eighty-year-old father—into prison. Second, and more serious, the chamberlain had removed every last vessel—from the humblest fishing boat to the largest ferry—from their side of the shore.

With no way to transport his troops across the narrow stretch of water, there was nothing for the fuming Nicephorus to do but sit down and wait for something to develop. Fortunately for him, events were swiftly overtaking the beleaguered head chamberlain. Nicephorus's brother, Leo, managed to escape from Constantinople by climbing through some drainage pipes, and his octogenarian father somehow slipped from Bringas's clutches and fled to the sanctuary of the Hagia Sophia. When the unpopular chamberlain's guards arrived and tried to seize the elderly man, the congregation erupted in a rage. Grabbing anything that was handy—including bricks, rocks, and demolished pews—they came roaring out into the streets and began skirmishing with the imperial guards. Pushed back into the surrounding streets, the chamberlain's forces held their own until a well-aimed flowerpot, launched by a woman from a nearby roof, struck the captain in the head, killing him instantly.

Three days of furious fighting followed, during the course of which Bringas completely lost control of the city. In the chaos, an illegitimate son of Romanus I Lecapenus named Basil was able to seize the imperial fleet and send it to pick up the waiting Nicephorus. At the sight of the great general riding through the Golden Gate on a massive white horse, dressed in his finest golden armor, the fury of the mob turned to cheers. Escorting Nicephorus to the Hagia Sophia, the crowd watched him dismount and kneel before the high altar as the patriarch gently placed the imperial crown on his lowered head.

The new emperor of Byzantium was one of the most qualified men ever to sit on the imperial throne and seemed to have been born to lead. Still energetic in his early fifties, he had held the supreme command over the army for the last nine years and was used to giving orders and getting results. He unfortunately wasn't gifted with a single ounce of charm, barking commands at his courtiers and insulting everyone he disagreed with, but the empire needed a firm hand at the helm, and there was no one better to steer the rudder. Unpleasant, boorish, and rude he may have been, but (if only by virtue of the fact that they didn't know him yet) he was extremely popular with his subjects, and Theophano welcomed him as her children's protector.

Their relationship must have been somewhat awkward. Strictly religious to the point of asceticism, Nicephorus couldn't have been less suited to the pleasure-loving twenty-two-year-old Theophano, but he soon fell hopelessly in love and, ignoring a previous vow of chastity, proposed to her within the month. Whether she actually loved him or not, Theophano needed him, and she gratefully accepted, taking her place beside him on the throne.

Marital bliss, however, could only keep the emperor in Constantinople for so long. He was always happiest on campaign, and, in any case, there were too many enemies on the frontiers to relax his vigilance. The caliphate was showing encouraging signs of weakness, and now was the time to press the advantage. Earlier that year, Nicephorus had sent his brilliant nephew John Tzimisces probing into Syria, and the young man had met exemplary success. Impatient to join him, the emperor gathered his army and set out, alerting his nephew by lighting a series of signal fires that carried news of the advance to the distant Taurus Mountains within a few hours. The first target was the ailing emir of Aleppo, who had been raiding imperial territory for decades. The Muslims took one look at the size of the imperial army bearing down on them and tried to negotiate, but Nicephorus ignored the panicked offer of tribute and stormed his way into Cilicia to conquer Tarsus. That same summer, the imperial forces cleared the Arabs from Cyprus. Two years later, Nicephorus brought the city of Aleppo to its knees, reducing the once-powerful emirate into a vassal state.

The emperor returned in triumph to the capital with a glittering reputation and a new confidence in the empire's power and prestige. He had humbled those who raised swords against him in the East and had demonstrated clearly enough that Byzantium was not to be trifled with. Unfortunately for the empire, however, it had enemies on all sides, and the very traits that had served Nicephorus so well in the East would betray him in the West and bring nothing but disaster.

Against the forces of Islam, it was war to the death—something for which Nicephorus's grating personality was perfectly suited—but when it came time to deal with the Christian powers to his west, his complete lack of tact became a glaring weakness. When diplomats from the German emperor Otto I mistakenly addressed him as king of the Greeks, Nicephorus had them thrown into a dungeon, nearly plunging both empires into a war. Things went from bad to worse when ambassadors from the Bulgarian king Peter arrived in Constantinople asking for their traditional small tribute.* Asking incredulously if they thought he was a slave who needed to pay tribute to a "wretched" people, the emperor had them slapped rudely in the face and told them to go back to their boorish king. Tell him, Nicephorus said, that I will soon come in person to pay you the tribute you deserve.

The emperor immediately gathered his army, ignoring the frantic appeals from the Bulgarian king. Several fortresses along the Bulgarian frontier were stormed, but one look at the dense woods and twisting ravines of Bulgaria was enough to give Nicephorus second thoughts. Advancing into such territory was asking to be ambushed; there were other ways to punish the uppity Bulgarians without risking his own troops. Sending messengers armed with a copious amount of Byzantine gold to Russia, Nicephorus bribed the Russians to do his fighting for him.

The Viking prince of Kiev, Svyatoslav, eagerly led his shambling horde across the border, crushed the Bulgarian army, captured King Peter, and impaled twenty thousand of those who resisted for good measure. Unfortunately for the empire, this rather easy victory only whetted the Russian appetite, and the prince of Kiev was soon hungrily eyeing Byzantine territory. In his anger, Nicephorus had merely exchanged a weak neighbor for a strong, aggressive one; but by the time he realized what he had done, it was too late.

---

*The tribute was used to defray the cost of a Byzantine princess at the Bulgarian court, enabling her to live in a manner befitting her station.

In any case, Nicephorus Phocas was now distracted by a quarrel with the church. He had been aware of its growing worldliness for some time (while marching on campaign through Byzantine lands, it was hard to miss the vast, uncultivated ecclesiastical estates) and numerous discussions with his best friend—a monk named Athanasius—convinced him that something needed to be done. Nicephorus had been annoyed at the patriarch ever since the man had refused to consider his request that soldiers who died fighting the Muslims should be considered martyrs, so, with his typical abruptness, the emperor promulgated several sweeping decrees.* The sprawling wealth of monastic houses had denied the state its due tax and corrupted the church for long enough. No longer would military veterans (or anyone else) be allowed to donate their land to huge ecclesiastical estates. The monks who had taken vows of poverty should live as their ancestors did in simple monasteries located in remote corners away from the hustle and bustle of busy life, not in sumptuous houses filled with breathtaking frescoes and surrounded by vineyards and fields tilled by serfs. The emperor sent his loyal friend Athanasius to Greece to endow a monastery on the slopes of Mount Athos, as an example of what a monastic community should be.† Then, as a final twist of the knife, he made it autonomous of the patriarch, answering directly to the throne.

With his domestic affairs thus put in order, the emperor left once again for the East in 968. This time his aim was to eliminate the Muslim power that kept trying to take over Armenia. Marching into the little Armenian town of Manzikert, he annihilated the Arab emi-

---

*The patriarch's refusal was the seminal moment in Byzantine history when it rejected completely the idea of "holy warriors." The West, of course, would come to a different conclusion during the Crusades.

†The monasteries of Mount Athos—the "Holy Mountain"—survive to this day, an island of the Byzantine world untouched by time or the ravages of modern development. Set on the stunningly beautiful Athonite peninsula, these twenty monasteries form an autonomous community—and they still fly the eagle flag of Byzantium.

rate and liberated the province. Turning south, he swept into Syria, easily taking the major cities of Emesa and Edessa, and in 969 managed to reconquer Antioch—the ancient capital of Syria and seat of one of the five great patriarchates of the Christian Church. Not since the reign of Heraclius had an emperor set foot in the city, and it's fitting that Nicephorus—whose name meant "bringer of victory"—would be the one to recover it. Gazing south, he briefly considered marching on to the Holy City, Jerusalem, but the campaigning season was nearly over, and a famine was plaguing both Byzantine and Arab lands. After twelve years of unbroken success, he could afford to postpone the conquest of Jerusalem for another year. It would still be there with the spring, and surely he deserved a rest. Swinging his great army around, the emperor marched wearily—but triumphantly—to his capital.

Yet for all his victories, Nicephorus was increasingly unpopular at home. In addition to his naturally abrasive personality, his attacks on ecclesiastical wealth had alienated the church, while the crippling taxes he levied to pay for his unending wars had lost the support of everyone else. His hated brother, Leo, had already been caught trying to artificially increase the price of wheat during a famine, and it was now widely believed that he was plotting to murder Theophano's young sons, Basil and Constantine. The emperor may not have been personally involved with these charges, but he took no action against his brother, further tarnishing his damaged reputation. Widely blamed for the rising cost of food and (rather unfairly) a poor harvest, Nicephorus became a virtual recluse. Alarmed by a prophecy that he would be killed in the Great Palace by one of his own citizens, he built a large wall separating it from the city, barricading himself inside. When he ventured out onto the streets at all, he had to brave torrents of abuse and even the occasional (poorly aimed) brick thrown at his head. Trying to reduce tensions, the emperor scheduled a mock battle inside the Hippodrome, but a rumor spread that he intended to slaughter the population, and the sight of drawn swords sparked a stampede, which left several hundred spectators crushed in its wake. Not surprisingly, Nicephorus escaped the oppressive climate of the capital at every opportunity, but this in turn earned him an enemy more formidable than any he had met on the battlefield.

His wife, Theophano, now twenty-eight and completely bored with an austere and absent husband, had fallen madly in love with his nephew John Tzimisces. The dazzling young general was everything that her husband wasn't. Dashing and intelligent with blond hair and piercing blue eyes, he was gracious and charming, irresistible to women—especially the lonely, cloistered empress. When John fell out of favor and was relieved of his command, it was the work of a moment for Theophano to force her adoring husband to recall him to Constantinople. There, under the cover of darkness, the two lovers met in the empress's wing of the palace and plotted one of the foulest murders in Byzantine history.

On a bitterly cold night, fifteen days before Christmas, the conspirators struck. Assassins slipped into the palace disguised as women and were hidden by Theophano in several unused rooms to wait for nightfall. Just before midnight, John arrived and was hauled over the walls in a basket, as a heavy snow began to fall. Drawing their swords, the assassins crept to the imperial bedchamber and burst into the room, only to discover the emperor's bed empty. Thinking they had been betrayed, the group panicked, and several conspirators attempted to leap off an upper balcony into the sea below. Just as the rest were turning to flee, however, a traitorous eunuch pointed out the figure of the sleeping emperor. He was (as usual) stretched out on a leopard skin on the floor.

Rushing over, the conspirators began to kick Nicephorus awake, striking him in the face with a sword as he tried to rise. The confused emperor was sent sprawling backward into the icons surrounding his blankets, his face covered in blood. Trying unsteadily to gain his feet, he was hauled roughly from the floor and thrown in front of Tzimisces, who shouted abuse at the bleeding man and ripped out handfuls of his beard. Barely conscious, Nicephorus implored the Virgin Mary for mercy, but this only served to enrage his assailants further. Smashing his jaw with the handles of their swords, they knocked out his teeth, torturing him until John finally gave the order to dispatch him with a hammer.

After lopping off the head, the conspirators threw the rest of the battered corpse out of a window. While one of the assassins went running through the palace with the severed head to discourage any retaliation from the imperial guard, the rest spread out into the snowy streets shouting that the tyrant had been overthrown. John himself, meanwhile, headed to the imperial throne room and pulled on the purple boots reserved for the emperor. At the sight of him wearing the imperial regalia, whatever resistance was left collapsed. The imperial guards dropped their swords and knelt obediently, hailing Tzimisces as emperor of the Romans.

The next day, some manner of decorum was restored when Nicephorus's headless corpse was quietly interred in the Church of the Holy Apostles. It was an ignominious end for a man who had served his empire so faithfully, but though few mourned him in the capital, posterity kept his name alive. His legend inspired generations of Byzantine and Bulgar poets, who celebrated his exploits in the epic poetry of the frontier. The church beatified him, and the monks of his monastery on Mount Athos continue to venerate him as their founder to this day.* Those who visited his tomb, tucked away in a quiet corner of the imperial mausoleum, could reflect that the great warrior emperor was summed up neatly with the wry inscription on his sarcophagus. Nicephorus Phocas, it proclaimed, YOU CONQUERED ALL BUT A WOMAN.

The lady in question made a show of being the grieving widow, but by now everyone knew how the emperor had died, and, in an unfortunate example of the vicious double standard in tenth-century Byzantium, blame for the entire sordid affair fell squarely on Theophano's shoulders. The empress was by no means innocent, but she was hardly the femme fatale that popular opinion made her. Deeply in

---

*Descendants of his family can still be found living in Greece and southern Lebanon.

love with John and desperate to protect her son Basil II, she was profoundly shocked when her lover abruptly threw her out of the palace and had her shipped off to a lonely exile. The patriarch had made it quite clear to Tzimisces that if he wanted to be crowned, he must first get rid of the despised Theophano, and the ambitious young man was only too happy to comply.

Surprisingly enough, given the excessive brutality and illegality of his rise, John's coronation was a calm affair, unsullied by riots or protests. This undoubtedly had something to do with his announcement that rioting would be punished with instant death, but most of the subdued capital was genuinely quite fond of their charismatic new emperor. He was already known for his generosity—a reputation he improved by distributing his vast fortune to the poor as a condition of his penance—and when he rather disingenuously executed two of his coconspirators for the murder of Nicephorus, most citizens considered the matter at rest.

There was something irresistible about John Tzimisces. Having learned the art of war at the feet of his uncle, he combined Nicephorus's military prowess with an infectious conviviality that endeared him to everyone he met.* There was a new vitality in the air, a feeling that anything could be accomplished now that the disagreeable emperor was dead and a true statesman had taken his place. The only ones who seemed to object to the change on the Byzantine throne were the Phocas family, but they did so more out of a sense of duty than passion. Nicephorus's nephew Bardas Phocas raised the obligatory standard of revolt, but it failed to attract wide support, and when Tzimisces' best friend Bardas Sclerus showed up with an army, Phocas quietly accepted exile on a pleasant Aegean island.

While his subordinates mopped up any traces of resistance to his rule, the emperor busied himself by drilling an army to deal with the

---

*Tzimisces was known for his ability with the bow and—if his primary biographer is to be believed—he would also frequently perform the impressive feat of vaulting himself over three horses to land in the saddle of the fourth.

mess his predecessor had left in the Balkans. The Russians were increasingly arrogant and bellicose, making no secret of the fact that they intended to invade Byzantine territory. "Don't trouble yourself with coming to us," they informed Tzimisces when they heard of his preparations, "we will soon enough be at your gates."

If it was war the Russians wanted, John I Tzimisces was only too happy to comply. Leading forty thousand troops on a lightning march, he surprised a Russian advance force near the Bulgarian capital of Preslav and wiped it out, then put the city under siege. After a few days of lobbing pots of Greek fire over the walls, the Byzantines smashed their way in, liberating the captured Bulgarian king.* The furious prince of Kiev mustered a huge army, but a few months later John managed to surprise it as well, leaving forty thousand dead on the blood-soaked field. The humiliated prince withdrew from Bulgarian territory a broken man, leaving the ravaged country for the last time.†

It didn't remain free for long. Bulgaria had been a constant thorn in the imperial side ever since the terrible Krum had seemingly appeared out of nowhere several generations before, and John intended to end the threat once and for all. After a year spent forcing its main cities to submit, the emperor formally annexed Bulgaria, extinguishing the dynasty of Krum. Western Bulgaria still clutched a fragile independence, governed by four sons of a local governor collectively calling themselves the Sons of the Count, but they were surrounded and weak, and John left them in place as he turned to pressing business in the East.

The empire would undoubtedly have been better served if Tzimisces had finished the conquest of Bulgaria, but the emperor was deeply troubled by reports from Syria. The Fatimids of Egypt, by far the most dangerous of the Muslim powers, had largely filled the power vacuum left by the collapsing Abbasid caliphate and were now

---

*His gratitude at being rescued was presumably tempered somewhat when John personally seized the crown jewels and renamed the city Joannopolis, after himself.
†On his return trip, the Russian prince was ambushed by the Pechenegs and, like the unfortunate emperor Nicephorus I, had his head made into a drinking cup.

threatening imperial territory. After easily defeating a Byzantine army sent to check them, they put Antioch under siege in the fall of 972, hoping to absorb all of Syria. Clearly, the time had come to turn the Byzantine sword against the Saracen.

Leaving the president of the Senate (the same Basil Lecapenus who had enabled Nicephonus II Phocas to seize power) in charge of the city, John I Tzimisces marched out of the Golden Gate at the head of his army at the start of 974. Riding a powerful white charger, resplendent in his finest armor, with his "Immortals" streaming out behind, the emperor embarked on one of the most impressive military campaigns in the empire's long history.* Starting in the northern part of modern-day Iraq, he forced the panicked emir of Mosul to pay him a hefty tribute, reducing the second most powerful emirate to the status of a client state. Not bothering to conquer the now-defenseless Baghdad, Tzimisces turned south into Syria, where the Fatimid army besieging Antioch fled in terror at his approach. But John hadn't raised his great army simply to watch his enemies momentarily retreat, and he surged down the Mediterranean coast. One by one the cities of Syria and Palestine fell. Baalbek, Beirut, and Damascus opened their gates, and the coastal cities of Tiberias, Acre, Caesarea, and Tripoli sent enormous tribute. No stronghold or fortress could resist the power of imperial arms—after three hundred years in abeyance, the Byzantine eagle had returned, and it wasn't in a conciliatory mood. After triumphantly entering Nazareth, the city where Jesus had spent his childhood nearly a thousand years before, Tzimisces rode the short distance to Mount Tabor, climbing its slopes to visit the site of Christ's transfiguration. Like Nicephorus Phocas before him, the emperor considered pressing on to Jerusalem but decided against it. His main aim had been to weaken the Fatimids, not to add territory to the empire. When the time came to restore the Holy

---

*The Immortals were an elite cavalry unit chosen for their bravery and skill. They continued to be the backbone of the Byzantine army until the reign of Alexius I, more than a century later.

City to Christian control, he would return, but that was a task for another day. Making the momentous decision to turn his victorious army around, Tzimisces made his luxurious way home.

Had the emperor extended his hand and returned Jerusalem to Orthodox control, he could have accomplished the great dream of the eastern Christians in Palestine. Instead, they would wait in vain for more than a century, while imperial power failed and the West launched the Crusades to restore the city to Christendom.

In the fall of 975, however, Byzantium still knew only triumph, and John I Tzimisces was content to haul the spoils of his campaign back to the capital, secure in the knowledge that he had made the empire stronger than it had been for nearly four centuries. On every side, its enemies were cowed and fleeing, and nothing seemed beyond the ambition of its grasp.*

The triumphant return to Constantinople was spoiled by only one thing. When the emperor inquired about who owned the vast lands he was passing through, mile after mile the answer was always the same—the chamberlain Basil Lecapenus. The easygoing Tzimisces hadn't been as assiduous as his predecessors at restricting the growth of aristocratic land, but the excessive wealth infuriated him, and he made it known that the moment he arrived at the capital, he would conduct a full investigation. Determined not to let that happen, the terrified chamberlain did the only thing he could think of. Welcoming the emperor with every show of enthusiasm, he slipped some poison into his food. Within days, it had done its work. John I Tzimisces had joined the ranks of his uncle and Julian the Apostate—emperors with such promise who had been cut down in their prime. The Christians of the Holy Land were left feeling bitter and abandoned, and, far away in Cairo, the Fatimids breathed a sigh of relief. The great conqueror was dead.

---

*Tzimisces had given his niece in marriage to the western emperor Otto II, and in doing so had succeeded in uniting the ruling dynasties of both empires for the first time since Theodosius I in the fourth century. The idea of restoring a single, undivided empire suddenly didn't seem quite so far-fetched.

19

::

BASIL THE BULGAR SLAYER

From the day that the King of Heaven called upon me to become the Emperor . . . no one saw my spear lie idle . . . O man, seeing now my tomb here, reward me for my campaigns with your prayers.
— Inscription on the tomb of Basil II

The astonishing thing about the Macedonian dynasty was that its greatest emperors were actually pretenders, men without blood ties to the throne who claimed that they were "protecting" the interests of the legitimate heirs. Romanus I Lecapenus, Nicephorus II Phocas, and John I Tzimisces had been so brilliant, so dazzling, that it was tempting to forget the shadowy figures they had displaced. Unremembered and unnoticed as he might be, however, Basil II, the son of Romanus II and the scheming Theophano, had been quietly growing up and now, at eighteen, was ready to rule as well as reign. Standing in his way was the formidable obstacle of the head chamberlain, the man who had so recently caused the great Tzimisces' demise. After a lifetime spent in the highest corridors of power, Basil Lecapenus knew everyone and everything in administration and wasn't about to relinquish effective control to a boy who had never shown even the slightest will or ability to rule.

A patronizing chamberlain determined to keep him a puppet, however, was the least of Basil II's problems. The last twelve years had seen two remarkable warrior-emperors lead Byzantium to an unprecedented place in the sun, and many in the empire began to wonder if perhaps a battle-hardened warrior should be at the helm instead of a youth whose only qualification was an accident of birth. After all, who could argue that any of the generals who had usurped the Macedonian dynasty weren't better emperors than the legitimate Romanus II? Hadn't most of their greatest rulers—from Julius Caesar to John Tzimisces—justified their power not by heredity but by strength in arms?

The idea was a seductive one, and when the general Bardas Sclerus rose in revolt saying just that, he was met with a roar of approval. When he crushed a loyalist army sent to stop him, all of Asia Minor saw visions of imperial glory and hailed him as emperor. The rebels suffered a minor setback when the imperial navy destroyed their transports, but their mood was still buoyant when they reached the Bosporus and stared across the water at the Queen of Cities.

In the capital, the eunuch Basil Lecapenus was starting to panic. For the moment, the navy was keeping the rebels at bay, but he knew all too well how easily an army could slip across the narrow stretch of water. The only experienced general who stood a chance against the veteran Sclerus was Bardas Phocas—a man whose ability was second only to his well-known desire to seize the throne—but he was currently in exile for attempting to do just that. Putting the imperial army in Phocas's grasping hands wasn't much better than handing the empire to Sclerus, but Basil didn't have any other choice. Recalling the exiled general, the chamberlain entrusted the empire to his care and sent him off to fight the rebel army.

For three years, the rival Bardases fought a series of inconclusive battles, with the rebel Sclerus generally proving the better commander but unable to conclusively defeat his wily opponent.* The matter was finally decided when the frustrated rebel foolishly accepted an offer of single combat against the huge Bardas Phocas. After

---

*Bardas Sclerus and Bardas Phocas had a tangled history. When Phocas first rebelled against his cousin Tzimisces, it had been Sclerus who had extinguished his military career by defeating him and sending him into exile. There was certainly no love lost between the two, but their fates were oddly linked until the end of their lives.

ending the war with a massive blow to his opponent's head that sent Sclerus crashing heavily to the ground, Phocas scattered the rebels and returned to Constantinople in triumph. The wounded Sclerus recovered, but he was a spent force, and he fled to Baghdad to avoid the emperor's wrath. After eight long years of exile, Bardas Phocas could now bask in the welcome role of savior of the empire, and for the moment the imperial gratitude was enough. Riding east to battle the Saracens, Phocas planned to cover himself in glory and bide his time until the moment was right to seize the throne.

By 985, Basil Lecapenus could congratulate himself on having brilliantly played off the empire's enemies against one another, and at the same time on having kept the legitimate emperor as a puppet. It was therefore a complete surprise to him—and everyone else—when the formerly passive Basil II suddenly struck without warning. Accused of conspiring against the emperor, the bewildered chamberlain was dragged from his bed in the middle of the night and placed under house arrest as his lands were confiscated and his vast wealth absorbed by the treasury. After twenty-five years as a crowned puppet, the son of Romanus II had finally claimed his inheritance.

Eager to prove himself, Basil II found an excellent excuse for a military adventure in Bulgaria. Thanks largely to Byzantium's distraction, Bulgaria had somehow managed to resurrect itself from its ruined state and expand at imperial expense. A remarkable man named Samuel, the youngest and most capable of the so-called Sons of the Count who had defied Tzimisces, had assumed the title of tsar—the Slavic version of Caesar—and declared a second Bulgarian empire. Conducting summer raids into northern Greece, the tsar managed to capture several key cities, damaging Byzantine prestige and inciting more of his countrymen to join him. Outraged by the temerity of this jumped-up peasant and determined to prove himself worthy of his glorious predecessors, Basil II gathered an army sixty thousand strong and headed for the magnificent Bulgarian city of Sofia.

The campaign was a disaster from the start. After several weeks of annoying the citizens of Sofia with an ineffectual siege, Basil II gave up and started the long march home. Traveling through a mountain pass called the Gates of Trajan without bothering to scout ahead, his army blundered into an ambush by the amused tsar, who had been watching for just such an opportunity. Leaving his insignia behind, the emperor managed to escape, but most of his army was cut to pieces. The twenty-eight-year-old Basil II had stumbled badly, and when he returned to Constantinople, frightened and humiliated, the damage to his prestige was immediately apparent.

To old Bardas Sclerus, watching from the safety of the caliph's court in Baghdad, it was obvious that he had been right all along. The bumbling boy in Constantinople who happened to have the right parents didn't deserve the throne after all, and with his incompetence now starkly revealed, surely an old warhorse like himself would be welcomed with open arms. The caliph was only too happy to provide funding for a campaign that promised to be extremely disruptive to his powerful neighbor, and so, loaded down with money, Bardas Sclerus made his third bid for the throne.

Annoyingly enough for the hopeful pretender, when he reached Asia Minor he discovered that his old rival Bardas Phocas had also rebelled. Rather than fight it out, the two decided to bury the hatchet and pool their resources, but this proved to be just a ruse, and the moment Sclerus lowered his guard Phocas had him arrested and thrown into a dungeon. With that unpleasantness behind him, Bardas Phocas gathered his cheering army and lumbered off toward Constantinople. Unfortunately for the rebels, however, Phocas lacked a navy, and when they reached the Bosporus it was to find the imperial fleet patrolling both coasts.

But nothing seemed able to dent Bardas Phocas's optimism. He was well aware that the master of Constantinople was a mere boy of twenty-eight whose only military experience had been to get his army annihilated in an ambush. Bardas Phocas, on the other hand, had seen a lifetime of impressive victories on the field, and historians were even now writing of him that "whole armies trembled at his shout."

In the capital, Basil II knew the deck was stacked against him.

He had lost his best troops in the ill-advised Bulgarian campaign, and the emboldened Tsar Samuel was raging unchecked through the Balkans, threatening to overrun the entire peninsula. Something clearly needed to be done soon, but even if the emperor somehow managed to scrape together an army, there wasn't anyone to lead it— certainly not a general of Phocas's caliber. The only solution was to enlist a formidable ally, and fortunately there was one close at hand. The emperor contacted the Russian prince Vladimir and offered the hand of his sister in exchange for an alliance.

The staid imperial court was horrified. As Basil's own grandfather Constantine VII had pointed out, Byzantine princesses "born in the purple" ranked with Greek fire as state treasures never to be handed over to its enemies. Furious patricians pointed out that no Roman princess in the history of the empire had ever been given to a pagan barbarian, and certainly not to one who already had plenty of wives and several hundred concubines. Now Basil II was threatening to trample Byzantine pride under the feet of the uncivilized Slavs. But neither the outraged cries of the court nor the anguished sobs of his sister had any effect on the emperor. Marriage in the imperial family had always been more of a political than a personal matter, and when Vladimir eagerly sweetened the deal by agreeing to provide six thousand huge Norse warriors in addition to being baptized, Basil's protesting sister was hastily bundled off to await her new husband's pleasure.*

---

*Vladimir had been interested in changing religions for some time. According to legend, he sent ambassadors to the major surrounding religions to help him decide. Islam was rejected for being without joy (especially in its rejection of alcohol and pork!), and Judaism was rejected since the Jews had lost their homeland and therefore seemed abandoned by God. Settling on Christianity, he sent his men to discover if the Latin or the Greek rite was better. It was hardly a fair fight. The ambassadors to the West found rather squat, dark churches, while their compatriots in Constantinople were treated to all the pageantry of a Divine Liturgy in the Hagia Sophia. "We no longer knew," they breathlessly reported back to Vladimir, "whether we were in heaven or on earth." The Russian prince was convinced. Within a year, he had been baptized, and Russia officially became Orthodox.

The arrangement may have offended popular sentiment in the capital, but Basil was quite pleased with himself when he saw the blond giants that Vladimir sent. Armed with massive double-bladed axes, and subject to the famous *beserker* rages, they were splendidly terrifying. The emperor was so impressed that he made them his personal bodyguards—a permanent position he called the Varangian Guard.* After slipping across the Bosporus at night with his new force, Basil launched a ferocious dawn attack on the unsuspecting rebel camp. While flamethrowers spraying Greek fire spread chaos, the emperor went crashing through the tents, slaughtering everyone he could find. Those rebels who weren't half asleep or drunk stumbled to their feet, only to be greeted by the horrible sight of the Norse warriors lopping off the limbs of men and beasts with a hideous efficiency. In a matter of hours, the killing was over, and though Phocas himself was away with a large part of the army besieging a city, Basil II could at last claim a victory in the field.

A few months later, the newly confident emperor got a chance to face his rival directly, and to the surprise of nearly everyone involved, he turned out to be a considerably better general than the aging Bardas Phocas. Seeing his imperial dreams slipping away just when they were within his grasp was too much for the old rebel, and he roared out a challenge of single combat, charging toward the emperor and wildly swinging his sword above his head. Before he had closed half the distance, a sudden seizure gripped him and Phocas fell heavily from his saddle. The watching imperial guards leaped on the paralyzed general, chopping off his head, and at the sight of their master's gruesome death, the rebel army disintegrated.

The great revolt was broken, but it wasn't quite over. The mo-

---

*The term "Varangian" means "men of the pledge," and they would be famously loyal to the throne (though not always to its occupant). On the night of their sovereign's death, they had the curious right to run to the imperial treasury and take as much gold as they could comfortably carry. This custom enabled most Varangians to retire as wealthy men and ensured a steady stream of Norse and Anglo-Saxon recruits.

ment she heard of her husband's death, Phocas's widow set the imprisoned Bardas Sclerus free, and the surviving rebels flocked to his standard. The old general accepted the acclamations of his troops, and for a moment it looked as if the civil war would drag on, but Sclerus was a tired, broken man, by now nearly completely blind. After a brief show of resistance, he happily accepted the emperor's offer of a fancy title and a comfortable estate. When the two met to discuss their treaty at one of the emperor's sumptuous villas, Basil was surprised to see that the celebrated general was a rather sad-looking, bent old man who had to be supported on either side in order to walk. After graciously pretending that the whole rebellion had been a simple misunderstanding, Basil asked his guest for advice on how to prevent dissension in the future. The answer, he was told, was to declare a virtual war on those of noble birth. "Exhaust them with unjust exactions, to keep them busy with their own affairs. Admit no woman to the imperial councils. Be accessible to no one. Share with few your most intimate plans."*

No emperor in the long and illustrious history of the empire would ever take such advice closer to heart. The vicious civil wars had left their scars on Basil II, wiping away the carefree spirit he had shown as a youth and leaving a hard, untrusting man in its place. Surrounded by his Varangian Guard, he dedicated himself unswervingly to the service of the empire. Nothing—neither the outcries of the aristocracy nor the spears of his enemies—would be allowed to get in the way.

By strengthening the empire's land laws, Basil II forced the nobility to return—without compensation—any land they had taken since the reign of Romanus Lecapenus. He also decreed that if a peasant couldn't pay his taxes, his rich neighbors would have to come up with the money for him. Predictably, the nobility howled with outrage, but Basil II ignored them. His entire life had been spent in the shadows of overpowerful aristocrats; their grasping ambitions had

---

*Michael Psellus, *Fourteen Byzantine Rulers* (London: Penguin, 1966).

troubled the Macedonian dynasty for long enough. Now that he was firmly in control, he meant to see that they would never have the opportunity to do so again.

By the spring of 991, the emperor was finally secure enough to begin the great endeavor of his life. He hadn't forgotten the humiliations of the Gates of Trajan, or how Samuel had laughed at Byzantine arms, and the time had come to tame the Bulgarian wolf. He moved with an agonizing slowness—there was no point in risking another ambush. Every route was checked and double-checked, and close tabs were kept on possible escape routes.

Tsar Samuel watched it all with some amusement from the safety of the mountains. He had no reason to fear a man he had so effortlessly beaten years before, and if the emperor's army was large, he could take comfort from the fact that it would soon be gone. The empire was a large place, with enemies on every side. All he had to do was stay out of the way and before long a crisis on some far-flung frontier was sure to force the Byzantines to leave. The tsar had seen invaders like this emperor before—one moment all flash and thunder, and the next moment gone.

Sure enough, less than a year after Basil had entered Bulgarian territory, a breathless message reached him that the Fatimids were besieging Aleppo and threatening Antioch. Those cities—and all of northern Syria—were on the brink of surrender, but there seemed little hope of reaching them in time since the journey would take the better part of three months. Basil II had so far only moved with glacial slowness, but he had spent his life surprising people and with the help of eighty thousand mules (one for each soldier, another for each man's equipment) he made the trip in an extraordinary sixteen days. Terrified by the Byzantine army that had seemed to materialize out of thin air, the Fatimid army fled, and Basil II marched triumphantly down the coast, conquering the city of Tripoli for good measure.

When the emperor returned home, it was to find that Tsar Samuel had taken advantage of his absence to overrun Bosnia and

Dalmatia, even raiding as far south as the Peloponnese. With virtually any other ruler on the Byzantine throne, Samuel's strategy of hiding in the hills until the danger had passed would have worked brilliantly. Against Basil II, however, the tactic only prolonged Bulgarian suffering. True enough, Basil had none of the panache or brilliance of his two predecessors, but he was far more dangerous than either of them. Other men campaigned from the middle of the spring to the end of the summer, but on returning to face the tsar, Basil II stayed in the field year-round, equally impervious to the freezing snow and the blazing sun. With his grinding, methodical nature, he never lost patience or resolve. Year after year, Bulgarian cities were sacked and their crops burned as the emperor relentlessly hunted Tsar Samuel. Finally, after nearly twenty years of defeats and devastating invasions, the Bulgarian army took a last stand. On the morning of July 29, 1014, the two armies clashed in a valley at the foot of the Belasica Mountains, and the result was a crushing Byzantine victory.

Samuel escaped to a nearby fortress, proclaiming that he would carry on the fight, but Basil was in no mood to let that happen. He had fifteen hundred prisoners blinded—sparing one eye in every hundred men so that they could lead their sightless companions back to the tsar. Mutilation had always been the preferred Byzantine treatment of its dangerous enemies, but never on such a scale, and from it Basil earned the nickname that is still celebrated in the street names of modern Greece. Down through the centuries the emperor would thereafter be known by the sobriquet *Boulgaroktonos*—the "Bulgar Slayer."

The ragged horde shuffled its way to the city of Prespa in modern-day Macedonia, where Samuel was staying. The horrible sight was even more devastating than Basil intended. Their very presence was a constant reminder of Samuel's humiliation, and their care was an added burden that the ravaged state couldn't afford. When they appeared before their tsar, the terrible sight was too much for the broken Samuel to bear. He turned his face to the wall and expired in shame two days later. The second Bulgarian empire struggled on for another four years without its founder, but the handwriting was on the wall, and in 1018 Basil II entered the Bulgarian capital and received its complete surrender.

For the first time since the Slavs had invaded the empire four centuries before, the entire Balkan Peninsula was under imperial control. Basil II had spent more than half his life in its conquest, capping a remarkable resurgence of Byzantine power brought about by the extraordinary Macedonian dynasty. The empire had almost doubled in size, emerging as the strongest power in the Mediterranean, and its new territories would not be easily relinquished. Unlike his predecessors, Basil II understood that quick gains seldom lasted unless they were properly consolidated and governed. Under previous emperors, conquered peoples had been made perfectly aware that they were second-class citizens, but now Bulgarian nobles were given Byzantine wives and imperial titles, and taxes were helpfully relaxed in regions that had been devastated by war. Such examples of good governance certainly reduced tensions and strengthened ties to Constantinople, but above all it was the emperor's refusal to indulge in unnecessary risks that contributed the most to maintaining peace. When the Fatimid caliph ordered all churches in his territory destroyed in 1012, Basil refused to take the bait—although he could certainly have extended Byzantine power into Palestine and even Egypt. Instead, he responded with an economic blow, banning all trade with the Fatimids until they saw the error of their ways. Only when they allied with Armenia to attack the empire did he come sweeping down to sack a few cities and panic the caliph. When it came to war, Basil was always willing but never eager to fight.

In one area only did the great emperor disastrously fail. Absorbed by the cares of state, he never produced an heir, but though this would prove to be calamitous for the empire, it didn't appear so in his lifetime. By 1025, in the steady hands of its all-powerful emperor, the Byzantine eagle was triumphant on virtually every frontier. Its enemies were scattered and broken before it, and only in Sicily did the

Muslim foe continue to resist. Hoping to correct that final oversight, the seventy-year-old emperor gathered a vast army and sent it under the care of a eunuch to await his arrival in Calabria. Basil II, however, never arrived. After a sixty-four-year reign—longer than any other monarch in Roman history—he died, fittingly enough, while planning the campaign.

Constantine the Great had set up twelve massive sarcophagi around his own magnificent tomb in the Church of the Holy Apostles, and the bodies of the greatest Byzantine emperors were traditionally laid to rest inside them. In 1025, there was one last unused sarcophagus, and by all rights Basil should have been buried there; but according to his own wishes, the body was taken to a church in Hebdomon just outside the city walls. Though there were few emperors who better deserved to be buried alongside the giants of the past, his final resting place was somehow fitting. He had always remained aloof from his citizens, never allowing himself to become distracted from the all-important task of running the empire. He had bent foreign rulers to his will, humbled his enemies, and provided a shield for the poor against the clutches of the aristocracy. Yet for all that, he was oddly distant, inspiring admiration in his subjects, but never love. His mind had always been uniquely un-Byzantine, cast more in the mold of his Spartan ancestors than the murky theological speculations of his peers. As the old rebel had advised him so many years ago, no woman or man was ever offered a share in his burdens. Through all the trials of his reign, he remained splendid but remote—surely the loneliest figure ever to sit on the Byzantine throne.

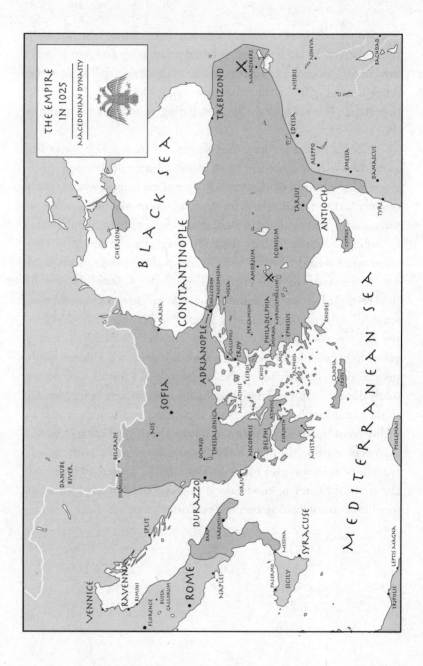

THE EMPIRE
IN 1025

MACEDONIAN DYNASTY

BLACK SEA

MEDITERRANEAN SEA

CHERSON

DANUBE
RIVER

SIRMIUM

BELGRADE

NIS

SOFIA

OCHRID

ADRIANOPLE

VARNA

CONSTANTINOPLE

CHALCEDON

NICOMEDIA

NICEA

TROY

GALLIPOLI

THESSALONICA

NICOPOLIS

CORFU

DELPHI

LEROS

MT. ATHOS

DURAZZO

ATHENS

CORINTH

MISTRA

PERGAMUM

PHILADELPHIA

SMYRNA

LAODICEA/LADICEA

EPHESUS

SAMOS

PATMOS

CHIOT

RHODES

AMORIUM

ICONIUM

MANZIKERT

TREBIZOND

EDESSA

NISIBIS

NINEVA

BACHDAD

ALEPPO

EMESSA

DAMASCUS

ANTIOCH

TARSUS

CYPRUS

TYRE

CANDIA
CRETE

PTOLEMAIS

LEPTIS MAGNA

TRIPOLIS

SYRACUSE

MESSINA

SICILY

PALERMO

NAPLES

ROME

BRUTA
GALLORUM

FLORENCE

RIMINI

RAVENNA

SPLIT

TARENTUM

BARI

VENNICE

20

::
::

THE MARCH OF FOLLY

The empire that Basil II left behind him was indeed glorious, stretching from the Danube in the west to the Euphrates in the east. No power in western Europe or the Middle East could approach it; its gold coin, the *nomisma,* was the standard currency of trade—and had been for centuries—and its Islamic enemies were cowed and crumbling. The Christian powers of Europe looked up to it as their great protector, and more than one German emperor traveled to southern Italy, where the imperial borders touched, to seek recognition of their titles.* Those from western Europe who traveled to the imperial markets or cities found a world drastically different from the one they had left behind. Medieval Europe was locked in feudalism, with little chance to escape grinding poverty. Peasants spent their lifetimes toiling on land they didn't own, and medicine offered "cures" to the sick that were often as lethal as the disease. The poor subsisted on a diet of coarse, dark bread and cheese, and were lucky to reach the age of thirty-five. Communication between cities was slow, travel was dangerous, and writing was restricted to the rich and powerful. The church provided what little education was available, but only if a literate priest could be found.

---

*They were also deeply impressed by its sophistication. In 1004, a Byzantine aristocrat named Maria sparked enormous interest in Venice by eating with an ancient Roman double-pronged golden instrument. Touted as the latest word in sophistication, the device became enormously popular, and soon the fork was common throughout the West.

In the East, by contrast, wealth poured into the imperial treasury, the population boomed, and famine seemed to be a thing of the past. Men flush with the excitement of new fortunes seemed to be everywhere, carried about in their sedan chairs, endowing lavish public buildings, and playing polo on the broad public avenues. Confidence was in the air, and it was contagious. The addition of the Bulgarians, the Serbs, and the Russians to the cultural mix had added layers of diversity, but society—and the church—had never been more unified. Iconoclasm, the last great heresy to afflict the Byzantine church, had been settled for nearly two centuries, and the church and the state were infused with a spirit of cooperation. Education once again became a way for ambitious young men to advance, and vast libraries became a status symbol.

There had always been a guarded respect for the pagan classics of antiquity, but with paganism long dead and no longer a threat, there was a new appreciation of the secular classics. A spirit of humanism swept through the empire, and scholars began to consciously emulate the styles of antiquity. Copies of the literature of ancient Greece and Rome became highly valued, and clergy and laymen alike began to dutifully reproduce the dazzling masterpieces. This was among the finest gifts that the empire bequeathed to posterity. Since Egypt—and the source of papyrus—had long been lost to the empire, the crumbling old manuscripts were copied onto more durable and readily available parchment. This in turn enabled the literature to survive. Despite the general destruction that followed the collapse of the empire, most of the Greek classics that are extant today come down to us through Byzantine copies of this period.

The emperors, of course, had always had access to the peerless imperial libraries, but now they began to see a general promotion of schooling as one of their roles. By the time of Basil II's death, Constantinople was home to brilliant poets, jurists, and historians—a glittering collection of literati that wouldn't be equaled in the West until the last days of the Renaissance.

It was a pity that Basil II didn't leave anyone worthy of receiving such a glorious inheritance, but, unfortunately for Byzantium, the cultural flowering that had given the empire such a splendid educated class had also made its court arrogant and insulated, utterly convinced that they knew how to govern the empire better than anyone else. Basil's death left power unexpectedly in their hands, and they deliberately chose weak and pliable emperors, interested more in keeping their newfound power than in what was best for the state. Ironically enough, this shortsighted policy of putting such mediocrities on the throne guaranteed their own decline. Ruthless taxation once again fell on the poor without burdening the rich, and the land laws of the Macedonian emperors were abandoned, leaving the peasants at the mercy of their predatory neighbors. The rich gobbled up virtually all of the land in their vast estates, while their contacts at court ensured that it was held tax free. Foolish emperors, confronted with a virtually independent aristocracy and now seriously short of funds, exacerbated the problem by devaluing their gold coins—a step the empire had managed to avoid for nearly seven hundred years. The value of the currency collapsed, sending inflation spiraling, and Byzantium's prestige plummeted as international merchants abandoned the worthless coins.

Small farmers were virtually driven to extinction, frequently ending up as serfs on their own lands, and since military veterans could no longer afford to farm, the entire system of the peasant-soldier collapsed.* The Byzantine army, now dangerously weakened, was forced to rely on mercenaries, and important commands were given to worthless political appointments. Foreign wars and political chaos fell like hammer blows on the rudderless empire, striking against both its spiritual and temporal strength. In the short space of fifty years, it was rocked by two tragedies that sapped its strength and undermined its foundations. Though the empire lasted for another

---

*The normal Byzantine practice was to settle veterans on the frontier who would provide a well-trained militia in exchange for land. This had the great advantage of lowering the cost of defense without seriously degrading the empire's safety and had worked magnificently for years.

four centuries, it never fully recovered from the impact of these twin disasters.

The first, and more damaging, blow fell in 1054 and severely impaired relations with the West. The crisis that culminated that year had been building to a head for decades, and was by now nearly inevitable. Underneath the thin veneer of Christian unity that joined the lands of the old Roman Empire lay the deep divisions of an East and a West that had been drifting apart for centuries. Of the five great patriarchs of the Christian Church, four were in the East, and there the Greek love of disputation had kept the church somewhat decentralized. The patriarch of Constantinople may have been the closest to imperial power, but he was also the youngest of the patriarchs, and the older, more prestigious bishops in Antioch, Alexandria, and Jerusalem zealously guarded their autonomy. Important decisions were made—as they always had been—by means of a council in which the whole voice of the church could be expressed. In the West, where the only patriarch was that of Rome, the pontiff had grown weary of the endless eastern speculation and heresy, and had begun to see himself as the final authority in Christendom. After all, hadn't Christ himself "handed the keys of heaven" to Peter, the first pope, with the words "on this rock I will build my Church"? Clearly, the pope was not merely the "first among equals" as the easterners taught, but the undisputed head of the church.

The crisis was precipitated when the stubborn patriarch Michael Cerularius wrote a letter to Pope Leo IX, addressing him as "brother" instead of "father" and comparing him to Judas for adding the word *filioque* to the Nicene Creed. This was an old—and rather intemperate—argument that had split the church for generations. According to the original version of the creed—the central statement of Christianity—the Holy Spirit emanated from God the Father. So it had remained until the late sixth century when the word *filioque* ("and the son") was added by the Spanish church in an attempt to emphasize Christ's divinity to their Arian, Visigothic overlords. The Eastern Church could, of course, sympathize with the *spirit* of the Spanish addition (they had after all fought the same battle against the Arians), but to their minds only the authority of a full council could alter the creed, and this arbitrary addition was therefore a vile heresy made all the more shocking when the pope officially endorsed it.* The Scriptures are mostly silent on the topic of the Trinity, making it virtually impossible to resolve an argument about the relationship of its members. Both sides dug in their heels on the issue, and now the patriarch's letter to the pope ripped aside the church's veil of unity to expose its deep-seated divisions for the entire world to see.†

It was at this moment of rancor that the Byzantine emperor Constantine IX invited the pope to send some legates to Constantinople to discuss a military alliance against their mutual enemies. The pope accepted the invitation, but, unfortunately for everyone involved, he chose a virulently anti-Greek cardinal named Humbert to act as his representative. Humbert arrived in Constantinople ready to be insulted, and was soon given ample opportunity when the equally insufferable Patriarch Cerularius refused to see him. Annoyed by the oily Greek food, drafty accommodations, and poor hospitality, Humbert spent his time castigating his hosts for the eastern practices of allowing priests to marry, using leavened bread in the Eucharist, and eating meat during Lent. Tempers were soured further when news arrived in late April that the pope had died, depriving Humbert of what little authority he had, and making his entire infuriating mission pointless. Demanding an audience with the patriarch, the cardinal requested permission to leave, but Cerularius gleefully refused, keeping the enraged Humbert under virtual house arrest. For two months, the

---

*The western church certainly took its time in adopting the Spanish version. As late as the ninth century, Pope Leo III posted the original wording of the creed outside the entrance to Saint Peter's, and in 880 John VIII had remained completely silent when Constantinople had condemned the addition.

†This split between Rome and Constantinople can most plainly be seen in modern Serbia and Croatia. Though both are Slavic countries that speak the same language, they had the misfortune to fall into opposing religious camps. Croatia allied itself with Rome and became a Catholic power, writing the common language in the Latin alphabet, while Serbia joined the Orthodox orbit and uses Cyrillic.

papal legate fumed in Constantinople, but by July 16, 1054, with no end to his containment in sight, he had had enough. Marching into the Hagia Sophia, Humbert solemnly placed a note of excommunication on the high altar. Turning around, he shook the dust symbolically off his feet and left the building, vowing never to return. The damage done in that moment was equaled only by its tragically unnecessary circumstances. Christendom would never be united again, and it was the disgruntled representative of a dead pope without a single shred of authority who had dealt the blow.

A few weeks later, the patriarch returned the favor by convening a council that excommunicated the West right back. Each side hoped the other would back down, but it was too late—relations were permanently sundered. The pope maintained that the Latin Church was the "Catholic" or "universal" one, while the patriarch made the same claim, arguing that the Greek rite was "Orthodox" or "true."

Christendom had been ripped in half, and Byzantium was now dangerously and terrifyingly alone. From now on, the powers to its west would offer no succor, and the empire would have to face the enemies to its east with only its own diminishing resources.

The weakened empire still had its army, but it was no longer the peerless fighting force that had made it the superpower of the Mediterranean. Years of neglect since Basil II's death had reduced it to virtual impotence, and the court, terrified of a military uprising, did its best to weaken it further—even taking the insane step of disbanding the local militias that guarded the frontiers. Outwardly, the empire may have looked glorious, but on the inside it was rotten and hollow, waiting for an enemy to break the brittle shell. Trapped in the firm grip of squabbling aristocrats, the throne was unlikely to produce a figure capable of undoing the damage, and Byzantium was given no chance to recover its strength.

While the empire was still reeling from its struggle with the papacy, a new and devastating enemy made its military weakness all too apparent. The Seljuk Turks had already taken the Muslim world by surprise. Originally a central Asian nomadic tribe, they spread over

Iran and Iraq, managing to seize Baghdad in 1055, replacing the weak and crumbling Abbasid caliphate. After crossing the undefended Byzantine frontiers, by 1067 they were looting their way through Armenia virtually unopposed. Combining the hunger of nomads in search of plunder and pastureland with the predatory aggression of jihadists, the Seljuks were unlike anything the Byzantines had seen before. Their mounted raiders struck fast and without warning, making it difficult to know where to concentrate the defenses. The unwieldy empire was used to dealing with states and armies, not roving bands slashing across their borders. In any case, the humiliated, demoralized imperial army could no longer offer much resistance.

Emperor Romanus Diogenes was a determined if not a gifted general, and when the Seljuks crossed the border in strength during his reign, he somehow managed to push them back across the Euphrates. Unfortunately for the empire, the small victory awakened all the aristocratic courtiers' old fears that a strong emperor would restrict their privileges. By the time the Turks returned the next year and seized a small Armenian fortress in the town of Manzikert, support for the emperor had begun to dangerously erode.

Oblivious to the mounting dissension, Romanus marched out with his army, determined to evict the Turks from Christian lands once and for all. On August 26, 1071, the two armies met, and the most fateful battle in Byzantine history began. Despite massive defections from his unreliable mercenaries, the emperor managed to push the Turks back, but at a critical moment his scheming nobles betrayed him and withdrew. The cream of the army was slaughtered on the spot, and Romanus Diogenes was captured and forced to kiss the ground while the sultan, Alp Arslan, rested a boot on his neck.

The humiliation of an emperor groveling in the dust seemed to many later Byzantines as the awful moment when everything started to go wrong, but if it marked the beginning of their final decline, then it was the Byzantines themselves who were to blame. The battle could easily have been avoided. At Manzikert, the sultan had tried to come to terms, but the petty nobles had refused his offers and insisted on being the authors of their own destruction. And while the loss of prestige and manpower after the battle were bad enough, they could have been recovered from. It was the behavior of the aristocrats afterward that truly wrecked Byzantium. After fleeing from the scene of their defeat, the nobility escaped to spread chaos throughout the empire, unleashing civil war in their vain attempts to seize control of the sinking Byzantine ship. Rival claimants to the throne rose up in a bewildering succession and were overthrown just as quickly by yet another general with imperial dreams.

Now that the facade had cracked, the frontiers of the empire collapsed with alarming speed. In Italy, the Norman adventurer Robert Guiscard conquered Bari, ending more than five centuries of Byzantine rule in its ancestral land. In the East, the Turks came pouring into Asia Minor, and instead of trying to stop them, ambitious generals tried to use them as mercenaries in their own bids for power. Unreliable troops switched sides with alarming frequency, and famine followed in the wake of armies that trampled fields and seized crops. Within ten years, the Turks had overrun thirty thousand square miles of Asia Minor virtually unopposed, robbing the empire of the source of most of its manpower and grain. Except for thin strips along the Black Sea coast and the Mediterranean, Anatolia was lost forever, along with any hope of a long-term recovery for the empire as a whole. Even if a strong emperor came along, there were no longer any reserves of men or material to draw upon. The empire was dying, and instead of helping, foolish men insisted on fighting over its corpse.

When the Turks broke into Chrysopolis on the Asian side of the Bosporus in 1078 and burned it to the ground, the end of the empire seemed at hand. The army was shattered and broken, and the government was in the hands of privileged, arrogant men who had jealously guarded their own interests, undermining any emperor who showed a glimmer of ability. In only fifty-three years, these men had nearly wrecked the empire with their irresponsibility and greed, squandering a bursting treasury and sitting idly by while the empire lost more than half its territory. The only hope of deliverance now for the impoverished and miserable citizens was that one of the squabbling generals would emerge a clear victor and at least bring order to the disintegrating state.

It would take a man of rare abilities to restore some measure of life to the sad and shattered Byzantium, but on Easter Sunday of 1081, that man arrived. After pausing long enough to enjoy the acclamations of the crowd, a thirty-three-year-old general named Alexius Comnenus walked into the Hagia Sophia and received the crown from the patriarch. The task ahead of him was nearly insurmountable, but Alexius was energetic and shrewd, and he would prove to be among the greatest men ever to sit on the Byzantine throne.

21

THE COMNENI RECOVERY

Alexius I Comnenus was an unlikely savior. A member of the aristocratic ranks that the Macedonian dynasty had struggled so long to suppress, he seemed at first to be just another usurper in a long line of meddlesome nobles that had brought such ruin to imperial fortunes. It was true that Alexius had an unrivaled military reputation—in his early twenties, he had fought at Manzikert, and he hadn't lost a battle since—but he had risen to power in the usual way by overthrowing his short-lived predecessor instead of by fighting the Turks. The motley army he commanded was so full of foreign mercenaries that the moment he brought them inside the walls of Constantinople they started looting the city, and a full day passed before he could bring them under control. Some of Constantinople's older citizens might well have shaken their heads and muttered that there was indeed nothing new under the sun.

It was hardly an auspicious start, but worse was yet to come. Within a month of Alexius's coronation, word reached him that a terrible force of Normans had landed on the Dalmatian coast and was heading toward the port city of Durazzo. If they took the city, they would have direct access to the thousand-year-old Via Egnatia and with it a straight invasion route to Constantinople.

The Normans were no ordinary wandering band of adventurers. The descendants of Vikings, these *Northmen* were the success story of the eleventh century. While their more famous brothers in Normandy had battered their way into Saxon England under the command of

William the Conqueror, the southern Normans had batted aside a papal army, held the pope captive, and managed to expel the last vestiges of the Roman Empire from Italy. Led by the remarkable Robert Guiscard, they had invaded Sicily, capturing Palermo and thoroughly broken Saracen power over the island. Now, having run out of enemies at home, and with his appetite whetted for imperial blood, the irascible Guiscard turned his attention to the far more tempting prize of Byzantium.

Upon arriving before the walls of Durazzo, Guiscard cheerfully put the city under siege, but its citizens were well aware that Alexius was on his way and showed no inclination to surrender. After a few months of ineffectual assaults, Robert withdrew to a more defensible position. On October 18, the emperor arrived with his army. The force Alexius had managed to gather in such a short period of time was impressively large, but it suffered from what was by now the traditional Byzantine weakness. The core of the army as always was the elite Varangian Guard, but the rest was an undisciplined, ragtag collection of mercenaries whose loyalty—and courage—was at best suspect. The only consolation for Alexius was that the Varangians, at least, were eager for battle.

Fifteen years before, a Norman duke had burst into Anglo-Saxon England, killing the rightful king at Hastings and placing his heavy boot on the back of anyone with a drop of Saxon blood. Many of those who found life intolerable as second-class citizens in Norman England had eventually made their way to Constantinople, where they had enlisted with their Viking cousins in the ranks of the Varangian Guard. Now at last they were face-to-face with the foreigners who had despoiled their homes, murdered their families, and stolen their possessions.

Swinging their terrible double-headed axes in wicked arcs, the Varangians waded into the Norman line, sending their blades crunching into any man or horse that got in their way. The Normans fell back in the face of such a ferocious assault, but Alexius's Turkish mercenaries betrayed him, and he was unable to press the advantage. The moment the Norman cavalry wheeled around, the bulk of the imperial army scattered, and the exposed and hopelessly outnumbered Varangians were surrounded and butchered to a man. Alexius, bleeding from a wound in the forehead, kept fighting, but he knew the day was lost. Soon he fled to Bulgaria to rebuild his shattered forces.

The empire had proven as weak as Guiscard had hoped, and with the cream of the Byzantine army gone, there was seemingly nothing to fear from Alexius. By the spring of 1082, Durazzo had fallen along with most of northern Greece, and Guiscard could confidently boast to his men that by winter they would all be dining in the palaces of Constantinople. Unfortunately for the invader's culinary plans, however, Alexius was far from finished. The ever-resourceful emperor knew he couldn't hope to stand toe-to-toe with Norman arms, but there were other ways to wage war, and in his capable hands diplomacy would prove a sharper weapon than steel.

Guiscard had been all-conquering in southern Italy, but his meteoric career had left numerous enemies in its wake. Chief among them was the German emperor Henry IV, who held northern Italy in his grip and nervously watched the growth of Norman power in the south. When Alexius sent along a healthy amount of gold with the rather obvious suggestion that a Norman emperor might not be a good thing for either of them, Henry obligingly invaded Rome, forcing the panicked pope to beg Guiscard to return at once. Robert wavered, but more Byzantine gold had found its way into the pockets of the Italians chafing under Norman rule, and news soon arrived that southern Italy had risen in rebellion.* Gnashing his teeth in frustration, Guiscard had no choice but to withdraw, leaving his son Bohemond to carry on the fight in his place.

Alexius immediately attacked, cobbling together no fewer than three mercenary armies, but each one met the same fate, and the

---

*One of Alexius's more unsung contributions to Byzantium was in restoring the gold content of its coins and thereby ending the vicious inflation that was crippling its economy.

emperor accomplished nothing more than further draining his treasury. Even without their charismatic leader, the Normans were clearly more than a match for his imperial forces, so Alexius began a search for allies to do the fighting for him. He found a ready one in Venice—that most Byzantine of sea republics—where the leadership was as alarmed as everyone else about the scope of Guiscard's ambitions. In return for the help of its navy, Alexius reduced Venetian tariffs to unprecedented (and from native merchants' perspectives rather dangerous) levels, and gave Venice a full colony in Constantinople with the freedom to trade in imperial waters. The concessions virtually drove Byzantine merchants from the sea, but that spring it must all have seemed worth it as the Venetian navy cut off Bohemond from supplies or reinforcements. By this time, the Normans were thoroughly exhausted. It had been nearly four years since they had landed in Byzantine territory, and though they had spectacularly demolished every army sent against them, they were no closer to conquering Constantinople than the day they arrived. Most of their officers were unimpressed by the son of Guiscard and wanted only to return home. Encouraged by Alexius's shrewd bribes, they started to grumble, and when Bohemond returned to Italy to raise more money, his officers promptly surrendered.

The next year, in 1085, the seventy-year-old Robert Guiscard tried again, but he got no farther than the island of Cephalonia, where a fever accomplished what innumerable enemy swords couldn't, and he died without accomplishing his great dream.* The empire could breathe a sigh of relief and turn its eyes once more to lesser threats from the East.

The Muslim threat—much like the Norman one—had recently been tremendously diminished by a fortuitous death. At the start of Alexius's reign, it had seemed that the Seljuk Turks would devour what was left of Asia Minor. In 1085, Antioch had fallen to their irre-

---

*Though his body was carried off and interred in Venosa, Italy, the charming town of Fiscardo—where he died—still bears a corrupted form of his name.

sistible advance, and the next year Edessa and most of Syria as well. In 1087, the greatest shock came when Jerusalem was captured and the pilgrim routes to the Holy City were completely cut off by the rather fanatical new masters. Turning to the coast, the Muslims captured Ephesus in 1090 and spread out to the Greek islands. Chios, Rhodes, and Lesbos fell in quick succession. But just when it appeared as if Asia was lost, the sultan died and his kingdom splintered in the usual power grab.

With the Norman threat blunted and the Muslim enemy fragmented, the empire might never have a better opportunity to push back the Seljuk threat—and Alexius knew it. All the emperor needed was an army, but as the recent struggle with the Normans had shown, his own was woefully inadequate. Alexius would have to turn to allies to find the necessary steel to stiffen his forces, and, in 1095, he did just that. Taking pen in hand, he wrote a letter to the pope.

The decision to appeal to Rome was somewhat surprising in light of the excommunication of forty-one years before, but most of those involved in that unfortunate event were long dead, and tempers had cooled in the ensuing decades. The emperor and the pope might quibble occasionally about theological details, but they were members of the same faith, and it was as a fellow Christian that Alexius wrote Urban. As a gesture of goodwill to get things off on the right foot, the emperor reopened the Latin churches in Constantinople, and when his ambassadors reached Pope Urban II, they found the pontiff to be in a conciliatory mood. The appalling Turkish conquests had profoundly shocked him, and the sad plight of eastern Christians under Muslim rule could no longer be ignored. No record of the conversation that followed has survived, but by the time the pope made his way to France a few months later, a grand new vision had formed in his mind. Islam had declared a jihad to seize the holy places of Christendom and spread its faith into Europe; now it was time for a grand Christian counteroffensive. On November 18, the pope mounted a huge platform just outside the French city of Clermont and delivered one of the most fateful speeches in history.

The Saracens, he proclaimed, had come storming out of the deserts to steal Christian land and defile their churches, murdering Christian pilgrims and oppressing the faith. They had torn down the Church of the Holy Sepulchre in Jerusalem and forced innumerable believers to convert to Islam. The West could no longer in good conscience ignore the suffering—it was the sacred duty of every Christian to march to the aid of their eastern brothers. The Saracens had stolen the city of God and now righteous soldiers were needed to drive them out. All those who marched with a pure heart would have their sins absolved.

The moment the pope finished speaking, the crowd erupted. Medieval Europe was filled with violence, and most of those gathered were painfully aware of how much blood stained their hands. Now, suddenly, they were offered a chance to avoid the eternal damnation that in all likelihood awaited them by wielding their swords in God's name. A bishop knelt down on the spot and pledged to take the cross, and within moments the papal officials had run out of material for those who wanted to sew crosses on their clothing as a sign of their intentions. France, Italy, and Germany were swept up in crusading fever as Urban traveled spreading the message, and peasants and knights alike flocked to his banner. So many responded that the pope had to begin encouraging some to stay home to take in the harvest and avert the danger of a famine. Not even in his wildest dreams had he imagined such a groundswell.

The sheer scale of the response electrified the pope, but it horrified Alexius. The last thing he needed was a shambling horde of western knights descending on his capital. What he really wanted were some mercenaries who recognized his authority, while the pope had given him what was sure to be an undisciplined rabble that listened little and demanded much.

And there were plenty of other reasons to mistrust the crusaders. Not only had the pope cleverly substituted Jerusalem for Constantinople as the object of the holy war, but he had also neglected to mention Alexius in any of his speeches, putting the Crusade firmly under his own control, and reinforcing the idea that the pope—not the emperor—was the supreme authority in Christendom. Furthermore, the whole idea of a "holy" war was an alien concept to the Byzantine mind. Killing, as Saint Basil of Caesarea had taught in the fourth century, was sometimes necessary but never praiseworthy, and certainly not grounds for remission of sins. The Eastern Church had held this line tenaciously throughout the centuries, even rejecting the great warrior-emperor Nicephorus Phocas's attempt to have soldiers who died fighting Muslims declared martyrs. Wars could, of course, be just, but on the whole diplomacy was infinitely preferable. Above all, eastern clergy were not permitted to take up arms, and the strange sight of Norman clerics armed and even leading soldiers disconcerted the watching hosts.

These strange western knights were obviously not to be trusted, and some Byzantines suspected that the true object of the Crusade was not the liberation of Jerusalem at all, but the capture of Constantinople. Anyone who doubted that only needed to look at the nobles who were already on their way, for foremost among the crusading knights was Bohemond—the hated son of Robert Guiscard.

The first group of crusaders to arrive before the gates of the city didn't improve Alexius's opinion of them. After the pope had returned to Italy, other men had taken up the task of preaching the Crusade, fanning out to spread the word. One of them, a rather unpleasant monk named Peter the Hermit, traveled through northern France and Germany, preaching to the poor and offering the destitute peasants a chance to escape their crushing lives. After attracting a following of forty thousand men, women, and children who were too impatient to wait for the official start date, Peter led his shambling horde to Constantinople. When they reached Hungary, it became apparent that many had joined the Crusade for less than noble reasons, and neither Peter nor anyone else could control them. Looting their way through the countryside, they set fire to Belgrade and stormed the citadel of any town that didn't turn over its supplies. At the city of Nish, the exasperated Byzantine governor sent out his troops to bring them into line, and in the skirmish ten thousand crusaders were killed. By the time Peter and his "People's Crusade" reached Constantinople, they were looking less like an army than a rabble of hungry, tired brigands. Knowing that they wouldn't stand a chance against the Turks, Alexius advised them to turn back, but they had come too far by now and were firmly convinced of their invulnerability. They were already becoming a headache—taking whatever they pleased and looting the suburbs of Constantinople—so with a final warning Alexius ferried them across to Asia Minor.

The People's Crusade came to a predictably bad end. The crusaders spent most of the next three months committing atrocities against the local Greek population—apparently without noticing that they were fellow Christians—before blundering into a Turkish ambush. Peter the Hermit managed to survive and make his miserable way back to Constantinople, but the rest of his "army" wasn't so lucky. The youngest and best-looking children were saved for the Turkish slave markets and the rest were wiped out.

The main crusading armies that arrived over the next nine months bore no resemblance to the pathetic rabble that Peter had led. Headed by the most powerful knights in western Europe, they were disciplined and strong, easily doubling the size of any army Alexius could muster. The logistics of feeding and handling such an enormous group were a nightmare, made especially difficult by the fact that neither they nor Alexius trusted the other an inch. Obviously, the emperor had to handle the situation with extreme care. Since these westerners valued oaths so highly, they must all be made to swear their allegiance to him, but it had to be done quickly. Arriving separately, they were small enough to be overawed by the majesty of the capital, but if they were allowed to join together, they would undoubtedly get it into their heads to attack the city. Constantinople had been a temptation to generations of would-be conquerors before them; why would crusaders prove any different?

The emperor was right to be alarmed. Constantinople was unlike any other city in the world, more splendid and intoxicating than any the westerners had ever seen. To a poor knight, the city was impossibly strange, dripping in gold and home to a population nearly twenty times that of Paris or London. The churches were filled with mysterious rites that seemed shockingly heretical, and the babble of dozens of exotic languages could be heard on streets choked with merchants and nobles dressed in bright silks and brilliant garments. The public monuments were impossibly large, the palaces unbearably magnificent, and the markets excessively expensive. Inevitably, there was a severe culture clash. The Byzantines the crusaders met treated them like barely civilized barbarians, resenting the swarms of "allies" who had looted their cities and stolen their crops, while the crusaders in response despised the "effeminate" Greeks arrayed in their flowing robes and surrounded by perfumed eunuchs who needed westerners to do their fighting for them. Annoyed by the cloying ceremony of the Byzantine court, most of the crusading princes at first treated the emperor with barely concealed contempt—one knight even went so far as to lounge impudently on the imperial throne when Alexius entered to meet with him. The emperor, however, was quite capable of holding his own. With a shrewd mixture of vague threats and luxurious gifts, he managed to procure an oath from each of them. Few arrived eager to pledge their loyalty, although some were compliant enough (Bohemond in particular was a little too willing to swear), but in the end virtually every leader agreed to return any conquered city to the empire. Only the distinguished Raymond of Toulouse stubbornly refused the exact wording, substituting instead the rather nebulous promise to "respect" the life and property of the emperor.

By the early months of 1097, the ordeal was over and the last of the crusaders had been ferried across the Bosporus and settled on the Asian shore. For Alexius, the feeling was one of extreme relief. The armies that had descended on his empire had been more of a threat than a help, and even if they were successful in Anatolia, they would most likely prove more dangerous than the currently disunited Turks. In any case, all that he could do now was wait and see what developed.

As soon as they landed, the crusaders headed for Nicaea, the ancient city that had witnessed the first great council of the church nearly eight centuries before. The Turkish sultan who had wiped out the People's Crusade was more annoyed than alarmed, assuming that these recent arrivals were of the same caliber. Instead, he found an army of hardened knights mounted on their powerful horses, encased in thick armor that rendered them completely impervious to arrows. The Turkish army shattered before the first charge of the crusader heavy cavalry, and the stunned sultan hastily retreated.

The only thing that marred the victory for the crusaders was the fact that the garrison of Nicaea chose to surrender to the Byzantine commander—who promptly shut the gates and refused to let them enjoy the customary pillaging. Such behavior by the Byzantines was perfectly understandable since the population of Nicaea was predominantly Byzantine Christian, but to the crusaders it smacked of treachery. They began to wonder if the emperor might not be confused between his allies and his enemies—especially when the captured Turks were offered a choice between service under the imperial standards or safe conduct home. For the moment, the crusaders muted their criticism, but their suspicions didn't bode well for future relations with Byzantium.

Alexius was more than happy to ignore western knighthood's injured pride, because he was fairly certain that they stood no chance against the innumerable Muslim enemies arrayed against them. Against all expectations in Constantinople, however, the First Crusade turned out to be a rousing success. The Turkish sultan tried again to stop the crusaders, but after two crushing defeats, he ordered their path stripped of supplies and left them unmolested. After a horrendous march across the arid, burning heart of Asia Minor, the crusaders reached Antioch and managed to batter their way inside. No sooner had they captured the city, however, than a massive army under the Turkisn governor of Mosul appeared, and the crusaders—now desperately short of water—were forced to kill most of their horses for food. Alexius gathered his army to march to their defense but was met halfway by a fleeing crusader, who informed him that all hope was lost and that the city had most likely already fallen. Realizing that there was nothing to gain by sacrificing his army, Alexius turned around and returned to Constantinople.

The crusaders, however, hadn't surrendered. Inspired by the miraculous discovery of a holy relic, they had flung themselves into a last-ditch offensive and managed to put the huge army to flight. Continuing their advance, they reached Jerusalem in midsummer, and on July 15, 1099, successfully stormed the Holy City. Many crusaders wept upon seeing the city that they had suffered so much to reach, but their entry into it unleashed all the pent-up frustrations of the last four years. Few of the inhabitants were spared—neither Orthodox, nor Muslims, nor Jews—and the hideously un-Christian bloodbath continued until early the next morning.

It was the work of several weeks to cleanse the city of the stench of rotting bodies, and by that time the crusaders had chosen a king. By the oaths they had all taken, they should have returned the city—along with everything else they had conquered—to the Byzantine Empire, but there was no longer any chance of that. As far as they were concerned, when Alexius had failed to relieve them in Antioch, he had revealed himself to be treacherous, releasing them from their vows. Bohemond had already seized Antioch, setting himself up as prince, and the rest of their conquests were now broken up into various crusader kingdoms. If the emperor wanted to press his claims to their lands, then he could do so in person with an army at his back.

Alexius was more than happy to let Palestine go. A few Christian buffer states in lands that had been lost for centuries might even be a good thing. But having his enemy Bohemond installed in Antioch was more than he could swallow. Long regarded as the second city of the empire and site of one of the great patriarchates of the church, Antioch had been lost to the Turks only fifteen years before. Its population was thoroughly Orthodox, its language was Greek, and its culture was Byzantine through and through. But even when Bohemond added insult to injury by tossing out the Greek patriarch and replacing him

with a Latin one, there was little Alexius could do. The emperor had
used the distraction of the Crusade to recover most of northwestern
Asia Minor—including the cities of Ephesus, Sardis, and Philadelphia—
but his armies were stretched out, and there was no hope of extending
his reach into Syria.

It seemed as if Bohemond was free to make as much mischief as
he liked, but in the summer of 1100 he stumbled into a Turkish ambush and spent the next three years locked away in a distant prison.
No fewer than three crusading armies were sent to rescue him, but
when they as usual ignored Alexius's offer of guides and advice, they
were easily cut to pieces by the Turks. This didn't stop them from
blaming the emperor for their failures, however, and when the furious
Bohemond was ransomed at last, he found plenty of support in Europe for a new offensive against Byzantium.* The bitter flower of mistrust and hostility was now in full bloom, its roots deeply embedded in
the cultural gulf between the East and the West. To the eyes of Europe, it seemed as if the true enemy of the crusader states wasn't Islam
at all but the grasping, duplicitous Byzantium. The emperor had done
nothing at all to help the crusaders when they were trapped in Antioch and had restricted access to imperial cities, but he had given Muslim prisoners all consideration (even to the point of receiving meals
without pork) and treated them as valuable allies. In Constantinople,
on the other hand, Alexius's original suspicions now seemed justified
after all—the crusading spirit was nothing more than a new twist on
an old story. The foreigners had come with words of support and talk
of brotherhood, but in the end they only wanted to conquer. Now
Alexius would face a new army, led by his old enemy Bohemond.

From the beginning of his invasion, Bohemond tried to repeat
his father's success. After landing in Epirus with an army thirty-four

---

*He managed to escape from Byzantine territory by concealing himself in a coffin
with a decaying rooster to provide an appropriate aroma. While his supporters
wept and dressed in mourning clothes, Bohemond's "coffin" was smuggled onto a
ship and delivered safely to Rome.

thousand strong, he immediately marched up the Dalmatian coast and besieged the mighty city of Durazzo. But Byzantium was no longer the fractured weakling it had been twenty-five years before, when Robert Guiscard had brought his Normans crashing into the empire. A quarter of a century under a single ruler had given the empire the great benefit of stability, uniting the various noble families under a single command. A measure of prosperity had returned, and with it a deeper loyalty to the government in Constantinople. With morale suitably high, Durazzo easily resisted the attack, and a Byzantine fleet cut off Bohemond from his supplies. Alexius leisurely made his way from Constantinople with an army, obliging the Norman to defend against attacks from his rear as well as from the city. By the end of the year, Bohemond's men were starving and, as usual in an army camp, suffering from malaria as well. The exhausted and humiliated crusader was brought before the emperor, where he humbly agreed to an unconditional surrender. After returning to Italy in shame, Bohemond died three years later without ever daring to show his face in the East again.

Alexius had refurbished the tarnished imperial reputation and been more successful than any could have hoped at the start of his reign, but he was now nearing sixty and rapidly aging. Suffering from an acute form of gout, he was more concerned with consolidating what he had recovered than with new battles against the Turks. Trying to bring relief to his subjects, he eased the tax burden on the poor, building them a vast free hospital and homeless shelter in the capital to provide for all their needs. Concerned by the growing power of Venice within the empire, he offered the same commercial treaties to Pisa, hoping that the two maritime republics would balance each other out. In 1116, there was time for one final campaign against the Turks; he completely routed the sultan's troops, ending the regular attacks on the Byzantine coast. By the terms of the resulting treaty, the Greek population of the Anatolian interior immigrated to Byzantine territory, escaping enslavement but ensuring the Islamification of Asia Minor.

By the time he returned victorious from his campaign, the emperor clearly didn't have much longer to live. Forced to sit up in order to breathe, and swollen with disease, he lingered on until August 1118, finally dying in his bed with his family by his side.* He had been a brilliant emperor and deserved to be buried in the Church of the Holy Apostles alongside the greatest of them, but instead he chose to be interred in the quiet little chapel he built along the seawalls.† The thirty-seven years he spent on the throne had given the empire a comforting stability just when it needed it the most, and had laid the foundation for a return to prosperity and strength. The full-scale collapse had been halted, and the emperor had even managed to recover the rich coastal lands along the Mediterranean and the Black Sea. With a little more cooperation and goodwill between his people and the crusaders, Alexius almost certainly could have recovered the interior of Asia Minor as well. With the heartland of Anatolia restored to the empire, the damage done by Manzikert would have been effectively undone, and a much stronger Byzantium would have existed to deny the Turks a foothold in Europe. The following centuries would see plenty of capable and ambitious men on the imperial throne; if they had been given access to the resources of Asia Minor, they could perhaps have prevented the five hundred years of enslavement that awaited half of Europe. But the poisonous relations between Byzantium and the crusaders were not Alexius's fault, and he can hardly be blamed for their deterioration. The Crusade could very well have overwhelmed the fragile imperial recovery, but he had handled it deftly and had accomplished more than any had dared to hope. Not all of his successors would have his skill—or be so lucky.

Long after the last crusaders left Constantinople, the impact of

---

*Among them was his daughter Anna Comnena, who wrote the *Alexiad*—perhaps the most entertaining Byzantine account of the life and times of Alexius.

†The church is still there, tucked unobtrusively into the surrounding masonry, and though it's now in ruins (and not entirely uninhabited), no tomb has ever been found. Perhaps Alexius sleeps there still in some undiscovered vault, dreaming of happier days.

their passing reverberated in the imperial capital. Though the first experience left a bitter taste in the mouths of both sides, the rather pampered court was nevertheless impressed by the superb physical prowess of their brutish guests. In many cases, these swaggering men were their first intimate glimpses of the faraway West, and though the crusaders were uneducated and rough, there was a savage magnificence in the way these men of iron held themselves.

When the Second Crusade, led by the crowned heads of Germany and France, made its way through the capital during the reign of Alexius's grandson Manuel, something in the pageantry of the age of chivalry caught the rich Byzantine imagination. It became fashionable for wealthy ladies to sport western-style dress, and the emperor Manuel even held jousting tournaments, horrifying his watching court by entering the lists himself.*

The fad for all things western, however, carried with it the tinge of superiority that all older civilizations feel toward younger, threatening ones. The wealthy might amuse themselves by aping these exotic strangers and their barbaric customs, but they felt little real warmth or understanding for their western colleagues. No matter how proficient these knights were at war, at heart most Byzantines considered them to be nothing more than jumped-up barbarians, incapable of true parity with the spiritual and temporal glory of Constantinople. The Roman Empire might have lost a good deal of its material luster, but it remained a shining beacon of learning and civilization in a darkened world, and no so-called king or prince from the barbaric West could ever really cross that divide.

Such lofty claims of glory seemed to be true enough under the Comnenian emperors, as the empire's recovery continued. Alexius's son John the Beautiful humbled the aggressive king of Hungary and forced the Danishmend Turks to become his vassals. When the stub-

---

*Unlike earlier Roman emperors who entered Olympic games or gladiatorial contests assured of victory (Nero, Commodus), Manuel was apparently quite proficient at jousting. According to Byzantine accounts, in one tournament he managed to unhorse two famous Italian knights.

244 / LOST TO THE WEST

bornly independent princes of Armenia continued to defy him, the emperor marched into Armenia and carted them off to Byzantine prisons for safekeeping. This display of imperial power brought the squabbling crusader kingdoms into line, and the prince of Antioch even presented himself before the emperor and pledged his humble allegiance. A hunting accident cut short John the Beautiful's promising reign, but his even more brilliant son Manuel took up where his father had left off. The arrogant prince of Antioch, mistaking the new emperor's youth for weakness, demanded that several fortresses be immediately turned over to him, only to have Manuel appear like lightning before the city, terrifying the populace. The other crusader kingdoms got the message and hurried to declare that the emperor was their overlord. When Manuel rode into Antioch in 1159 to personally assume control of it, the leading dignitaries of the crusader world—including the king of Jerusalem—marched obediently behind him. Three years later, the Seljuk Turks accepted vassal status in exchange for Manuel's promise to leave them alone; in the West, Serbia and Bosnia were annexed by the crown. Byzantium seemed to have recovered from Manzikert and reclaimed its prestige.

There were, however, ominous clouds on the horizon. The empire's reputation in the West had not been particularly high since the First Crusade, but it worsened significantly with the unmitigated failure of the second. Though the debacle was hardly the fault of Byzantium, French and especially Norman crusaders returned home with alarming tales of Byzantine duplicity and shocking imperial treaties with the Muslim enemy.* The fact that the crusaders had repeatedly ignored Manuel's advice to avoid the Turks by traveling along the safer

---

*The Germans elected to ignore Manuel's advice and march by the quickest route and were ambushed almost immediately, virtually eliminating the Teutonic army from the struggle. Under the command of the French, the remaining crusaders made the mind-boggling decision to attack Damascus—the one Muslim power that was allied with them—invading at the height of summer. By July 28, 1148, after only five days of a disastrous siege, the various leaders abandoned the attempt in disgust and returned to their homes.

coastal routes was conveniently overlooked; the treaty with the sultan was damning enough. Clearly, the heretical Greeks cared nothing for the Christian cause in the East and were secretly trying to undermine the crusaders' success.

Even more dangerous than Byzantium's blackened reputation in the West, however, were the deteriorating relations with Venice. The Italian city-state had built up quite a commercial empire largely at Byzantine expense, and its increasingly arrogant attitude was unacceptable to the rank-and-file native merchants whose trade was being strangled. One could hardly walk the streets of the capital without running into an insufferable Venetian, and there were many who wished the emperor would send them all back to their lagoon. Surely an empire as glorious and mighty as Byzantium didn't need to have its merchants crowded out by foreigners and its wealth diverted to some far-off city. John the Beautiful had tried to curb Venetian influence by refusing to renew their trading rights, but he had only succeeded in starting a war in which the hopelessly decrepit Byzantine navy couldn't even participate. After a few months of having his coasts burned and trade disrupted, John swallowed his pride and gave in to Venetian demands, having accomplished nothing more than increasing the bitterness on both sides. His son Manuel as usual had better luck. In 1171, the emperor, in an act equal parts foolishness and bravery, simply arrested every Venetian in the empire and seized their merchandise, ignoring the outraged protests. The Venetian ambassador Enrico Dandolo was indignantly recalled (though not before losing the use of an eye), and the powerful navy took his place. Once again, the two nations were at war, but this time the Byzantines didn't even have a navy, since John had disgustedly cut funding to it several years before. Incredibly, however, Manuel's luck held. The plague broke out among the Venetian ships and the war effort collapsed. The poor doge returned to Venice—bringing the plague with him—and was brutally killed by an angry mob.

The Venetian stranglehold on the empire's sea commerce was broken, but it was a Pyrrhic victory. For the moment, the republic was content to lick its wounds and nurse its bruised ego, but memories were long on the Venetian lagoon. Thirty-two years would pass, but Venice—and Enrico Dandolo—would have their revenge.

Buoyed by a certain amount of grudging international respect, and now seen once again as a great power of the Aegean and the Balkans, Byzantium paid little attention to the animosity that was building against it. Seemingly capable of raising vast armies by "stamping its foot," the empire had cowed its enemies in the East and imposed its will over its provinces in the West. Manuel was so confident of its power that he had even written to the pope, offering in effect to act as the sword arm of the church. But the strength of Byzantium was largely an illusion, built by the smoke and mirrors of three brilliant emperors. The erudite and flashy Manuel may have looked every inch an emperor and impressed all he met with the breadth of his learning, but his victories lacked any real substance. The crusader princes and kings promised him allegiance, but that disappeared with the departure of his armies; and though the Turks had become his vassals, that only lulled the empire to sleep. Without Asia Minor restored to the empire, Byzantium lacked the resources for a permanent recovery, but with one calamitous exception, none of the Comnenian emperors ever attempted to reconquer their lost heartland. Their wars were only defensive, reacting to outside threats instead of trying to repair the extensive damage done by Manzikert.

Manuel's greatest mistake was his failure to evict the armies of Islam from Anatolia. At the start of his reign, the Danishmend Turks were broken and squabbling, and the sight of the imperial army seemed enough to cow the Seljuks. After humbling the crusader kingdoms, Manuel could have turned his sword against the Turks, but instead he accepted their vassalage and turned his back on them for nearly a decade. The moment the imperial armies left the region, the Seljuks invaded Danishmend territory, easily overcoming their weakened enemies. For the first time in nearly a century, Turkish Asia Minor was once again united under a single strong sultan. Instead of quarreling, divided enemies, Manuel now faced a united, hostile front.

In 1176, he tried to correct his mistake, marching with his army to attack the Turkish capital of Iconium, but was ambushed while crossing the pass of Myriocephalum. After nearly a century of rebuilding, the imperial army had been as powerless against the Turks as ever, and its reputation had been irrevocably broken. Imperial strength was revealed as nothing more than a monstrous sham, an illusion based on the emperor's dazzling style but without real substance.

Manuel lived on for four more years, even managing to ambush a small Turkish army as revenge for his great disaster, but his spirit was diminished, and the tides of history were running against Byzantium. In the fall of 1180, he fell mortally ill, and on September 24 he died, bringing the brilliant century of the Comneni to a close. His death was as most of his life had been: an example of exquisite timing. Having presided over the pinnacle of Byzantine prestige, he exited just as the empire's power dissolved and the sky grew dark, leaving his successors to face the storm. Those watching his funeral procession unknowingly caught the final glimpse of imperial glory as it faded from view. After Manuel, the entire house of cards came tumbling down.

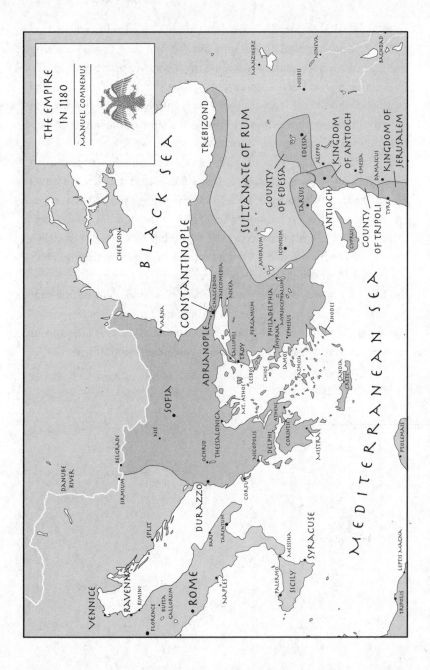

THE EMPIRE
IN 1180
MANUEL COMNENUS

BLACK SEA

CHERSON

VENNICE
RAVENNA
RIMINI
FLORENCE
BUSTA
GALLORUM
ROME
NAPLES
SPLIT
PARI
TARENTUM
DURAZZO
CORFU
PALERMO
SICILY
MESSINA
SYRACUSE
TRIPOLIS
LEPTIS MAGNA

DANUBE
RIVER
SIRMIUM
BELGRADE
NIS
SOFIA
OCHRID
THESSALONICA
NICOPOLIS
DELPHI ATHENS
CORINTH
MISTRA
MT. ATHOS
LESBOS
CHIOS
SAMOS
PATMOS

VARNA
ADRIANOPLE
CONSTANTINOPLE
GALLIPOLI
TROY
CHALCEDON
NICOMEDIA
NICEA
PERGAMUM
PHILADELPHIA
SMYRNA MYRIOCEPHALUM
EPHESUS
RHODES
CANDIA
CRETE

TREBIZOND

SULTANATE OF RUM

AMORIUM
ICONIUM

MANZIKERT

NISIBIS

NINEVA

BAGDAD

COUNTY
OF EDESSA
EDESSA
ALEPPO
KINGDOM
OF ANTIOCH
TARSUS
ANTIOCH
EMESA
CYPRUS
DAMASCUS
COUNTY
OF TRIPOLI
TYRE

KINGDOM OF
JERUSALEM

PTOLEMAIS

MEDITERRANEAN SEA

22

::

SWORDS THAT DRIP WITH
CHRISTIAN BLOOD

The speed at which the empire collapsed took even its citizens by surprise. In the past when Byzantium was threatened, great leaders had arrived to save it, but now it seemed as if the imperial stage was conspicuously absent of statesmen. Manuel's twelve-year-old son, Alexius II, was obviously incapable of dealing with the looming problems facing the empire and could only watch as the Turks advanced unopposed in Asia Minor, the brilliant Stefan Nemanja declared independence for Serbia, and the opportunistic king of Hungary detached Dalmatia and Bosnia from the empire. Some relief arrived when Manuel's cousin Andronicus seized the throne, but he proved a deeply flawed savior, fully earning his nickname of Andronicus the Terrible.* Gifted with all the brilliance but none of the restraint of his family, he understood only violence, and though he cut down on corruption, his rule quickly descended into a reign of terror. Nearly demented with paranoia, he forced Manuel's son to sign his own death sentence, had him executed, and, in a final act of depravity, married the eleven-year-old widow. After two years, the people of the capital could take no more and in suitably violent fashion put a new emperor on the throne.

---

*By the time he came to the throne he had already seduced no fewer than two of his nieces.

For all his faults, Andronicus the Terrible had at least preserved some sort of central authority in the empire. Isaac Angelus—the man who took his place—founded the dynasty that would throw away the empire's remaining strength and preside over its complete breakup. Unaccustomed to enforcing his will on others, Isaac sat back while the authority of the central government crumbled. Governors became virtually independent, and friend and foe alike began to realize that Constantinople was impotent. The Aegean and Ionian islands, safely outside the reach of the decaying navy, rebelled almost immediately, and the Balkans slipped forever out of Byzantium's grasp.

The empire's misery was compounded by the worsening situation in the Christian East. The Muslim world was united under the brilliant leadership of a Kurdish sultan named Saladin, and the squabbling crusader kingdoms could put up little resistance. In 1187, Jerusalem fell, and inevitably the West launched another Crusade to retake it, again using Constantinople as a staging point. The presence of foreign armies passing through the capital was dangerous at the best of times, but Isaac would have been hard pressed to have handled the situation more poorly. When the German ambassadors arrived to discuss transport to Asia Minor, Isaac panicked and threw them into prison. The enraged German emperor Frederick Barbarossa threatened to turn the Crusade against Constantinople, and the blustering Isaac caved completely, immediately freeing the prisoners and showering them with gold and apologies.

This shameful behavior went a long way toward confirming the abysmal Byzantine reputation in the West and thoroughly disgusted the emperor's beleaguered subjects. Whatever support Isaac had left crumbled away when he made the insane decision to officially disband the imperial navy and entrust the empire's sea defenses to Venice. Seeing his moment to strike, Isaac's younger brother Alexius III ambushed the emperor and his son and—after blinding the emperor—threw them both into the darkest prison he could find.

Unfortunately for the empire, the new emperor proved to be a good deal worse than his brother. Capturing the throne had taken most of his energy, and now he couldn't be bothered to actually govern. While the Turks marched up the Byzantine coastline in Asia Minor and Bulgaria expanded in the west, Alexius III busied himself in a search for money to fund his lavish parties—even stooping in his greed to stripping the old imperial tombs of their golden ornaments.

As the emperor plundered his own city, Isaac in his black cell was dreaming of revenge. His own escape was impossible and, since he was blind, quite pointless, but if his son Alexius IV could break free, there might yet be justice. Somehow the old emperor made contact with his supporters in the city, and in 1201, two Pisan merchants were able to smuggle the young prince out. Fleeing to Hungary, Alexius IV stumbled onto an unexpected sight: a new crusading army was on the march.

The Third Crusade hadn't been a success. After sacking the Seljuk capital of Iconium, the fearsome German emperor Frederick Barbarossa had drowned in a freak accident while crossing the Saleph River in southeastern Anatolia.* Without him, the German army panicked and melted away, with some soldiers even committing suicide in their desperation. The English and French armies, on the other hand, arrived in much better condition, and—led by the dashing Richard the Lion-Hearted—they were ready to fight. Repairing the damage done to the crusader kingdoms was tedious work, though, and Richard had no patience. After a year spent conquering the coastline, he was terribly bored with the entire thing. Jerusalem seemed as unreachable as ever, the crusaders were squabbling mercilessly, and the French king (he rightly suspected) was plotting against him.

---

*Like King Arthur in Britain, a legend soon grew up that Barbarossa wasn't dead but merely asleep in the brooding mountains of Germany. He will arise— so the story goes—when ravens cease to fly, and restore Germany to her ancient greatness.

After hastily patching up a truce with his Muslim rival—the gallant Saladin—Richard sailed off to find another adventure, announcing before he left that any future Crusade should be directed against Egypt—the "Achilles' heel" of the East.

Richard's reputation was so great in Europe that the German leaders of the Fourth Crusade decided to take his advice and capture Jerusalem via Egypt. This, of course, meant that the entire army would need to be transported across the Mediterranean, and there was only one place that could provide enough ships for an entire Crusade. Gathering their courts, the princes of Europe headed for Venice.

The islands in the Lagoon of Venice had a long and tangled history with the empire. Originally composed of refugees from the Lombard invasion of Italy in the sixth century, the collection of islands that made up Venice was administered by the imperial governor of Ravenna and drew heavily on the Byzantine culture around it. The church on its oldest island, Torcello, had been paid for by the emperor Heraclius, the main cathedral of Saint Mark's was a loose replica of the Church of the Holy Apostles in Constantinople, and Venetian sons and daughters were regularly sent for education—or spouses—to Byzantium. Even the title of "doge" was a corruption of the original imperial title of *dux,* or duke. Recent years, however, had seen more competition than cooperation between the republic and the empire, and the latest heavy-handed treatment of Venetian traders by the Comnenian emperors still grated on Italian nerves.

This was especially true of the doge who greeted the crusaders in 1202. He was none other than Enrico Dandolo—the ambassador who had vainly protested the emperor Manuel's seizure of all Venetian property within the Byzantine Empire thirty years before. Now in his nineties and completely blind, the old doge masked a fierce intelligence and an iron will behind his seemingly frail frame. Here was an opportunity not to be missed for the calculating Dandolo. Venetian claims for lost property were still outstanding, and the insults endured at the hands of the empire had lost nothing in the intervening years. Now, at last, however, was a chance of revenge.

First, he agreed to build the necessary ships, but only in return for an enormous sum. Unfortunately for the crusaders, turnout for the expedition was embarrassingly low, and they could only come up with little more than half of what they owed. Dandolo shrewdly cut off food and water to the Christian army now trapped on the lagoon awaiting its navy, and when they were appropriately softened up, he smoothly proposed a solution. The Kingdom of Hungary had recently ousted Venice from its protectorate over the city of Zara on the Dalmatian coast. If the crusaders would only consent to restoring this city to its rightful owners, payment of the sum could be postponed. The pope instantly forbid this blatant hijacking of the Crusade, but the crusaders had little choice. A few soldiers trickled away, disgusted by the thought of attacking a Christian city, but the majority uneasily boarded their ships and set sail. The terrified citizens of Zara, bewildered that they were under attack by the soldiers of Christ, desperately hung crosses from the walls, but it was to no avail. The city was broken into and thoroughly looted; it seemed as if crusading zeal could sink no lower.

It was at Zara that the fugitive Alexius IV joined the Crusade. Desperate for support, he was willing to say anything to free his father and overthrow his uncle, and he rashly promised to add ten thousand soldiers to the Crusade and pay everyone at least three times the money owed to Venice. As a final incentive, he even proposed to place the Byzantine church under Rome's control in return for the Crusade's help in recovering his crown.

Perhaps no single conversation in its history ever did the empire more harm. Enrico Dandolo knew perfectly well that the Byzantine prince's wild offers were pure fantasy. Central authority in the empire had been collapsing for decades, and the frequent revolts combined with a corrupt bureaucracy incapable of collecting taxes made it virtually impossible to raise any money—much less the lavish sums offered by Alexius IV. The old doge, however, sitting amid the ruins of Zara, had begun to dream of a much larger prize, and the foolish Byzantine would make the perfect tool. He had probably never intended to attack Egypt at all, since at that moment his ambassadors were concluding a lucrative trade agreement in Cairo. Dandolo ostensibly agreed to redirect the Crusade to Constantinople, and to those soldiers squeamish about attacking the premier Christian city, he smoothly pointed out that the Greeks were heretics and that by placing Alexius IV on the throne they would be restoring the unity of the church. The pope frantically excommunicated anyone who considered the idea, and some drifted disgustedly away; but the Venetian doge was persuasive, and again most of the soldiers dutifully boarded their ships. The Fourth Crusade was now firmly under Dandolo's control.

Alexius III had already proved lazy and corrupt, and he now showed that he was a coward as well. The moment the crusading army showed up beneath Constantinople's walls, he fled for Thrace—taking the crown jewels with him—and left the capital to its fate. The dumbfounded inhabitants of the city watched as the crusading fleet dismantled the massive chain protecting the imperial harbor and launched a ferocious attack against the lower, vulnerable seawalls. Soon they came pouring into the city, setting fire to every house they found. In the imperial palace, the terrified courtiers realized that there was only one way to stop the invaders. These terrible westerners had come to topple the usurper and restore the rightful emperor, so they hurriedly sent someone to fetch Isaac from the dungeons. Within moments, the blind, bewildered emperor had been mounted on the throne with a crown perched precariously over his remaining wisps of hair, and messengers were speeding toward the crusader camp to inform them that their demands had been met. Alexius IV was solemnly crowned alongside his father, the treaty he had made with the Crusade was ratified by both of them, and the crusaders withdrew across the Golden Horn to await their reward.

Old emperor Isaac may have been blind—and thanks to his prison stay more than a little mad—but he realized at once that his son had made impossible promises to these western thugs. It wasn't long before Alexius IV came to the same conclusion. Emptying the treasury and confiscating most of his citizens' wealth only managed to raise half the sum, and by Christmas of 1203 his popularity matched that of the Antichrist. He had brought nothing but calamity to the city from the moment he had appeared with these barbaric savages in tow, and now he was bleeding them white. If only, some of his citizens mused, this unsatisfactory emperor had remained in his prison cell, none of this would have happened.

The crusaders had an even lower view of Alexius IV. To them, he was a pathetic figure, and a liar to boot. They couldn't believe that the ruler of such a magnificent city of grand monuments and soaring buildings would have trouble raising the sums promised. Surely the emperor could snap his fingers and raise ten times the amount offered. Enrico Dandolo was not the least bit interested in the promised reward, but he smoothly played on the crusader fears, suggesting that Alexius IV was holding out on them, stonewalling while he prepared his army to resist. The emperor, he said, was a treacherous snake whose promises were worthless. The only way they would see their reward now was war.

While Enrico Dandolo steered the crusaders inexorably to war, Constantinople finally shook off its lethargy. There were many who wished to see the Angeli gone, but it was a remarkable figure named Alexius Murtzuphlus who finally acted.* He rushed into the emperor's quarters at midnight, shook his drowsy sovereign awake, and told him that the entire city was howling for his blood. Promising to spirit the terrified emperor to safety, Murtzuphlus instead rushed him into the arms of his co-conspirators, who shackled the youth and threw him into the dungeons where his father, Isaac, already waited. The reunion between the two of them was understandably bitter, and this time it was also short, since Murtzuphlus was taking no chances. Isaac Angelus, old and ailing, was easily dispatched; but after

---

*Murtzuphlus means "downcast" or "depressed." Alexius's real name was Ducas, but since he had unusually bushy eyebrows that gave him a permanently despondent look, he was universally known by the nickname Murtzuphlus.

poison failed to achieve the desired result with his son, Alexius IV was strangled with a bowstring.

In another time and place, Murtzuphlus would have made a fine emperor. In his mid-sixties, but still vibrant and decisive, he infused his citizens with a new spirit, shoring up walls, setting aside food, and posting guards on the ramparts. But his forces were too spread out, the walls were too long, and his enemy too numerous. On Monday, April 12, 1204, spurred on by Dandolo's whispers, the crusaders again attacked, hurling themselves against the same stretch of seawalls that had proved vulnerable before. Murtzuphlus, who had sensibly raised the height of the walls, seemed to be everywhere at once, racing along the ramparts to encourage his men where the fighting was thickest, but within a few hours several towers had fallen and a group of French soldiers managed to smash open a gate. The crusaders poured into the breach, and from that moment on the city was doomed. The Varangians surrendered, and after a valiant attempt to rally his men the emperor realized that all was lost, and slipped out of the Golden Gate to plan a counterattack.

The moment Murtzuphlus fled, any semblance of Byzantine resistance collapsed. The crusaders, however, fearing a last stand in the crowded warren of streets, set fire to as many buildings as they could, hoping to keep the inhabitants at bay. Most of them had never dreamed of a city so large and were staggered by its sheer size. Palaces and magnificent churches rose up on every side in cascading rows of wealth, manicured pleasure gardens sprawled luxuriously down to dappled harbors, and grandiose monuments seemed to stretch out around each corner. A French chronicler, disbelieving the evidence of his own eyes, wrote that more houses were burned in the fires they set than could be found in the three greatest cities of France combined. The great crusading princes were just as astonished as their men. Overwhelmed by Constantinople's vastness, they called a halt to the slaughter when night fell, thinking that a city of such size couldn't possibly be conquered in less than a month. That night the invaders camped in one of Constantinople's great forums, resting in the shadow of brooding monuments to long-lost Byzantine greatness.

The citizens of Constantinople awoke the next morning to find their city still burning, but they hoped that the worst of the violence was at an end. The nightmare, however, had only just begun. The proud city on the Bosporus had stood inviolate since the days of the Roman Empire's strength, a great beacon of light in a swiftly darkening world. Unrest and turmoil may have stained its streets, threats and privations may have dimmed its luster since Constantine had made it his capital nearly nine hundred years before, but alone among the cities of antiquity it had never felt the sting of a foreign conqueror's boot. Its libraries still brimmed with lost Greek and Latin writings, its churches were packed with priceless relics, and its palaces and squares were adorned with wondrous works of art. The city was unlike any other in the world, the last jewel in the Roman crown, and when the crusaders awoke that Tuesday morning, they fell on it like wolves.

Armed bands went roving through the city in an orgy of destruction. Nothing was sacred in the frenzied search for riches. Tombs were smashed open, reliquaries had their contents flung aside, and priceless manuscripts were hacked apart to extract the jeweled coverings. Churches were desecrated, women defiled, and palaces pulled down. Neither the living nor the dead were spared. The lid of Justinian's magnificent sarcophagus was cracked open, and though the sight of his preserved corpse gave the vandals a momentary pause, it couldn't stop them from hurling it aside to get at the golden vestments and silver ornaments.

For three days, the fire and the looting continued unabated, and what escaped the clutches of one was inevitably claimed by the other. When silence finally settled on the shocked and shattered city, even the crusaders were taken aback by the amount of plunder. No city, one of them wrote, had produced such loot since the creation of the world.

Of all the crusaders, only the Venetians thought to preserve—not destroy—the priceless artifacts that had fallen into their power. They knew beauty when they saw it, and while the rest of the army hacked apart classical statues, melted down the precious metals, and divided the spoils, the Venetians sent back the works of art to adorn their city on the lagoon.*

For Dandolo, it had been a remarkable triumph. Venetian commercial power was guaranteed for the foreseeable future, and her main rivals of Pisa and Genoa were completely excluded. The old doge had effortlessly hijacked the armed might of Europe and used it to his advantage, disregarding threats of excommunication along the way and ensuring Venetian greatness for decades to come. But in doing so he had perpetrated one of the great tragedies of human history. Byzantium, the mighty Christian bulwark that had sheltered western Europe from the rising tide of Islam for so many centuries, had been shattered beyond repair—wrecked by men who claimed that they were serving God. Blinded by their avarice and manipulated by the doge, the crusading leaders broke the great Christian power of the East, condemning the crippled remnants—and much of eastern Europe—to five centuries of a living death under the heel of the Turks.

After the events of the Fourth Crusade, the already deep divide between East and West stretched into a yawning chasm that was truly irreconcilable. The crusading spirit, which had started out as a desire to help Christian brothers in the East, was revealed as a horrendous mockery. In the name of God, they had come with hardened hearts and cruel swords to kill and maim, to plunder and destroy—and in the work of a moment they had broken the altars and smashed the icons that generations of the faithful had venerated. Once the riches drifted away and the palaces subsided in ruins, the West eventually lost interest and turned away, but the East never forgot. Watching the crusaders

---

*Where a large part of it still remains. One Venetian in particular climbed on the Carceres—the monumental gate to the Hippodrome—and removed four life-size bronze horses. Once shipped to Venice, they were brought to Saint Mark's, where they can still be seen today.

walk their charred and blackened streets, the Byzantines knew that these men with the cross sewn brightly over their armor could no longer be considered Christians at all. Let the powers of Islam come, they thought. Better to be ruled by an infidel than these heretics who made a mockery of Christ.

23

THE EMPIRE IN EXILE

When Pope Innocent III was informed of the sacking of Constantinople, he understood at once the damage that had been done. Furiously excommunicating everyone who had taken part, he wondered aloud how the dream of church unity could ever now occur. How could the Greeks, he wrote to his legates, ever forgive their Catholic brothers, whose swords still dripped with Christian blood, and who had betrayed and violated their holiest shrines?* Eastern Christians, he concluded with good reason, now detested Latins more than dogs.

The new masters of Constantinople, meanwhile, seemed determined to increase the native resentment. In a hastily cleaned Hagia Sophia, where a few days before a prostitute had been mockingly perched on the patriarchal throne, a Latin emperor was crowned, and the feudal arrangements of the West were forced on the corpse of the Byzantine Empire. The various nobles were rewarded with large estates, and a patchwork of semi-independent kingdoms replaced the single authority of the emperor. A crusader knight seized Macedonia, calling himself the king of Thessaloniki, and another set himself up as

---

*Exactly eight hundred years later, in 2004, Pope John Paul II apologized—though the Fourth Crusade was hardly the fault of the pontiff—to the patriarch of Constantinople when the latter paid a visit to the Vatican, expressing pain and disgust even at a distance of eight centuries.

the lord of Athens.* Not even in its most advanced decay had the Byzantine state been as powerless as the Latin one that took its place.

Remarkably enough, given the deplorable state of the capital, the vast majority of Byzantines in the countryside were reasonably well off. As the central authority of the emperors had weakened in the years before the Fourth Crusade, the towns and villages of Byzantium had flourished. Merchants of the West, the East, and the Islamic world converged in fairs held throughout the empire, where they displayed exotic wares from as far away as Russia, India, China, and Africa. The urban population boomed, and since the corrupt and paralyzed imperial government was unable to collect taxes, the wealth stayed in private hands. Emperors could no longer afford their lavish building programs as the treasury dried up, but private citizens could, and the cities became showpieces for personal fortunes. A new spirit of humanism was in the air, along with an intellectual curiosity. Byzantine art, which had been stylized for centuries, became suddenly more lifelike; writers began to depart from the cluttered, archaic styles of antiquity; and individual patrons of the arts sponsored vibrant local styles in the frescoes and mosaics of their villas. The spirit of Byzantium was flowering even as imperial fortunes declined, and not even the terrible trauma of the Fourth Crusade could dampen it for long.

Despite the resilience of its culture and economy, the empire's power seemed irretrievably lost. Alexius Murtzuphlus had tried to organize a counteroffensive with his fellow emperor-in-exile Alexius III, but his idiotic colleague had betrayed him, and the crusaders had flung Murtzuphlus to his death from the top of the Theodosian column. In remote Trebizond on the shores of the Black Sea, the grandsons of Andronicus the Terrible declared themselves the rightful emperors; while at Epirus, the great-grandson of Alexius Comnenus

---

*Virtually the only armed opposition came from a local brigand named Leo Sgurus. After four years of struggle Leo was trapped on top of the acropolis of Corinth, and, rather than surrender, he decided—in a scene worthy of Hollywood—to commit suicide by riding his horse over the side of the citadel.

claimed the same thing. The most powerful and important fragment of the empire, however, was centered at Nicaea, where the patriarch crowned Alexius III's son-in-law Theodore Lascaris as emperor.

As refugees and wealth poured into the Nicene haven of the Orthodox faith and Byzantine culture, the crusader's Latin Empire of Constantinople grew progressively weaker. Within a year, a Bulgarian army had effectively broken its power, destroying its army, capturing the impotent emperor, and allowing Theodore Lascaris to reconquer most of northwestern Asia Minor. Instead of confronting the obvious danger of Nicaea, however, successive Latin emperors concentrated on extracting wealth from the citizens of Constantinople, abandoning themselves to the pleasures of palace life.

Only the threat of the Seljuk Turks at their rear prevented the Nicaean emperors from further exploiting Latin weakness; but in 1242, a terrifying Mongol horde suddenly appeared, and the situation dramatically changed. Smashing the Turkish army sent against him, the Mongol khan forced the Seljuk sultan to become his vassal and extracted a promise of an annual tribute of horses, hunting dogs, and gold. The Mongol horde seemed poised to descend on Nicaea next, but it unexpectedly withdrew the next year, leaving the Seljuks crippled in his wake. To the relieved Byzantines, it seemed as if God had delivered them from certain destruction, and perhaps even given them a powerful new ally. Nestorian Christians who had been expelled from the Byzantine Empire had reached Mongolia in the seventh century, and though the khans had yet to embrace a major religion, several high-ranking Mongols—including the daughter-in-law of Genghis Khan—were Christian. In any case, whether they were well disposed to Christianity or not, the Mongols' timely attack finally left Nicaea free to pursue its dream of recapturing Constantinople.

Through careful diplomacy and military displays, Nicaea slowly built up the pressure on the tottering Latin Empire. By now the crusader kingdom had virtually shrunk down to Constantinople itself, and the capital lived under a perpetual shadow of gloom, with its deserted streets and dilapidated palaces. Its humiliated emperor

Baldwin II was so impoverished that he'd been obliged to sell off the lead from the roof of the imperial palace—which was now in a tumbledown state of advanced decay—and in his desperate search for money had even begun to pawn the few relics that had survived the sack. By 1259, when a dashing young general named Michael Palaeologus was crowned in Nicaea, Baldwin was barely clinging on to power, and few doubted the general would recover the city. The only question was when.

Nicaea was not without its own turmoil. The thirty-four-year-old Michael Palaeologus had come to power only after the regent was brutally hacked to death during the funeral service of his predecessor, but by the time Michael was crowned on Christmas day, his empire was infinitely more powerful and vibrant than its Latin counterpart. In the summer of 1261, Michael neutralized the threat of the Venetian navy by signing a treaty with their archrivals Genoa, and sent his Caesar, Alexius Strategopoulos, to see how strong Constantinople's defenses were. When the Caesar arrived outside the city in July with eight hundred men, some farmers immediately informed him that the Latin garrison—along with the Venetian navy—was away attacking an island in the Bosporus. Hardly believing his luck, Strategopoulos hid until nightfall in a monastery near the Pege Gate, easily escaping detection by the laconic defenders. Upon discovering a small, unlocked postern gate nearby, the Caesar sent through a handful of men who quietly overpowered the guards and opened the main gate. On the morning of July 25, 1261, the Nicaean army poured into the city, shouting at the top of their lungs and beating their swords against their shields. Emperor Baldwin II was so terrified by the noise that he left the crown jewels behind, fleeing to the palace of the Bucoleon, where he was somehow able to find a Venetian ship and make good his escape. Within hours, it was all over. The Venetian quarter was burned to the ground, and the returning Venetian navy was too busy rescuing its loved ones to fight back.

For the Latins inside the city, there was no thought of resistance, only of panicked flight. Scattering in all directions, they hid in churches, disguised themselves as monks, and even leaped into the sewers to avoid detection. When they cautiously emerged, however, they found that there had been no massacre. The Byzantines had come home not to plunder but to live. The bedraggled Latins hurried quietly down to the harbors and boarded the returning Venetian ships, glad that Byzantines had shown more restraint in victory than their own crusading predecessors.

The incredible news reached Michael Palaeologus where he was asleep in his tent, nearly two hundred miles away. Refusing to believe that his forces had captured the city until he had seen Baldwin's discarded scepter, Michael hurried to take possession of the capital that he had long dreamed of but never seen. On August 15, 1261, he solemnly entered through the Golden Gate and walked to the Hagia Sophia, where he was crowned as Michael VIII. After fifty-seven years in exile, the Byzantine Empire had come home.

The city that Michael VIII triumphantly entered was a pale shadow of its former self. Charred and blackened houses stood abandoned on every corner, still sagging and in ruin from the sack more than five decades before. Its churches were despoiled and dilapidated, its palaces decayed, and its treasures dispersed. The formidable Theodosian walls were badly in need of repair, the imperial harbor was completely unprotected, and the surrounding countryside was devastated. Its weary citizens had little hope for relief from a throne that had seen—from Irene in 780 to Alexius Murtzuphlus in 1204—half of its occupants overthrown. Worst of all, however, the old unity of the Byzantine world had vanished—the splinters of the empire in Trebizond and Epirus remained stubbornly independent, sapping the already diminished strength of Byzantium. The only hope of salvation seemed to be from the West, but the Fourth Crusade had severely ruptured western relations.

If anyone had a chance of repairing the damage, however, it was Michael VIII. Not yet forty, he was energetic and vibrant, hiding a fierce intelligence behind a convivial smile. Boasting an impressive imperial lineage of no fewer than eleven emperors and three dynasties among his ancestors, he was well connected, able, and smarter than anyone else around him. His first task was to restore the city's shattered morale, and he did so with a whirlwind of construction, repairing walls and rebuilding churches. In the upper gallery of the Hagia Sophia, the emperor commissioned a stunning mosaic of Christ flanked by Mary and John the Baptist—perhaps the finest piece of art that Byzantium ever produced. A massive chain was stretched across the imperial harbor to protect it from enemy vessels, and the moats around the land walls were cleared. Knowing the value of propaganda, the emperor designed a new flag and sent it fluttering from every parapet and tower in the city. Though the eagle had been the symbol of the Roman Empire since Gaius Marius had chosen it thirteen hundred years before, most banners before Michael bore either Constantine's cross or the *Chi-Rho*—the first two Greek letters of Christ's name. Now the emperor added a great golden eagle, double-headed with two crowns—one for the interim capital of Nicaea and one for Constantinople. Those who saw it could swell with pride and remind themselves that Byzantium had been a mighty empire embracing two continents, looking both east and west. Perhaps under the dashing Michael VIII it would be so again. The imperial enemies were scattered and disunited, and an immediate offensive just might catch them on their heels.

At the head of his small, battle-hardened army, Michael VIII had soon pushed back a marauding Bulgarian army and forced the Byzantine despot of Epirus to submit to the empire. By 1265, he had conquered most of the Peloponnese from its Latin overlords and even managed to clear the Turks out of the Meander valley. The next year, however, a new player appeared on the international stage, and everything was thrown into confusion.

The Norman Kingdom of Sicily had dominated Italian politics for a long time, but by 1266 its energy was exhausted. Pope Urban IV, wanting a friendlier hand at its helm, invited Charles of Anjou, the younger brother of King Louis IX of France, to seize the kingdom. If the pope wanted a neutral power to his south, however, he could hardly have made a worse choice. Charles was cruel and grasping, and after beheading his sixteen-year-old opponent in a public square, he immediately began planning to enlarge his domains. His schemes were given an unexpected boost when Baldwin II, the exiled and rather pathetic Latin emperor of Constantinople, offered to give him the Peloponnese in exchange for help regaining the throne. The delighted Sicilian king immediately began levying heavy taxes to support the war effort and searching for allies, forming an anti-Byzantine league with Venice.

Knowing his small army and decrepit navy would stand no chance against his united enemies, Michael VIII turned to diplomacy, adroitly managing to keep them at bay. Venice was bought off with greater trading privileges within the empire, and a few letters hastily written to King Louis persuaded the French king to restrain his headstrong younger brother. For the moment, the voracious Charles was forced to sit on his hands, but the French king died in 1270, and Charles gleefully invaded. Sicilian arms were irresistible, but once again Michael VIII outthought his opponent. Writing to the pope, the emperor cleverly dangled the promise of a union of the churches before the pontiff's eyes in exchange for bringing Charles to heel.

The ploy worked and Charles was recalled, but Michael was playing a dangerous game. He was well aware that his subjects would never accept domination by the hated Roman church, and he couldn't keep stalling the pope indefinitely. For three years, the emperor smoothly dodged the papal representatives; but by 1274, Pope Gregory X got tired of waiting and sent an ultimatum to Constantinople—either implement the union immediately or face the consequences. There was little that Michael VIII could do. Asking only that eastern practices be left alone, he submitted his church to the authority of the pope.

The firestorm in Constantinople was both unsurprising and immediate. The patriarch angrily refused to ratify the hated document, and most of Michael's subjects felt bitterly betrayed. The emperor had not only dangerously weakened his throne, but he had also handed the

Orthodox powers of Serbia and Bulgaria the perfect bit of propaganda. Each could now invade imperial territory at will and claim to be fighting for tradition and truth. Any such invasion, Michael well knew, would receive dangerous support from his outraged subjects. But he had removed the justification of papal support from any future attack by Charles, and that for Michael VIII was worth the price of popular unrest. In any case, he didn't intend to sit idly by while his enemies pounced. When Bulgaria invaded, trying to exploit the weakness, Michael simply invited the Mongol Golden Horde into Bulgaria. The Mongol advance crippled the kingdom, dealing Bulgaria a blow from which it never recovered.

Charles of Anjou had been seriously checked, but he wasn't beaten yet. If his grand alliance had foundered on Byzantine treachery, then it must be more solidly rebuilt. Venice was easily seduced. She was always looking to her own advantage, and the rights Michael VIII had granted to Genoa were cutting deeply into her profits. A victory for Charles would mean the banishment of the Genoese upstarts—an irresistible attraction for the Lion of Saint Mark's. The only thing restraining Charles was papal displeasure, but the resourceful king overcame even this seemingly insurmountable obstacle. Pope Gregory X died in 1276, and through steady interference and intimidation Charles managed to have a French cardinal elected pope who hated the Byzantines almost as much as he did.* In 1281, the French pope sent a letter to the stunned Byzantine emperor informing him that he had been excommunicated on the grounds of his subjects' continued resistance to Catholicism. The emperor could hardly believe the news. He had sacrificed his popularity and invited charges of impiety and betrayal for nothing. Now Venice and Sicily were firmly

---

*The pope is best known to posterity for his role in the life of a young Italian adventurer. On his election in 1271, Gregory received a letter from Kublai Khan asking for oil from a lamp in the Church of the Holy Sepulchre. The pontiff entrusted it to the young Marco Polo—whose lively account of the journey became one of the most famous books of the Middle Ages.

allied against him, and they would sail under the papal blessing. Not even the Fourth Crusade had such support.

Byzantium's only advantage was Michael VIII. In a brilliant bit of truly "byzantine" diplomacy, Michael reached out to Peter III of Aragon, urging him to invade Sicily. Peter was related to the dynasty that Charles of Anjou had evicted from power and considered Sicily his birthright. And thanks to vicious taxation and a copious amount of Byzantine gold, anti-French feeling on the island was at a fever pitch. Now, suggested Michael VIII, would be the perfect time for the Spanish savior to arrive.

Unaware of the storm that was gathering, Charles of Anjou left Sicily for the mainland of Italy to put the finishing touches on his army. In his absence, the island exploded. The revolt known to posterity as the Sicilian Vespers started innocuously enough on the outskirts of Palermo. As the bells of the church of Santo Spirito rang to call the faithful to Vespers on Easter Monday of 1282, an inebriated French soldier tried to seduce a Sicilian girl. To the outraged onlookers, it was the last straw. These boorish French had lorded it over them for long enough, growing fat off Sicilian labor. The enraged mob killed the offending soldier and fanned out through the streets of Palermo, venting nearly two decades of frustration on anyone with a drop of French blood. When the sun rose on Tuesday morning, there wasn't a Frenchman left alive, and the electrifying news of the revolt sped throughout the island. By May, French resistance had collapsed, and by the end of August Peter III had landed and taken possession of Palermo. Charles of Anjou furiously put several Sicilian ports under siege, but he had abused his former subjects for too long, and they preferred death to his return. Though he spent the rest of his life trying to recover the island, he was never successful, and in 1285 he died, a broken man.

Michael VIII never lived to see the death of his great enemy. With the threat of western aggression gone, the despot of Epirus was once again asserting his independence, and the emperor was determined to bring him into line. The fifty-eight-year-old emperor again led his troops toward battle, but he had gotten no farther than Thrace when he fell seriously ill. Thinking as always of his responsibilities, the dying emperor proclaimed his son Andronicus II to be his successor, and expired quietly in the first days of December.

He had been among Byzantium's greatest emperors, restoring its capital and dominating the politics of the Mediterranean. Without him, the empire would certainly have fallen to Charles of Anjou—or any number of watching enemies—and the Byzantine light would have been extinguished, its immense learning dispersed among a West not yet ready to receive it. Instead, Michael VIII had deftly outmaneuvered his enemies, founding in the process the longest-lasting dynasty in the history of the Roman Empire. Nearly two hundred years later, a member of his family would still be sitting on the throne of Byzantium, fighting the same battle of survival—albeit with much longer odds. Michael had done what he could to repair the imperial wreckage. He left behind valuable tools to continue the recovery: a small but disciplined army, a reasonably full treasury, and a refurbished navy. But for the savior of the empire, no gratitude awaited. Excommunicated by the pope, he died a heretic to the Catholic West and a traitor to the Orthodox East. His son buried him without ceremony or consecration in a simple, unmarked grave. Michael VIII's affronted subjects, however, would all too soon have reason to miss him. If Byzantium looked strong at his death, it was only because his brilliance had made it so. Without a strong army or reliable allies, its power was now purely diplomatic, and it needed hands as skillful as Michael's to guide it. Unfortunately for the empire, however, few of Michael's successors would prove worthy of him.

24

::

THE BRILLIANT SUNSET

"Qui desiderat pacem, praeparet bellum."
"If you want peace, prepare for war."
—VEGETIUS

The last two centuries of Byzantine history make, for the most part, rather discouraging reading. Against an increasingly hopeless backdrop, petty emperors waged destructive internal squabbles while the empire crumbled, reducing the once-proud state to a mere caricature of itself. There were, however, small moments of light to pierce the advancing gloom, rare individuals of courage and determination, struggling against the overwhelming odds, knowing full well that they were doomed. As the empire edged toward extinction, a cultural flowering occurred, a brilliant explosion of art, architecture, and science as if the Byzantine world was rushing to express itself before its voice was forever silenced. Sophisticated hospitals were built with both male and female doctors, and young medical students were given access to cadavers to learn the human body by dissection. Byzantine astronomers postulated on the spherical shape of the world and held seminars to discuss how light appeared to move faster than sound.

For the most part these advancing fields of physics, astronomy, and mathematics managed to peacefully coexist with the increasingly mystic Byzantine Church, but there were occasional tensions. The noted fourteenth-century scholar George Plethon composed hymns to the Olympian gods, and even went so far as suggesting a revival of

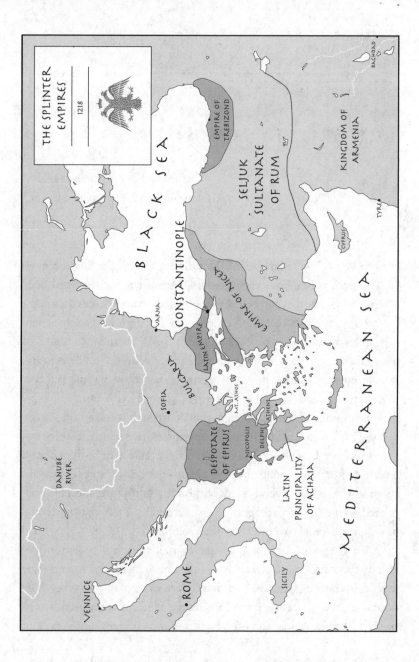

THE SPLINTER
EMPIRES

1218

BLACK SEA

EMPIRE OF TREBIZOND

SELJUK SULTANATE OF RUM

KINGDOM OF ARMENIA

CONSTANTINOPLE

EMPIRE OF NICEA

LATIN EMPIRE

VARNA

BULGARIA

SOFIA

CYPRUS

TYRE

MT. ATHOS

NICOPOLIS

DELPHI

ATHENS

DESPOTATE OF EPIRUS

LATIN PRINCIPALITY OF ACHAIA

DANUBE RIVER

MEDITERRANEAN SEA

SICILY

ROME

VENNICE

BAGHDAD

ancient paganism.* While this certainly didn't help the reputation of the sciences and tended to confirm the suspicion that excessive study in some fields weakened the moral fiber, Byzantine society at large remained remarkably open to new ideas. This spirit was seen most vividly in the decorations and new buildings of the capital. Perhaps the impoverished empire could no longer build on the grand scale of the Hagia Sophia, or even the more modest levels of the Macedonian dynasty, but what it lacked in splendor it made up for in originality. In Constantinople, a wealthy noble named Theodore Metochites embellished the church of the Chora Monastery with vivid frescoes and haunting mosaics, departing from the staid forms of past imperial art in a way that still has the power to catch the breath today. The Ottoman shadow may have been looming over the city, but even the threat of extinction couldn't cow the Byzantine spirit.

Ironically enough, it was partly Michael VIII's glorious reconquest of Constantinople that hastened the collapse. Once restored to their rightful capital, the focus of the Byzantine leaders shifted back to Europe. Concentrating on the all-important city, the myopic emperors turned their backs on Asia Minor, where the balance of power was rapidly changing. The Mongol sack of Baghdad in 1258 had broken the back of Seljuk power and a massive influx of Turkic tribes had come streaming in to fill the vacuum.† One of these groups, led by an extraordinary warlord named Osman, united several tribes and crossed into Byzantine territory. Calling his men "Gazi" warriors—the "swords of God"—Osman led a jihad aimed at nothing less than the

---

*He also suggested that a good way to deter adultery would be to force the guilty women to live as prostitutes (no word on the punishment for the men involved) while those who committed rape should be burned alive.

†As a Muslim, the Mongol warlord didn't want to shed the blood of the heir of Muhammad, so he had the caliph wrapped in a carpet before trampling him with a horse. The invaders then settled down to a thorough sack of the city. According to legend, so many books from its great library were hurled into the Tigris that the river ran black from the ink for six months. The story is an obvious hyperbole, but Baghdad has never been the same since.

capture of Constantinople. The terrified Byzantine population of Anatolia fled at his approach and was replaced with Turkish settlers, largely extinguishing the Greek presence in Asia Minor. After a short struggle, the ancient city of Ephesus fell and Osman's troops—now calling themselves Ottoman in his honor—shattered the weakened imperial army. Under his son Orhan, they took Bursa, at the western end of the Silk Road just across the Golden Horn from the capital, and then Nicaea and Nicomedia as well. Soon all that was left of the empire in Asia was Philadelphia and remote Trebizond on the Black Sea coast. Ottoman warriors could now stand in the waters of the Propontis and see the fluttering banners hanging from the churches and palaces of fabled Constantinople. The storied city was almost within their grasp. All they needed now was a way across.

Incredibly enough, this was conveniently provided by the Byzantines themselves, who seemed more interested in fighting over the fragments of their empire than protecting it from the obvious threat. By 1347, what was left of Byzantium was devolving into something resembling class warfare. A rebel patrician named John Cantacuzenus was attempting to seize the throne, and its current occupant responded by waging a successful public-relations war that branded John as a reactionary—the embodiment of the privileged class that had brought such ruin to the empire.* Across the empire, indignant cities expelled his troops. The citizens of Adrianople, anticipating the French Revolution by more than four centuries, massacred every aristocrat they could find and appointed a commune to rule the city.

Thrown back on his heels, Cantacuzenus invited the Turks into Europe, hoping to use their strength to seize Constantinople. The deal won Cantacuzenus his crown, but was disastrous for Europe, as what started as a trickle of Ottoman soldiers all too quickly became a

---

*There were the usual complaints of the poor against the rich, as well as the startling claim that allowing the wealthy and destitute to marry (a practice frowned upon) would eliminate poverty and lead to a utopian society of shared resources.

flood.* As the Turks crossed the Hellespont in ever-greater numbers to ravage Thrace, the bubonic plague returned to Constantinople after an absence of six centuries, adding the miseries of disease to the horrors of war. Spreading as it had before in the bodies of fleas and rats, it claimed the lives—according to one terrified account—of nearly 90 percent of the population.†

The one consolation for the huddled, miserable inhabitants of Byzantine Thrace was that the Turks had come as raiders, not settlers. Each winter, the marauding Ottomans returned across the Bosporus to their Asian heartland and left the weary peasants in peace. But even that small comfort disappeared in 1354. On the morning of March 2, a tremendous earthquake shattered the walls of Gallipoli, reducing the city to rubble. Declaring it to be a sign from God, the Turks swept in, settling their women and children and evicting the few Byzantines who hadn't already fled. The emperor frantically offered them a large amount of money to leave, but their emir responded that since Allah had given them the city, to leave would be a sign of impiety. The Ottomans had gained their first toehold in Europe, and they didn't intend to leave. Jihadists flooded across from Asia, and the weak and devastated Thrace fell easy victim to their advance. After a probing stab in 1359 convinced the Ottomans that Constantinople was out of reach, they simply surged around it. Three years later, Adrianople fell, surrounding the capital of eastern Christendom in an Islamic sea.

The Turkish emir left little doubt of his intentions. Moving the capital of the Ottoman Empire into Europe, he sold part of Adrianople's population into slavery and replaced the balance with settlers of Turkish stock. The rest of Thrace was subjected to the same treatment, and as most of its population was transferred to Anatolia, Turk-

*It was by this time a rather pathetic glass crown, since John's impoverished predecessor had pawned the real thing to Venice.
†In Europe, the black death, as it was called, carried off nearly a third of the population, but the Ottomans, far away from densely settled cities, were largely spared.

ish settlers came pouring in. The Ottoman tide seemed irresistible, and the mood in the capital was one of gloomy pessimism. "Turkish expansion . . ." one of them wrote, "is like the sea . . . it never has peace, but always rolls."*

Emperors and diplomats left for Europe to beg for help, but only the pope was interested, and the price for his aid was always the same. The eastern and the western churches must be joined, and the Orthodox must place themselves beneath the authority of Rome. This had already been proposed several times in the past, but always the people of Constantinople had disgustedly rejected it. John V, however, was desperate enough to attempt it again. In 1369, he knelt solemnly on the steps of Saint Peter's, accepted the supremacy of the pope, and formally converted to Catholicism.

The emperor's submission was a personal act that had no binding power on anyone else, and the only thing it accomplished was to embarrass John in the eyes of his subjects. The empire may have been distinctly shabby, but Byzantine dignity would never tolerate a willful submission to the hated Latin rite whose crusaders had so recently stained the streets of Constantinople with blood. The westerners had chased the Byzantines from their homes, murdered their families, and ruined their beautiful city. Even if the empire was now plainly doomed, asking its citizens to submit in their faith as well was too much. As far as they were concerned, no aid was worth that cost.

Despite John's conversion, the promised help from the West never arrived, but the Orthodox power of Serbia responded to the empire's plight. Marching down into Macedonia, they met the Ottoman army on the banks of the Maritsa River. The Turkish emir Murad—now calling himself sultan—won an overwhelming victory and forced Macedonia's squabbling princes to become his vassals. Determined to crush the Orthodox spirit, Murad swept into Dalmatia and Bulgaria, sacking their major cities and reducing their princes to

---

*Roger Crowley, *1453* (New York: Hyperion, 2005).

vassalage. A coalition of princes led by the heroic Serbian Stefan Lazar managed to keep the Ottoman advance from entering Bosnia, but in 1389, at the terrible battle of Kosovo, Tsar Lazar was killed and the last vestige of Serbian power was irretrievably broken. The only consolation for the people of the Balkans—whose fate was now sealed—was that Murad didn't survive the battle. A Serbian soldier feigning desertion was brought before the sultan and managed to plunge a sword into his stomach before being hacked apart by the sultan's guards.

Emperor John V had pinned all his hopes on Serbian help, and the disaster broke him. Writing to the sultan, he humbly offered to become an Ottoman vassal if only the sultan would spare his capital. Two hundred years before, Manuel I had made the Seljuk sultan his vassal; now John's young son Manuel II watched helplessly as his prostrate father reversed the situation. The anointed defender of Orthodoxy was now a servant of Christendom's greatest enemy.

It was at this moment of despair that another man of vision finally ascended the Byzantine throne. Manuel II had all the energy and political wisdom that his father so conspicuously lacked, and though he knew there was little hope for the empire, he was determined that it should expire with its head held high.

Never in its long history had the deck been so thoroughly stacked against Byzantium. The new Ottoman sultan Bayezid, a man whose speed in battle would soon earn him the nickname "the Thunderbolt," was more menacing than his father, Murad, had ever been. Ominously taking the title "Sultan of Rum" (Rome), he was determined to crush any thoughts of independence. Forcibly reminding the emperor of who his master was, Bayezid peremptorily summoned Manuel II to Asia Minor. Philadelphia, one of the seven cities of Revelation and the last Christian outpost in Anatolia, still resisted the Turks. Clearly relishing the agony it caused, Bayezid ordered Manuel to help reduce this final Byzantine city to ruin.

Manuel II had no choice but to participate in the final political extinction of the Christian East. The imperial writ now barely extended beyond the walls of Constantinople itself, and the emperor didn't have any illusions about the weakness of the Byzantine position. It could still claim a few ports on the Aegean and most of the Peloponnese, but such scraps hardly deserved to be called an empire. Any show of resistance against the overwhelming force of the Turks would almost certainly be suicidal, and the sultan was already dangerously hostile.

The campaign was mercifully short, and Manuel II was back in Constantinople in time to marry a Serbian princess named Helena Dragases the next year.* The emperor was willing to play the faithful vassal to keep the Ottoman wolf at bay, but Bayezid seemed determined to provoke a war. After increasing the tribute that the impoverished empire had to pay, the sultan ordered a huge Turkish quarter to be set up in Constantinople that was independent of Byzantine authorities and governed instead by Muslim judges. As if such humiliations weren't bad enough, the unstable sultan then took to bouts of arbitrary cruelty, mutilating several Byzantine ambassadors and screaming that he would kill his imperial vassal. By this time, Manuel II had had enough. There was no sense in trying to appease such an unpredictable monster. When Bayezid summoned him for a campaign against Transylvania, Manuel II slammed the gates shut in his face and prepared for war. A few months later, the Ottoman army appeared, and the siege began.

Despite the overwhelming power of the Ottoman forces, Bayezid suffered from the same weakness that many would-be conquerors of Constantinople had discovered before him. Without a navy, there was no hope of an effective blockade, and the land walls of the city were stout enough to resist any attempt thrown at them. To make matters worse, the furious sultan soon got word that his recent foray into Transylvania had awakened Hungary to the Turkish threat, and a new Crusade was lumbering on its way. Briefly raising the siege, Bayezid raced to the Bulgarian city of Nicopolis, somehow arriving

---

*Fortunately for posterity, the emperor left a lively account of his journey across the lost Byzantine heartland.

before the crusaders, and smashed their army to pieces. Ordering his men to lop off the heads of ten thousand prisoners, the sultan returned to Constantinople, conquering Athens and central Greece for good measure along the way.

By 1399, when the Thunderbolt returned, Manuel II was no longer in his capital. Taking advantage of the sultan's absence, the emperor had boarded a ship and headed to Europe. Landing triumphantly in Venice, he was given a warm reception, and wherever he went, from Paris to London, crowds flocked to see him. The emperor had come for assistance, but not to beg, and a Europe trembling in the first stirrings of the Renaissance greeted him with open arms. This tall, gracious figure seemed every inch an emperor, a worthy successor of Augustus or Constantine, and erudite into the bargain. Manuel's visit, so different from the one his father, John, had made just a few years before, brought up no mention of a union of churches, or of a humiliating submission. Manuel sat on the throne of the Caesars, and, no matter how debased that throne had become, its dignity was still unparalleled.

In terms of style, Manuel's European visit was a tour de force, but practically speaking it achieved as little as his father's had. There were some vague promises of support, but no one was in a hurry to help. Henry IV was too insecure on his English throne, the king of France was hopelessly insane, and the rest of Europe was still asleep to the danger. Manuel traveled from capital to capital in vain, stubbornly refusing to give up while there was the faintest hope. Just as he was succumbing to despair, salvation arrived from a most unexpected quarter. The electrifying news swept through Europe, quickly reaching Manuel II where he was staying in Paris. A great army from the east had invaded Asia Minor, and Bayezid had withdrawn to fight it. Constantinople was saved.

The rumors swirling in France had it that a mighty Christian king had arrived to save Byzantium, but this was only half true. The Turkic warrior Timur the Lame had been born in central Asian Uzbekistan more than sixty years before and had spent his life in the saddle at the head of a Mongol horde. His dream was to restore the glorious empire of Ghengis Khan, and to that end he unleashed his army in an extraordinary burst of conquest. By the year 1400, he had an empire that stretched from India to Russia and from Afghanistan to Armenia. Spies preceded his troops, spreading tales of his inhuman cruelty, weakening the morale of the defenders and spreading panic. In Damascus, he herded the citizens into the Grand Mosque and burned it to the ground; in Tikrit, he ordered each soldier to show him two severed heads or forfeit their own; and in Baghdad, he slaughtered ninety thousand civilians and built a pyramid out of their skulls. Lands he passed through became deserts, cities became ghost towns, and whole populations fled.

At the turn of the century, he crossed into Ottoman territory, bringing the enraged sultan speeding from his siege of Constantinople. When the two armies met outside of Ankara on July 20, 1402, the carnage was terrible. Fifteen thousand Turks fell, and the sultan himself was captured. Timur the Lame cheerfully took possession of Bayezid's harem and, according to some accounts, used the sultan as a footstool, carrying him before the army in an iron cage.* The Mongol warlord was now the master of Asia Minor, but he was restless and more interested in conquest than administration. After a few more outrages—he sacked Philadelphia and built a wall of corpses to commemorate it—he withdrew to invade China, leaving a shattered Ottoman Empire and a chaotic Anatolia in his wake.

Now was the moment to drive the Turks out of Europe, but as usual Manuel II could find many vague promises but no actual help to accomplish it. Whatever chance there was to turn the tide passed by forever the moment the new sultan arrived in Adrianople. Bayezid's

---

*Some contemporary accounts say the Mongol khan treated Bayezid with respect—or at least more respect than confining him to a cage—while others go to great lengths to describe the humiliation, relishing every detail. In any case, Timur the Lame had no use for the Ottomans, and abusing their conquered sultan certainly wouldn't have been out of character.

son Süleyman had survived the devastating Mongol attack, and he slipped across the Bosporus to take possession of the European provinces while his brothers fought it out in Asia Minor. Skillfully neutralizing his Christian neighbors by granting Venice and Genoa trade concessions, Süleyman contacted the Byzantine emperor and offered extraordinary terms. Manuel II was, of course, to be released immediately from the humiliation of vassalage; Thrace and Thessalonica were instantly returned to the empire, along with the monastic community of Mount Athos; and, as the final pièce de résistance, Süleyman offered to become Manuel's vassal.

On the warm afternoon of June 9, 1403, Manuel II entered triumphantly into Constantinople. He had left as the servant of the sultan and against all conceivable odds had returned the master. Crowds cheered him as he walked down the streets, church bells rang out jubilantly throughout the city, and a special service of thanksgiving was held in the Hagia Sophia. Despite Süleyman's subservient posturing, however, the Ottoman sultan had the better end of the bargain. With a few gulps of swallowed pride, he had gained a valuable respite. Byzantium was as weak as ever, and its newfound prestige was merely an illusion. A concerted effort by Christendom just might have been able to push the Turks out of Europe while they were still fragmented, but the Ottoman willingness to come to terms had lulled the European powers into a false sense of security. Convinced that the threat had been overblown, they turned their attentions elsewhere and left Byzantium terribly alone. It would've been better for the empire by far if Manuel had rejected Süleyman's terms.

The respite from Ottoman aggression was all too brief. In 1409, Süleyman's brother Musa crossed into his territory and besieged the city of Adrianople. Manuel II gave what aid he could to his vassal, but, after a brief struggle, Musa captured the city and strangled Süleyman. By 1411, the new sultan was at the walls of Constantinople, determined to punish the emperor for supporting the wrong side, and Manuel was only able to rescue the situation by encouraging

Mehmed—a third brother—to overthrow Musa. The siege was lifted and Musa succumbed in his turn to the bowstring, but once again Constantinople was subject to the Ottoman whim.

Fortunately for the empire, the cultured, sophisticated new sultan took an instant liking to Manuel, even referring to him as "my father and overlord," and loyally kept the peace. The emperor took advantage of the lull to shore up the imperial defenses, taking a tour of Byzantine territory, and building a six-mile-long wall across the Isthmus of Corinth—the Hexamilion—to cut off access to the Peloponnese. He remained on excellent terms with his Turkish counterpart, but the truce with Islam, Manuel II well knew, could never last for long, and sooner or later an Ottoman army would once again be at the gates.*

The invasion came sooner than the emperor expected. In 1421, the thirty-two-year-old Mehmed suddenly died, leaving his violent, unstable seventeen-year-old son Murad II as sultan. Such times of transition were inevitably chaotic, with rival claimants trying to seize power, and Constantinople was faced with the opportunity to support a usurper. Manuel II, now in his seventies and increasingly feeling his age, preferred to leave the Ottomans to sort it out and not risk antagonizing the eventual victor. His eldest son, John VIII, however, with all the confidence of youth, wanted to take a more aggressive stance and support a pretender. In the end, the weary emperor gave in, imperial support was thrown behind Murad's cousin Mustafa, and the Byzantines held their breath.

Manuel II had been wise to hesitate in risking the empire's neutrality. Mustafa was trapped by his cousin in Gallipoli and strangled,

---

*Understandably for a man whose empire was under almost constant attack from Islam, Manuel II abhorred the concept of conversion by the sword. A prolific writer, he left us a book called *26 Dialogues with a Persian,* which is a record of his debates on the subject with his Muslim counterparts. In 2006, Pope Benedict XVI quoted from it, arguing that violence had no place in faith. Ironically, the speech unleashed a firestorm of controversy in the Middle East, resulting in the destruction of some churches and several deaths.

and Murad furiously turned on Byzantium. Thessalonica was put under siege, the Hexamilion was demolished, and the Peloponnese was raided. By 1422, Murad was at the walls of Constantinople, demanding the city's immediate surrender. Manuel II was near death, but he had one final gift for his capital. Sending ambassadors to the sultan's youngest brother, the emperor convinced him that the time was right to make a bid for the throne. The annoyed sultan had no choice but to immediately deal with the threat. In exchange for a promise by the emperor to once again become a Turkish vassal, the siege was hastily lifted, and Murad raced to Asia Minor. Somehow Manuel II had successfully avoided extinction. Alone in a Turkish sea, the situation was no better now than it had been at the time of his coronation, but thanks to his ingenuity and cleverness, Constantinople had been saved. Manuel II could expire with his empire—however tenuously—at peace.

It didn't stay so for long. Manuel's oldest son, John VIII, was barely crowned before Sultan Murad II decided to besiege the city of Thessalonica. The hard-pressed Byzantine commander turned over the city to Venice in exchange for its protection, but in 1430 the Venetian governor decided the situation was beyond saving and calmly sailed away, wishing the defenders the best of luck. The hapless Byzantines managed to hold out until March, but the walls were finally breached and the Turks poured in, committing the usual atrocities.

Convinced that Constantinople would be next, John VIII left for the familiar attempt to drum up support in Europe, confident in his abilities to succeed where his predecessors had failed. The Turkish threat, he was quite sure, was now plain for anyone to see, and the West would certainly be motivated out of fear, if not altruism. Like his father and grandfather before him, however, John found that Europe was caught up in its own struggles and quite blind to any larger danger. England and France were locked in the Hundred Years War—Joan of Arc had been captured and burned by the English that same year—and everywhere else John went he received the same tired old response. Byzantium could receive no aid until the Orthodox Church submitted to Rome.

John VIII knew full well that his subjects would never accept such a thing, but he was desperate and promised the pope that he could convert the empire to Catholicism. The pontiff didn't quite believe him—he'd heard that promise too many times before—but the emperor was determined. After fourteen years of tortuous negotiations and diplomatic maneuvering, he gathered a group of intimidated eastern bishops and signed the decree of union at a council at Florence, officially joining the churches. The pope instantly promised armed help, and Hungary, well aware that it was the next nation on the Ottoman chopping block, agreed to lead the Crusade.

It was one thing to sign a document, however, and quite another to enforce it. John returned to his capital to find his actions universally condemned and his own position on the throne seriously undermined. Most of those who had signed the hated decree publicly retracted their signatures; the patriarchs of Alexandria, Jerusalem, and Antioch furiously repudiated it; and one of the emperor's brothers tried to seize the throne in the name of Orthodoxy.

With the church hopelessly divided and the citizens up in arms, everything now depended on the Crusade. Led by the Hungarian king Ladislas, along with the brilliant Transylvanian general John Hunyadi, the crusaders set off in 1443, sweeping into Bulgaria and conquering it within a few months. Murad II was so alarmed at having his Christian enemies united against him that he offered the crusaders a ten-year truce if they would withdraw. The Serbian contingent of the army accepted and returned home, but the rest, spurred on by the pope, plunged down to the Black Sea coast. At the little city of Varna, they found the enraged sultan waiting with an army nearly three times their size. The Turks broke before the first crusader charge, but disaster struck when, in a wild attempt to capture the fleeing Murad, King Ladislas was killed. The crusader army disintegrated in a panic, and in a few hours' time, the Christian army had ceased to exist.

The Hungarian regent John Hunyadi managed to regroup his

forces and keep the sultan busy for a few years, but by 1448 his army was effectively crushed. Watching sadly from Constantinople, John VIII, who had pinned all his hopes on help from the West, was completely broken. He had incurred the wrath of his people and the abasement of his throne, and divided the church in vain. Heartbroken and defeated, he was near death, but one final humiliation remained. On the sultan's return, the emperor was forced to present himself before Murad II and congratulate him on the victory that had sealed Constantinople's fate. Eleven days later, he was dead.

25

···

THE ETERNAL EMPEROR

We hope in the "blond" people to save us . . . We put our hope in the
oracles, in the false prophecies. We waste our time in worthless words.
—TIMOTHY GREGORY, *A History of Byzantium* (2006)

Within days of the funeral, Byzantine ambassadors were speeding on their way to the Peloponnese. There, at Mistra, in the vale of ancient Sparta, they found John's younger brother Constantine XI Dragases and informed him that he was now the emperor of Byzantium. The envoys had no authority to crown him—that had to be done by the patriarch in Constantinople—but a simple ceremony was held.* Boarding a Venetian galley—there were no Byzantine ones available—the last emperor of Constantinople made his way to the capital, making his formal entry on March 12, 1449.

Of all Manuel II's sons, Constantine was by far the most able. Charismatic and courageous, he was deeply conscious of Byzantium's long and glorious history, and he was determined to uphold its dignity. A true son of his father, Constantine considered appeasement to be another form of treachery. The armies of Islam had been beating against the capital's walls for centuries, and to cower before them as his brother and grandfather had done would only add humiliation to the eventual destruction.

The emperor, however, had no illusion about the odds against

---

*Today a double eagle carved into the floor of the cathedral of Agios Dimitrios in Mistra marks the place where the last Byzantine emperor was officially confirmed.

him. At forty-three, he had spent more than half his life fighting the Turks, and he knew his enemy well. Three years earlier, during the initial excitement of the Hungarian Crusade, Constantine had taken advantage of the Ottoman distraction to seize Athens and much of northern Greece from the Turks. After the collapse of the Crusade, Constantine had been left to face the full brunt of the sultan's anger alone. Murad II swept into Greece, capturing Athens and forcing the Byzantines to take refuge behind the six-mile-long Hexamilion. Safe behind the wall, Constantine expected to hold out for months, but the Turks brought with them a terrifying new weapon—several large cannons. The opening blast tore into the wall, roaring with terrible certainty that the world had changed. Defensive fortifications, no matter how grand, were now obsolete. The age of the cannon had begun.

The Hexamilion collapsed in a mere five days, and Constantine barely escaped with his life. The Ottomans burst into the Peloponnese, and only a fortuitous early winter snow that blocked the mountain passes spared the capital of Mistra. Fortunately for the empire, Murad II was more interested in conquering the Balkans than finishing off the remnants of Byzantium, so the Ottoman armies lumbered off to conquer Dalmatia, and Constantine XI was left in peace to rebuild southern Greece as best he could.*

By the time the new emperor made his entry into Constantinople, the city was a dim reflection of its former grandeur, shrunken behind its walls like an ebbing tide. The streets of the capital no longer murmured with the babble of a dozen languages, merchant ships no longer crowded the imperial harbors, and wealth no longer adorned its palaces and churches. From an imperial height of nearly

---

*To ensure the loyalty of Balkan magnates in his absence, Murad II often took their sons as hostages. One particular prisoner was the Transylvanian prince Vlad III, who amused himself in captivity by impaling birds on little sticks. Developing an intense hatred for the Turks in general and the young Sultan Mehmed II in particular, he devoted his life to keeping the Turks out of Transylvania. His cruelty soon earned him the nickname "Vlad the Impaler," but he always preferred his father's nickname of "The Dragon," and it is as Dracula—Son of the Dragon—that posterity remembers him.

half a million in Justinian's day, the population had fallen to around fifty thousand. Deserted fields choked with weeds now covered vast stretches of the city, and half-ruined buildings still slumped in their sprawling decay. And yet, for all that, there was a strange vibrancy in the air. The newly painted frescoes were not as sumptuous as they had been in the past, silver and gold no longer encrusted the icons, and grand mosaics no longer dazzled the eye, but there was a freshness and new vitality to the art that struck out against the waning imperial fortunes. Artisans and scholars found willing patrons in the swirling atmosphere, and new schools of art flourished in the monasteries scattered throughout the fragmented empire. Byzantium had lived in the shadow of the merciless Turk for centuries, and knew with a terrible certainty that it would be destroyed root and branch, but there was a determination to experience life in full even as the hour of doom approached. Materially, the empire may have been reduced to an insignificant speck, but intellectually and culturally it was blooming.

Constantine XI would have liked to give his subjects the welcome diversion of an imperial coronation, but such an event was out of the question. The patriarch was a known supporter of John VIII's Decree of Union joining the Orthodox and Catholic churches, and was therefore considered little better than a heretic by most of his flock. Having such a controversial figure crown him would almost certainly touch off widespread rioting. In any case, Constantine tacitly supported his patriarch's position. The emperor's sacred duty was to preserve his capital's independence, and if submission to Rome offered even the slightest chance of western aid, then it must be pursued. The last emperor of Byzantium would have to remain uncrowned.

While Constantine was negotiating the complex currents of Constantinople, Murad II was finding the capital of Dalmatia much more difficult to conquer than he had anticipated. Led by the Dragon of Albania—the charismatic Skanderbeg—the Dalmatians frustrated every Ottoman attempt at a siege. In 1451, Murad II gave up in disgust, announcing that the province couldn't be taken, and retired to Adrianople, where, to the immense relief of Byzantium, he died.

Church bells rang out in celebration throughout Constantinople. The new sultan, Mehmed II, was only nineteen years old, and when the emperor sent ambassadors to congratulate him on his accession, the sultan swore by the Prophet and the Koran that he would devote himself to peace with the empire for as long as he lived. Western powers nervous after the defeat of the Hungarian Crusade eagerly persuaded themselves to believe him. The young sultan, however, was a mass of contradictions. A poet and a scholar fluent in several languages, he was also an unstable tyrant capable of bestial cruelty. A brilliant organizer and strategist, he was so superstitious that he wouldn't attack without the blessing of an astrologer. Despite this hesitancy, however, there was a touch of Machiavellian decisiveness about him. On becoming sultan, he had strangled his infant half brother to avoid a potential threat, distracting the child's mother by inviting her to dinner. When the poor woman returned home and found her infant dead, she was given no time to grieve; instead, she was immediately married off to one of Mehmed's officers. In the sultan's mind such brutality was the only way to prevent a civil war, and he would later famously explain to his sons that fratricide was in the best interests of "world order." This example of the new sultan's character passed unheeded by the West. Europe and Byzantium were studiously looking the other way, happy to believe that peace between Islam and the empire was possible. They were soon to be disillusioned.

Mehmed II only managed to restrain himself for a matter of months before deciding to break his oath. Sending his engineers to the narrowest point of the Bosporus, where Asia is separated from Europe by only seven hundred yards, he crossed the thin sliver of water and set about demolishing the Byzantine town he found occupying the site. There on the spot where two thousand years before the Persian king Xerxes had crossed with his massive army to meet the doomed Spartan king Leonidas, Mehmed built a fortress. His grandfather had built a similar castle on the Asian side to command the straits, and now the two structures would effectively cut off Constantinople from the Black Sea. It was a blatant act of war, and the sultan didn't bother to disguise his intentions. When Constantine sent emissaries to remind Mehmed that he was breaking his oath and to implore him to at least spare the neighboring villages, Mehmed had the ambassadors executed.

As the walls of the new fortress rose ever higher, a young Hungarian named Urban entered Constantinople and offered his services to the emperor. A specialist in the design and firing of cannons, he offered to start producing guns for the Byzantines. Constantine XI was delighted. He'd seen the deadly new weapons firsthand at the Hexamilion and knew the terrifying power of these deafening monstrosities that could shatter stone and level walls. But there was simply no money to employ the young man. Somehow a stipend was scraped together to keep Urban in the city, but even that was soon exhausted, and the increasingly destitute Hungarian left to offer his services to the Turks.

Mehmed was only too happy to welcome Urban, and after showering him with gifts, he asked the Hungarian if his cannons could bring down a city wall. Urban knew full well what wall the sultan was referring to, and since he had spent long hours surveying Constantinople's famous defenses, he promised to make a cannon that would demolish the very gates of Babylon. Setting to work immediately, he soon produced a bronze monster that could fire a six-hundred-pound stone ball, and the delighted sultan had it mounted in his new fortress, announcing that any ship wishing to pass would have to stop and pay a toll. The Venetians protested that this would completely cut off trade on the Bosporus, but the sultan was in deadly earnest. When a Venetian ship tried to run the straits, Mehmed had it blasted out of the water. Dragging the shell-shocked crew from the waves, he had them executed, and then impaled their captain, mounting the corpse on the bank as a public warning.

The sultan was pleased with his new weapon, but he wanted a bigger one and ordered Urban to build a cannon more than twice as large. The Hungarian went back to his foundry and cast a twenty-seven-foot-long behemoth that could hurl a fifteen-hundred-pound granite ball more than a mile. This, Mehmed knew, was the key to a quick knockout blow to Constantinople that would allow him to conquer the city before the West would have a chance to organize a relief Crusade. The only problem now was transporting the great gun the 140 miles from the foundry in Adrianople to the walls of Constantinople. Carpenters and stonemasons were sent scurrying ahead, leveling hills and building bridges, while a team of sixty oxen and two hundred men pulled the cannon across the Thracian countryside at the lumbering pace of 2.5 miles per day. Mehmed himself set out with his army on March 23, 1453. Constantinople's doom was now at hand.

Constantine XI had done what he could to prepare—clearing out moats, repairing walls, and laying in provisions. He'd seen what the Turks did to conquered cities and understood that there was little chance of survival. One last hope remained: His brother John VIII had promised to join the churches, but an official service celebrating the union had never occurred. Now the pope sent a cardinal promising aid if the decree was formally read in the Hagia Sophia, and the emperor didn't hesitate. In a poorly attended service held in the great church, the officiating priest declared that the Orthodox and the Catholic churches were officially joined. The heavens, he proclaimed, were rejoicing.

The mood in the city was far from jubilant, but with certain annihilation approaching, there were no riots or public outcries. Two hundred archers had come with the cardinal, and there was the faint hope that perhaps more would arrive after the union was made official. Most of the population simply avoided the ceremony altogether and refused to enter any church "contaminated" by the Latin rite. They wouldn't add to the gloom by rioting, but they wouldn't abandon their traditions, either. That Easter, the Hagia Sophia sat strangely quiet and empty as the population drifted away to find churches that still maintained the Greek rite. Five days later, on April 6, the Turks arrived.

The Republic of Venice promised to send a navy to repel the Turks, but no ships were seen on the horizon, and even the most optimistic began to realize that Venetian aid was all words and no action. The appeal to the West had been in vain, and now an Ottoman army that seemed as numerous as the stars was at hand. Looking bitterly down on that vast sea of their enemies and knowing that the Latin Mass was being proclaimed in their beloved Orthodox churches, the Byzantines could ruefully reflect that they had paid the price of union without reaping its reward. The Venetians in the city all gallantly vowed to stay and help, but the gesture was spoiled when a short time later seven galleys carrying hundreds of desperately needed men fled the city under the cover of night. The only bright spot was the arrival of the brilliant siege expert Giovanni Giustiniani from Genoa with a private army of seven hundred highly trained soldiers. He had come to gallantly defend the city his namesake, Justinian, had once ruled, but his grand gesture couldn't dispel a terrible sense of foreboding. Added to Constantine's meager force, the Genovese brought the number of defenders to just under seven thousand men. These had to be spread over twelve and a half miles of land walls and defend the city from some eighty thousand Ottoman troops. Tension and worry hung thickly over the city, but there was no time to brood. Mehmed rode up to the gates as soon as he arrived and demanded an instant surrender. Receiving no reply, he opened fire on April 6.

The great gun roared, spitting flame, smoke, and a stone ball that made the thousand-year-old Theodosian wall shudder. For ten centuries, those walls had thrown back endless arrays of would-be conquerors, but the age of brick and mortar had passed, and the ancient defenses were subjected to a bombardment unprecedented in the history of siege warfare. The main cannon needed time to cool between each firing and could only be discharged seven times a day, but the sultan had other guns that could take up the slack. Stone balls mercilessly slammed into the walls, shattering the brick and occasionally bringing down whole sections. By the end of the first day, a large part of the outer wall was reduced to rubble, and the sultan ordered an assault. Constantine threw himself into the breach, somehow repulsing the successive attacks, and when night fell Giustiniani devised a way to repair the walls. Driving wooden stakes into the collapsed rubble to provide a loose form, he heaped the broken brick and stone into a makeshift wall. The next day, when the firing resumed, the rubble absorbed the cannonballs better than the solid walls and remained more or less intact. Taking heart, the defenders fell into a steady rhythm. By day, they would do their best to stay out of the way of the stone balls raining death all around them; by night, when the guns were at last silenced, they rushed out to repair the damage.

After forty-eight days of continuous bombardment on the vulnerable spot where the walls descended into the little Lycus River valley, a second attempt to take the city by storm proved just as unsuccessful. Once again the emperor led a heroic defense, and the frustrated sultan vented his anger by impaling his Byzantine prisoners in sight of the walls. Changing tactics, Mehmed decided to attack the imperial harbor where the seawalls were more vulnerable, and ordered his ships to ram the great chain, but it easily held. This was humiliating for the Ottomans, but the situation was made worse when three Genovese ships carrying a much-needed shipment of food to the beleaguered capital managed to smash their way through the Ottoman navy and slip into the harbor—despite Mehmed's furious order to sink them at all costs.

This public flouting of his authority threw the sultan into his usual rage. He had lost prestige and allowed his enemies to take heart; their cheers at the Genovese display could be plainly heard in the Turkish camp. This obviously couldn't be allowed to continue, so Mehmed prepared an ambitious response.

The entrance to the imperial harbor was protected by a great chain stretching from Constantinople to a tower in the Genovese colony on the opposite shore. Repeated attempts to force the chain had failed, but there were other options for someone of the sultan's limitless resources. In a stunning display of Turkish planning and organization, Mehmed transported seventy ships overland on greased logs, bypassed the Genovese colony, and dropped his fleet silently into the imperial harbor.

The fall of the harbor came as a physical blow to Constantine. Not only were the waters no longer safe for fishing, depriving the starving city of its one reliable source of food, but now there were another three and a half miles of walls for his stretched forces to defend. Both sides knew the end was surely at hand, and when Mehmed viciously beheaded more Byzantine prisoners in sight of the walls, the emotionally spent defenders responded by throwing their Turkish prisoners from the ramparts. It was war to the death. If the sultan showed no mercy, then he wouldn't be given any in return.

The one hope sustaining the defenders was that the promised Venetian fleet would arrive and save them, but as May dragged on, morale and hope began to fade. In desperation, Constantine had sent a ship to search for any sign of an approaching fleet, but after three weeks it returned and sadly reported that there was no sign of any help. Byzantium had been abandoned to its fate. The imperial ministers begged Constantine to flee and to set up a government in exile until the city could be retaken. The crusader empire had eventually collapsed, and the Ottomans would as well; the important thing was to keep the emperor alive. Exhausted but firm, Constantine refused. These were his people, and he would be with them to the end.

In the Turkish camp, Mehmed was preparing his troops for the final assault. The walls that his guns had been pounding were now heaps of rubble, and further bombardment could hardly achieve much more. His attempts at storming the city had resulted in horrendous casualties, and every day that he failed to take the city eroded his prestige. The time had come for a last push. Not bothering to keep the news from his weary opponents, he announced that on Tuesday, the twenty-ninth of May, the final attack would begin.

In Constantinople, the exhausted defenders had reached the breaking point. Subjected to a continuous hellish bombardment, they had to brave the Turkish guns by day and repair the walls by night. There was little time for rest, either emotional or physical, and tensions had begun to flare. But on that last Monday of the empire's history, the mood changed. There was no rest for the weary, of course, and work continued, but for the first time in weeks, the inhabitants of the city began to make their way to the Hagia Sophia. There, for the first and last time in Byzantine history, the divisions that had split the church for centuries were forgotten, Greek priests stood shoulder to shoulder with Latin ones, and a truly ecumenical service began.

While the population gathered in the great church, Constantine gave a final speech—a funeral oration, as Edward Gibbon put it—for the Roman Empire. Reminding his assembled troops of their glorious history, he proudly charged them to acquit themselves with dignity and honor: "Animals may run from animals, but you are men, and worthy heirs of the great heroes of Ancient Greece and Rome."* Turning to the Italians who were fighting in defense of Constantinople, the emperor thanked them for their service, assuring them that they were now brothers, united by a common bond. After shaking hands with each of the commanders, he dismissed them to their posts and joined the rest of the population in the Hagia Sophia.

There was no sleep that night for the emperor of Byzantium. He remained in the church to pray until all but a few candles were extinguished, rode out to say a final good-bye to his household, and then spent the rest of the night riding the walls, assuring himself that nothing else could be done. Upon reaching his post at the most vulnerable point in the walls, he dismounted and waited for the attack that he knew must come with the dawn. The sultan, however, chose not to wait for the sun. At one thirty in the morning, the quiet darkness was shattered with a tremendous roar. The Turkish guns erupted, crashing into a section of the wall and sending the defenders scrambling for cover. Within moments, a large gap had appeared, and Mehmed sent his shock troops into the breach before the Byzantines could repair it. For three hours, the onslaught continued, but thanks largely to the efforts of Giustiniani, they were repulsed each time. The Genovese commander seemed to be everywhere, encouraging the men and

---

*Nicol, Donald M. *The Immortal Emperor* (Cambridge: Cambridge University Press, 1992, p. 67).

shoring up the line wherever it wavered. By four in the morning, the exhausted Ottoman irregulars fell back, parting to let the main army pour in. Again the Turks came crashing into the Christian line, clawing their way over the dead and trying to smash their way inside. They fought with an almost maniacal fervor, each man eager to gain the sultan's favor on earth or rewards in paradise by perishing for his faith. They came within inches of forcing their way in, but Constantine appeared with reinforcements in the nick of time and beat them back. The exhausted defenders slumped wearily down as the defeated Ottomans withdrew, but again there was to be no rest. Sensing his enemies wavering, Mehmed sent in the Janissaries.

Much like the Varangians in the Byzantine army or the Praetorians of ancient Rome, the Janissaries were the elite fighting forces of the Turkish army. Made up of Christians who had been taken from their families while children and forcibly converted to Islam, they were fanatically loyal and expertly trained. Accompanied by the blaring sound of martial music, these disciplined troops came in an unbroken line, seemingly impervious to anything fired at them from the walls. Somehow they were beaten back, but during the assault Giustiniani was wounded when a crossbow bolt crunched through his chest armor. The wound wasn't mortal, but the stricken Giustiniani was too exhausted to continue. Constantine begged him to stay, knowing what would happen if his men saw him leave, but Giustiniani was adamant and had himself carried down to a waiting ship in the harbor.

The emperor's worst fears were immediately realized. The sight of their valiant leader being carried from the walls sparked a panic among the Genovese, and they began retreating through an inner gate just as the Janissaries launched another attack. In the chaos, the Turks overran several towers, butchering the panicked defenders who were now trapped between the walls. From his position by the Saint Romanus Gate, Constantine knew that all was now lost. With the cry "the City is lost, but I live," he flung off his imperial regalia and plunged into the breach, disappearing into history.

The carnage was terrible. Turkish soldiers fanned out along streets that were soon slick with blood, covering the ground so thickly with corpses that in some places it could hardly be seen. The Venetians and Genovese managed to get to their ships and escape—fortunately for them, the Turkish sailors blockading the harbor, eager to join in the looting, had all abandoned their ships—but the rest of the population was doomed. Women and children were raped, men were impaled, houses were sacked, and churches were looted and burned. The city's most famous icon—an image said to have been painted by Saint Luke himself—was hacked into four pieces, ancient statues were toppled and demolished, the imperial tombs were smashed open to have their contents tossed into the streets, and the imperial palace was left a ruined shell.

As Ottoman flags began appearing on the walls and even the Great Palace, the emotionally shattered inhabitants streamed toward the one place they had always felt safe. An old legend maintained that the Hagia Sophia wouldn't fall to the Turks, thanks to an angel who would descend from the nearby Column of Constantine to defend the faithful. Inside the cavernous building, a service of matins was being conducted, and the comforting chants echoing under the familiar golden icons reassured the refugees. But the ancient prophecies rang hollow—no angel appeared to save them, and even the massive bronze doors couldn't keep their berserk enemies at bay. The Turks smashed their way in, killing the priests at the high altar and butchering the congregation on the spot. A lucky few who appeared to be wealthy were spared for the slave markets, but they were forced to watch as the church was defiled. The patriarchal vestments were draped around the haunches of dogs while the Eucharist was thrown to the ground. A Janissary mockingly perched his cap on the crucifix, and the altars were tipped over and used as feed troughs for horses or even worse, as a bed to rape the women and children hostages. Anything that looked valuable was pried from the walls or smashed, and anywhere a cross could be found it was hacked out.

By the end of the first day, there was virtually nothing left to plunder and the twenty-one-year-old sultan called a halt to the slaughter. The Hagia Sophia was converted to a mosque, its glorious mosaics were painted over with geometric designs, huge wooden shields were hung with verses from the Koran, and a mihrab was hacked into the wall at an appropriate angle.* The bewildered population that was left found themselves prisoners in a city they no longer knew. Mehmed ordered the execution of all males of noble birth and sold the rest of his prisoners into slavery, presenting each of his main supporters with four hundred Greek children. He was especially anxious to find the body of Constantine to reassure himself that his great enemy was truly dead. Men were hastily sent to wade through the gore, washing corpses and examining severed heads. A body was found dressed in silk stockings embroidered with an eagle, but when Mehmed impaled the head and paraded it around the city, it failed to impress those who had known the emperor. Despite the sultan's best efforts, the body was never found. In death, if not in life, Constantine XI had eluded his oppressor's grasp.

After 1,123 years and 18 days, the Byzantine Empire had drawn to a close. The Divine Liturgy that had echoed from the great dome of the Hagia Sophia for nearly a millennium fell silent, and the clouds of incense slowly cleared from the desecrated churches of the city. The shocked and shattered Byzantines were now in permanent exile, but they could at least reflect that their empire had come to a glorious and heroic end. Their last emperor had chosen death over surrender or a diminishment of his ideals, and in doing so he had found a common grave among the men he led. Proud and brave, the iconic eighty-eighth emperor of Byzantium had brought the empire full circle. Like the first to rule in the city by the Bosporus, he had been a son of Helena named Constantine, and it was fitting that in his hour of need he had a Justinian by his side.

---

*A Muslim prayer niche that traditionally faces Mecca, indicating the direction for the faithful to face when they pray.

EPILOGUE: BYZANTINE EMBERS

King, I shall arise from my enmarbled sleep,
And from my mystic tomb I shall come forth
To open wide the bricked-up Golden Gate;
And, victor over the Caliphs and the Tsars,
Hunting them beyond the Red Apple Tree,
I shall seek rest upon my ancient bounds.
—DONALD M. NICOL, *The Immortal Emperor* (1992)

When the sun rose on the shattered capital of Christendom the following morning of Wednesday, May 30, 1453, the Ottoman conquest of the empire was all but complete. Constantine's squabbling brothers were still holding out in the Peloponnese and the descendants of Alexius Comnenus were still ruling in Trebizond on the Black Sea coast. But these were empty shells, splintered fragments existing at the whim of the sultan, and by the late summer of 1461, the last of them had surrendered. The Turks had at last fulfilled the cherished dream of Islam to claim the city, and its capture took a profound hold on the Ottoman psyche. Constantinople became the Ottoman capital in imitation of the mighty empire that had come before, and Mehmed took the title of Caesar, appointing a patriarch and clothing himself in the trappings of Byzantium.* The Turks never forgot the magic of that victory, and even today their

---

*The name was not officially changed to Istanbul until 1930.

flag still proudly displays a waning moon to commemorate how the early morning sky appeared on a Tuesday in 1453.*

The consciousness of the Orthodox world was also seared with the images of that terrible May, and over time memory began to transform into legend. The priests officiating in the Hagia Sophia when the Turks had burst in hadn't been slaughtered but had stopped in midchant and miraculously melted into the southern wall of the sanctuary. When the city was again in Christian hands, they would reappear and take up the service from where it had been interrupted. As for the last heroic emperor, he hadn't perished in the fighting but had been rescued by an angel and turned to stone. There, in a cave below the Golden Gate, the marble emperor awaits, like a Byzantine King Arthur, to return in triumph and once more rule his people. In the five centuries of Ottoman domination that followed, Constantine's doomed stand against impossible odds became the talismanic symbol of the Orthodox Church in exile. His statue still stands in Athens, sword arm defiantly raised, the first proto-martyr and iconic, unofficial saint of modern Greece.†

Byzantium's long resistance to Islam had finally ended in defeat, but in carrying on the struggle for so long, it had won an important victory. The great walls of Constantine's city had delayed the Muslim advance into Europe for eight hundred years, allowing the West the time it needed to develop. When the Ottoman tide washed over Byzantium, it was nearing its crest; the armies of Islam would soon falter before the walls of Vienna, and the Ottoman Empire would begin its long retreat from Europe.

The fall of Constantinople may have extinguished the last vestige of the Roman Empire, but the immense light of its learning wasn't snuffed out. Refugees streamed into western Europe, bringing with

---

*The crescent moon had actually been chosen by the citizens of Byzantium as the symbol of their city as early as 670 BC in honor of the patron goddess Artemis. Mehmed adopted it for his own banner and—once adapted to show a more appropriate waxing moon—it soon spread to become the official Islamic standard.
†The identification with the Byzantine past was also shown linguistically, since up until the nineteenth century the Greek word for themselves was *Romíoi*, not *Hellene*.

them the lost jewels of Greek and Roman civilization. The first blush of humanism was just stirring the West's collective soul, and it received Byzantium's precious gift with enthusiasm. Partial copies of Aristotle's works had been well known for centuries, but now Europe was introduced to Plato and Demosthenes, electrified by the *Iliad,* and captivated by Xenophon and Aeschylus. Byzantine émigrés tutored luminaries as diverse as Petrarch and Boccaccio and the wealthy Cosimo de' Medici was so impressed by a Byzantine lecturer that he founded the Platonic Academy of Florence. The result was a "rebirth" or "Renaissance," as it was soon called, during which western Europe was reintroduced to its own roots.

Other exiles fled to Russia, the last great free Orthodox state, and tried to re-create the Byzantine dream. The kings of those vast northern lands already had a Byzantine alphabet and an eastern soul, and they welcomed the newcomers, taking the title of tsar—their version of Caesar—and adopting the double-headed eagle as their symbol. Byzantine art combined with local styles and continued to flourish throughout the Balkans and the north. The Russians could never forget the dazzling vision of Constantinople that was passed on to them, and the yearning for it became the long unfulfilled dream of the Russian Empire. They drank so deeply of Byzantium that even Stalin, flushed with the victory of Communism, embraced its memory, passing along both the lessons of its history and the dark mistrust of the West that still haunts the Kremlin.

The greatest heir of Byzantium, however, is undoubtedly the Orthodox Church. Pressed into service by the forces of nationalism in the nineteenth and twentieth centuries, the church provided a cultural repository linking the peoples of the former empire with the glorious epochs of their past. Today the Byzantine eagle flutters proudly from the flags of nations from Albania to Montenegro, and though each state has its local version of the church, the heritage they all bear is Byzantine.*

---

*The eagle is also the symbol of Iraq and Egypt—a dim reflection of a time when Justinian's empire embraced most of the known world.

Only in the West was the story largely forgotten, though without Byzantium the history of the Middle East and Europe is at best incomplete and at worst incomprehensible. When the smoke cleared from the Turkish cannons that awful Tuesday, it revealed a world that had profoundly changed. The Middle Ages had ended, and western Europe was on the brink of an extraordinary cultural explosion. Only thirty-five years after the fall of Constantinople, Bartholomeu Dias rounded the Cape of Good Hope, opening up a sea route to India, and just four years after that, a little-known Italian explorer named Christopher Columbus—using a translated Byzantine text of Ptolemy's *Geographia*—discovered America.

In the heady Age of Discovery that was dawning, there was little room for the tangled memories of Byzantium. The great bastion that had sheltered Europe for a millennium sank into obscurity, and the word "Byzantine" became a caricature of its people, conjuring up images of unnecessary complexity and vaguely sinister designs. Such accusations were as undeserved as they were untrue, and successfully denied the West the lessons afforded by the empire's history and example. Though it sprang from the same cultural fountainhead that birthed western Europe, Byzantium found its own unique balance to the familiar tensions of church and state, faith and reason. Its empire stretched over lands long considered inherently unstable, and though it frequently stumbled, it left behind a legacy of stability and even unity for more than a thousand years.

The greatest tragedy in its vast and glorious tapestry is not the way in which it fell, but that it has been consigned to irrelevance, its voices unheeded and its lessons unlearned. For those who have eyes to see, however, the lonely Theodosian walls still stand, battered and abused, marching the long miles from the Sea of Marmara to the waters of the Golden Horn. There they serve as a fitting testament to that epic struggle five centuries ago, an unwavering reminder that the Roman Empire didn't expire in the humiliation of a little Augustus, but in the heroism of a Constantine.

SELECTED BIBLIOGRAPHY

PRIMARY SOURCES ::

330–600

The following two books have been of invaluable service in researching the conversion of Constantine the Great (especially Eusebius's account found in Maas), as well as theology, everyday life, and imperial edicts from the fourth century until the Muslim invasions of the seventh.

Lactantius. *De Mortibus Persecutorum,* J. L. Creed, ed. & trans. Oxford: Clarendon, 1984.
Maas, Michael. *Readings in Late Antiquity.* London: Routledge, 2003.

For the reign of Julian the Apostate I drew heavily on his principal biographer:

Ammianus Marcellinus. *The Later Roman Empire* (A.D. *354–378),* W. Hamilton, ed. & trans. New York: Penguin Classics, 1986.

as well as:

Wright, Wilmer C. *Julian: Volume III.* Cambridge: Harvard University Press, 2003.

The latter is a collection of letters and polemics that the emperor wrote throughout his public life, from first donning his armor in Gaul to leaving for his ill-fated Persian campaign in 363.

Procopius was of immense assistance in researching the reign of Justinian, both the official "Buildings" and "Wars" and of course the scandalous "Secret History."

Procopius. *Buildings.* H. B. Dewing, ed. & trans. Cambridge: Harvard University Press, 2002.

Procopius. *History of the Wars: The Persian War Books 1 & 2.* H. B. Dewing, ed. & trans. New York: Cosimo Classics, 2007.

Procopius. *History of the Wars: The Vandalic War Books 3 & 4.* H. B. Dewing, ed. & trans. New York: Cosimo Classics, 2007.

Procopius. *The Secret History.* G. A. Williamson, ed. & trans. London: Penguin Classics, 1966.

600–1000

This time period covers the Byzantine "dark ages" where literary sources become somewhat scarce. Fortunately the "Chronicle of Theophanes" sheds some much-needed light. This work by a ninth-century monk describes the rise of Heraclius and the empire's struggle for survival amid religious dissension and external attack. The two major epochs of the period—the Iconoclastic controversy and the rise of the Macedonian dynasty—are detailed in Alice-Mary Talbot's wonderful translations of *Leo the Deacon* and *Eight Saints' Lives.*

Talbot, Alice-Mary. *Byzantine Defenders of Images: Eight Saints' Lives in English Translation.* Washington, D.C.: Dumbarton Oaks, 1998.

Talbot, Alice-Mary. *The History of Leo the Deacon: Byzantine Military Expansion in the Tenth Century.* Washington, D.C.: Dumbarton Oaks, 2005.

Turtledove, Harry. *The Chronicle of Theophanes.* Philadelphia: University of Pennsylvania Press, 1982.

1000–1453

For the period from the First to the Fourth Crusades, I have depended on the lively eyewitness accounts provided by Anna Comnena, John Kinnamos, Michael Psellus, and Niketas Choniates for the Eastern perspective, and on Joinville and Villehardouin for the Western.

Choniates, Niketas. *O City of Byzantium: Annals of Niketas Choniates.* Trans. Harry J. Magoulias. Detroit: Wayne State University Press, 1986.

Comnena, Anna. *The Alexiad.* London: Penguin Classics, 1969.

Kinnamos, John. *Deeds of John and Manuel Comnenus.* C. M. Brand, ed. & trans. New York: Columbia University Press, 1976.

Psellus, Michael. *Fourteen Byzantine Rulers.* London: Penguin Classics, 1966.

Shaw, M. R. B. *Joinville and Villehardouin: Chronicles of the Crusades.* New York: Penguin, 1963.

SECONDARY SOURCES

The secondary sources that have been most helpful can be broken down into two groups—those that are overviews of Byzantine history and those that deal with specific periods. In the former category I have made most use of Warren Treadgold's exhaustive history and Lord Norwich's three-volume set. Timothy Gregory's work has also been important, and, of course, Edward Gibbon—though with a certain amount of salt. In the latter category, for the period of the Crusades, I was assisted by Jonathan Harris's work, and for the early Macedonian Dynasty by the great Steven Runciman. In detailing the final moments of the empire I am indebted to Roger Crowley and especially Donald Nicol for his excellent study on Constantine Dragases.

Crowley, Roger. *1453: The Holy War for Constantinople and the Clash of Islam and the West.* New York: Hyperion, 2005.

Gibbon, Edward. *The Decline and Fall of the Roman Empire.* 6 vols. New York: Random House, 1993.

Gregory, Timothy E. *A History of Byzantium.* Malden, MA: Blackwell Publishing, 2005.

Harris, Jonathan. *Byzantium and the Crusades.* London: Hambledon Continuum, 2006.

Nicol, Donald M. *The Immortal Emperor.* Cambridge: Cambridge University Press, 1992.

Norwich, John Julius. *Byzantium: The Apogee.* New York: Alfred A. Knopf, 2004.

———. *Byzantium: The Decline and Fall.* New York: Alfred A. Knopf, 2003.

———. *Byzantium: The Early Centuries.* New York: Alfred A. Knopf, 1989.

Runciman, Steven. *The Emperor Romanus Lecapenus and His Reign.* Cambridge: Cambridge University Press, 1929.

Treadgold, Warren. *A History of the Byzantine State and Society.* California: Stanford University Press, 1997.

APPENDIX

EMPERORS OF CONSTANTINOPLE

CONSTANTINIAN DYNASTY (324–363)

324–353 ..... Constantine the Great
353–361 ..... Constantius .... *Son of Constantine the Great*
361–363 ..... Julian the Apostate .... *Cousin of Constantius*

NON-DYNASTIC

363–364 ..... Jovian .... *Soldier, chosen on the battlefield*
364–378 ..... Valens .... *Brother of Western Emperor*
Valentinian

THEODOSIAN DYNASTY (379–457)

379–395 ..... Theodosius I the Great ...... *Soldier, chosen by Western*
Emperor Gratian
395–408 .... Arcadius .... *Son of Theodosius*
408–450 .... Theodosius II .... *Son of Arcadius*
450–457 ..... Marcian .... *Married Theodosius II's sister*

LEONID DYNASTY (457–518)

457–474 ..... Leo I the Thracian .... *Soldier, chosen by Eastern*
general Aspar
474 .... Leo II .... *Grandson of Leo I*
474–475 ..... Zeno .... *Son-in-law of Leo I*
475–476 ..... Basiliscus .... *Usurper, brother-in-law of*
Leo I

476–491 . . . . . Zeno (again)
491–518 . . . . . Anastasius I . . . . *Son-in-law of Leo I*

JUSTINIAN DYNASTY (527–602)

518–527 . . . . . Justin I . . . . *Commander of the Palace*
Guard
527–565 . . . . . Justinian I the Great . . . . *Nephew of Justin I*
565–578 . . . . . Justin II . . . . *Nephew of Justinian*
578–582 . . . . . Tiberius II . . . . *Adopted by Justin II*
582–602 . . . . Maurice . . . . *Son-in-law of Tiberius II*

NON-DYNASTIC

602–610 . . . . Phocas . . . . *Usurper, soldier of Maurice*

HERACLIUS DYNASTY (610–711)

610–641 . . . . Heraclius . . . . *Usurper, general from*
Carthage
641 . . . . Constantine III . . . . *Son of Heraclius*
641 . . . . Heraclonas . . . . *Son of Heraclius*
641–668 . . . . Constans II the Bearded . . . . *Son of Constantine III*
668–685 . . . . Constantine IV . . . . *Son of Constans II*
685–695 . . . . . Justinian II the Slit-Nosed . . . *Son of Constantine IV*
695–698 . . . . Leontius . . . . *Usurper, soldier of Justinian II*
698–705 . . . . Tiberius III . . . . *Usurper, Germanic naval*
officer of Leontius
705–711 . . . . . Justinian II (again)

NON-DYNASTIC

711–713 . . . . . . Philippicus . . . . *Usurper, Armenian soldier*
of Justinian II
713–715 . . . . . Anastasius II . . . . *Usurper, imperial secretary*
of Philippicus
715–717 . . . . . Theodosius III . . . . *Usurper, tax collector and*
son (?) of Tiberius III

ISAURIAN DYNASTY (717–802)

717–741 ..... Leo III the Isaurian .... *Usurper, Syrian diplomat of Justinian II*

741–775 ..... Constantine V the Dung-Named............... *Son of Leo III*

775–780 .... Leo IV the Khazar .... *Son-in-law of Leo III*

780–797 .... Constantine VI the Blinded .... *Son of Leo IV*

797–802 .... Irene the Athenian .... *Wife of Leo IV, mother of Constantine VI*

NICEPHORUS DYNASTY (802–813)

802–811..... Nicephorus I .... *Usurper, finance minister of Irene*

811 .... Stauracius .... *Son of Nicephorus I*

811–813 ..... Michael I Rangabe .... *Son-in-law of Nicephorus I*

NON-DYNASTIC

813–820..... Leo V the Armenian......... *Patrician and general of Michael I*

AMORIAN DYNASTY (820–867)

820–829 .... Michael II the Stammerer ... *Son-in-law of Constantine VI*

829–842 .... Theophilus .... *Son of Michael II*

842–855 .... Theodora.................. *Wife of Theophilus*

842–867 .... Michael III the Drunkard ... *Son of Theophilus*

MACEDONIAN DYNASTY (867–1056)

867–886 .... Basil I the Macedonian ...... *Armenian peasant, married Michael III's widow*

886–912 .... Leo VI the Wise .... *Son of Basil I or Michael III*

912–913..... Alexander .... *Son of Basil I*

913–959..... Constantine VII the Purple-Born................. *Son of Leo VI*

920–944 .... Romanus I Lecapenus .... *General, father-in-law of Constantine VII*

959–963 .... Romanus II the Purple-Born .... *Son of Constantine VII*

963–969 .... Nicephorus II Phocas .... *General, married Romanus II's widow*

969–976 .... John I Tzimisces .... *Usurper, nephew of Nicephorus II*

976–1025 ... Basil II the Bulgar-Slayer .... *Son of Romanus II*

1025–1028 .. Constantine VIII .... *Son of Romanus II*

1028–1050 .. Zoë .... *Daughter of Constantine VIII*

1028–1034 .. Romanus III Argyrus .... *Zoë's first husband*

1034–1041... Michael IV the Paphlagonian .... *Zoë's second husband*

1041–1042 .. Michael V the Caulker....... *Zoë's adopted son*

1042 .... Zoë and Theodora .... *Daughters of Constantine VIII*

1042–1055... Constantine IX Monomachus .... *Zoë's third husband*

1055–1056... Theodora (again)

NON-DYNASTIC

1056–1057 .. Michael VI the Old .... *Chosen by Theodora*

1057–1059... Isaac I Comnenus.......... *Usurper, general of Michael VI*

DUCAS DYNASTY (1059–1081)

1059–1067 .. Constantine X .... *Chosen by Isaac*

1068–1071 .. Romanus IV Diogenes ...... *Married Constantine X's widow*

1071–1078... Michael VII the Quarter-Short..................... *Son of Constantine X*

1078–1081 .. Nicephorus III Botaneiates.. *Usurper, general of Michael VII*

COMNENIAN DYNASTY (1081–1185)

1081–1118 ... Alexius I .... *Usurper, nephew of Isaac I*

1118–1143.... John II the Beautiful .... *Son of Alexius I*

1141–1180 ... Manuel I the Great.......... *Son of John II*

1180–1183 ... Alexius II .... *Son of Manuel I*
1183–1185.... Andronicus the Terrible ..... *Usurper, cousin of Manuel I*

ANGELUS DYNASTY (1185–1204)

1185–1195 ... Isaac II Angelus............. *Great-grandson of Alexius I*
1195–1203 ... Alexius III Angelus .... *Brother of Isaac II*
1203–1204 ...Isaac II (again) and son
            Alexius IV

NON-DYNASTIC

1204 .... Alexius V the
            Bushy-Eyebrowed .... *Usurper, son-in-law of*
                                      Alexius III

PALAEOLOGIAN DYNASTY (1259–1453)

1259–1282 ... Michael VIII .... *Great-grandson of Alexius III*
1282–1328 ... Andronicus II .... *Son of Michael VIII*
1328–1341 ... Andronicus III .... *Grandson of Andronicus II*
1341–1391.... John V .... *Son of Andronicus III*
1347–1354 ... John VI .... *Father-in-law of John V*
1376–1379 ... Andronicus IV............. *Son of John V*
1390 .... John VII .... *Son of Andronicus IV*
1391–1425 ... Manuel II .... *Son of John V*
1425–1448 ... John VIII .... *Son of Manuel II*
1448–1453 ... Constantine XI Dragases .... *Son of Manuel II*

ACKNOWLEDGMENTS

Like the individuals it chronicles, a book never occurs in a vacuum, and writing this one has left me indebted to several people. First and foremost is my brother, Anders, who was a tireless source of encouragement and without whom pen would never have been put to paper. I am also grateful to Tina Bennett for her constant, excellent advice and to my editor, Rick Horgan, for his insightful comments and for keeping me true to the original aims of the book. The manuscript could never have reached its final form without Julian Pavia's astute reading and has benefited immensely from his thoughtful questions. Many thanks also to Sam Freedman, David Morken, and to my students who endured the constant shoehorning of Byzantium into nearly every subject, but still asked questions. I am sincerely grateful as well to my parents for encouraging my love for the past, and to my siblings, Tonja, Pat, Nils, and Celine, for braving an endless stream of emperors and generals with unceasing support. Finally, I must thank my wife, Catherine, who has had to share me with Byzantium for far too long but whose enthusiasm for my work has never dimmed. Thank you all; your encouragement and guidance enabled this book to be written.

INDEX